No Schlock...Just Rock!

A Journalistic Journey
2003-2008

GREG PRATO

Printed and distributed by Greg Prato
Published by Greg Prato
All photos by Richard Galbraith [www.myspace.com/richardgalbraith].
Book design and layout by Linda Krieg
[www.myspace.com/lindakriegdesign].
Special thanks to Robert Prato Jr., for fine-tuning this book's title.
Copyright © 2009, Greg Prato.
All Rights Reserved.
First Edition, May 2009

ISBN: 978-0-578-02294-9

Contents

Foreword

Let's keep this short and sweet, shall we? No ramblings about how rock journalism is going to save the world or solve the economy problem…wait, I'm already rambling! OK, honestly, let's focus on this. No, really, I'm serious this time!

The book you're holding in your tidy hands is comprised of articles, reviews, and interviews that yours truly conducted for four UK-based mags from 2003 to 2008—Classic Rock, Guitarist, Metal Hammer, and Record Collector. In the process, I got to interview many of my favorite all-time rock n' rollers.

I'd imagine that quite a few of you who had the good taste to buy this book are familiar with my writing through my three books—'A Devil on One Shoulder and an Angel on the Other: The Story of Shannon Hoon and Blind Melon,' 'Touched by Magic: The Tommy Bolin Story,' and/or 'Grunge is Dead: The Oral History of Seattle Rock Music.' Well, you may find this next bit interesting—the "germs" of the ideas for all three books are included in *this* book, in the form of articles I did for Classic Rock (the grunge book can be linked to the Soundgarden feature, while the other two are traced to the obvious Melon and Bolin features).

You'll also find extra items added in that were deleted from the published articles (word counts can bring even the sturdiest of writers down to their knees), as well as an article that never saw the light of day, until now—the 'Stories Behind the Song' for Steely Dan's "Reelin' in the Years." Why was it not published? It remains a mystery. But fret not concerned readers and friends, I was indeed paid for the article.

For all of these articles, I put in a decent amount of work, and found it disheartening that these poor little buggers were in danger of being forgotten over the sands of time. So I figured a rescue mission was in order, and with a little effort and the proper amount of research, all were located, dusted off, and correctly put in order, for your unmitigated reading pleasure.

So, on that note, kick back, relax, adjust your iPod to the appropriate artist, read on, and most importantly...LONG LIVE ROCK N' ROLL!!!

Enjoy,
Greg Prato
New York, March 2008

p.s. Questions? Comments? Email me at gregprato@yahoo.com..

Classic Rock

Features

Blind Melon

Gala Performance

*In 1993, Blind Melon issued one of the year's most aired videos on
MTV, saw their debut album nearly top the U.S. charts, landed tours
alongside Guns N' Roses, Neil Young, Soundgarden, and Lenny Kravitz,
and gained a legion of fans. Two years later, it was all over. Classic Rock
chats with Brad Smith, Rogers Stevens, and Christopher Thorn about
the band's meteoric rise and rapid fall.*

It was a warm summer evening in 1993—July 9th in New Haven, Connecticut,
to be exact. A few buddies and I have made the trek from Long Island, New
York, to catch a performance by one of our favorite bands, Blind Melon, at
a venue called Toad's Place. One small problem … it turns out that it's a
21+ entry, and me and another chap are the only members of our "gang"
that fit the required age bill. Standing outside as the show time grows nearer,
it's looking pretty bleak, until we see a smallish, longhaired "hippie" looking
figure walking down the street with a backpack on.

"Hey guys," the friendly voice says, complimenting yours truly on
wearing a Primus t-shirt. This was the beginning of my brief but memorable
interaction with Blind Melon's singer, Shannon Hoon. Never mind that his
band was about to take the stage, he seemed more concerned when we voiced
our dilemma. "Don't worry, this is what's going to happen. When we go on,
someone inside is going to crack open that fire exit right there, then you guys
gotta bum rush the door." A few songs into the set, my friends and I are safely
inside the venue, with Hoon announcing from the stage that he's glad to see
that the "young people" had made it in.

After the show, we meet guitarist Rogers Stevens, a friendly chap who
like Hoon, likes to chat with fans. The subject comes up of how Blind Melon
appears to be on the verge of a big breakthrough. "If we do become big, we
won't change. Stick with us." As I travel back home that night (finally reaching
my destination at sunrise), I think about Stevens' words, which soon prove
prophetic. A few weeks later, everyone seems to want a piece of the band, as their

career is suddenly skyrocketing. Sadly, looking back several years later, this time period could probably be classified as the beginning of the end for the band.

Talking to three of the surviving Blind Melon members nearly ten years after their abrupt end (Stevens, guitarist Christopher Thorn, and bassist Brad Smith), you get a sense of regret and sadness that Blind Melon never got a chance to deliver on their potential. But you also get a feeling from its ex-members of being proud of their experiences together, and of their memories of working with Hoon. "We all had the same kind of background," remembers Smith, "Moving from a small town, and we kinda wore that on our sleeves. At the time, right before Nirvana and Pearl Jam dropped, it was unique for a band to have that kinda stance, and I think that was our draw and appeal from a lot of the industry folks. Y'know, 'These guys are fresh off the boat and they kick ass!'"

When Smith says his ex-bandmates came from small towns, he's not kidding, as such obscure locales as West Point, Mississippi (Rogers and Smith), Lafayette, Indiana (Hoon), Dover, Pennsylvania (Thorn), and Columbus, Mississippi (drummer Glen Graham) are linked to the band. None exactly known for spawning rock musicians. Stevens: "When Brad and I were doing high school bands, it wasn't so much that we were outcasts—people were completely baffled by what we were doing. I think they thought that we just lost or minds or something. And it wasn't that it got a bad response, it got *no response*. Other than, 'Well, we'll just let them do their thing, and they'll grow out of it.'"

But grow out of it they never did, as childhood pals Stevens and Smith hatched a rock n' roll plan. Smith: "We always got magazines like Hit Parader and Metal Hammer, and were like, 'Fuck it man, it's all happening in L.A.' We had big balls and little brains, and moved to Los Angeles to take our chance." Arriving on the west coast in 1989, Smith remembers his and Stevens' shock upon realizing that the music scene was anything but the rock haven painted in the press. "It was the remnants of the glam metal scene, which was ultra sad. I was depressed from the music scene, it was just horrible." But Smith found some solace when he found another like-minded musician, Christopher Thorn. "I moved out in '87 or '88, went on a bunch of auditions," reminisces Thorn. "I was in this sorta folk rock band, and that's how I met Brad. I placed an ad in the Music Connection, Brad called, and we became great friends."

It soon became obvious that the only way Stevens and Smith were going to assemble a band was to hunt down other transplants from outside states. Enter longhaired wild child Shannon Hoon. Having fronted bands back home in Indiana, Hoon built up such an extensive rap sheet with the local police that he was basically forced to flee the area. Only a few weeks after landing in Los Angeles, he crossed paths with Stevens. Smith: "Rogers had the first meeting with Shannon, called me up, and said, 'Brad, you gotta go down, right now, to the rehearsal space and meet this guy Shannon—I'm telling you, he's the guy, he's amazing.' He just seemed like a bro from Mississippi. I swear to God, it was like, 'Let's go smoke some weed and go out to the train trestle!' He was just completely unpretentious, unaffected by L.A. thus far, and he felt like one of us immediately."

Although they were taken by Hoon's musical talents straight away (Thorn: "He played 'Change' that night on the acoustic"), Stevens recalls an early introduction to their new singer's unpredictable and potentially volatile demeanor—"He talked a lot, he would *not shut up*. I remember that first night that we decided we were going to be in a band; we'd gotten really drunk. We were crashing at my apartment, and he tried to pick a fight with me! He got mad 'cause I was laughing at him—he said something really stupid. That was the thing about Shannon, he'd say everything that came into his mind. A lot of the times it would be like, 'Why did you say that?' So he was trying to get a cab back to Indiana! And then I'm laughing even more. Miraculously, he didn't throw a punch—it could've ended right there."

While the still-unnamed band was rehearsing with a local drummer, it was becoming apparent that they needed someone else more like them—in other words, someone from a small town. Enter Glen Graham, a longtime acquaintance of Stevens' from Mississippi. Stevens: "We fired this drummer, 'cause he didn't really fit in the group as far as the way he played and everything, so we called Glen. He drove out—he was getting ready to move to North Carolina, and he just made a left turn instead of a right turn, and drove to L.A." The only remaining matter of business was a band name, which Smith took care of, when he remembered a phrase his father used to call a few hippie neighbors back home in Mississippi—"Blind Melon."

A demo tape was soon recorded, and before the band even played a single show, numerous major labels were courting them. Stevens figures it was due to

Hoon's relationship with a certain fellow Indiana native. "I think Shannon's sister and [Axl Rose] were in school together. Labels jumped all over us 'cause of Shannon's connection with Guns N' Roses." Right around the time that the G n' R track 'Don't Cry' surfaced in 1991 (with Hoon duetting alongside Rose, and appearing in its video), Blind Melon was signed to Capitol Records. While they were given a fair amount of artist control, Stevens admits the main motivation for going with Capitol—"They paid us more money!"

Partying in L.A. soon began getting in the way of songwriting however, resulting in an unsuccessful stab at recording an EP with Neil Young's producer, David Briggs. Stevens: "At the time, we were immature, and I remember blaming him. In hindsight, that's not the case really—it was more our fault than anybody." With the tracks shelved, the quintet decided to relocate to the peace and quiet of Durham, North Carolina, where they would not be distracted by extracurricular activities. Renting a house that they would dub "Sleepyhouse," Blind Melon got to work. Smith: "We weren't going to leave and go out on the town, 'cause there's nothing to do in Durham, so we just played music, smoked weed, and everyone was into painting at the time. It was a blast. It was a very strange environment. Shannon tin foiled the windows, so it was always dark in there, with candles. Rogers didn't take off his pajamas for a week!"

Shortly after the dawn of 1992, Blind Melon found themselves recording their debut in a spot that was in the midst of a musical uprising—Seattle, Washington. Setting up shop at London Bridge Studios, Rick Parashar was hired to produce; the same gentleman whose name would soon be a fixture on the U.S. album charts (producing Pearl Jam's 'Ten,' Temple of the Dog's self-titled release, and Alice in Chains' 'Sap'). Smith: "I remember it being really easy. Apart from all our dope smoking and all the disagreements we may have had, we had our shit together musically. We would play two or three takes of a song, and that was it. There was no chopping on the tape machine—the only thing that maybe got overdubbed were some guitar solos and the lead vocals. So I look back on those times and I'm like, 'There's a real sense of musical purity and performance to that record.' I think that's what's missing from today's records—'Blind Melon' really captured that."

Instead of recording the album from beginning to end, the band accepted an offer to open up for Public Image Limited, Big Audio Dynamite, and Live on MTV's 120 Minutes Tour that spring. While Blind Melon's southern rock jams and long hair may have seemed out of place with the other bands, Stevens has nothing but fond memories of the tour. "The Big Audio Dynamite guys were pros at knowing how to have fun on the road, and we got to be friends with Live. It was all a new experience to us—we went into it completely wide eyed. We were definitely the low men on the totem pole, but I think people were pulling for us, 'cause we had kinda an underdog situation—we didn't have an album out. John Lydon was really cool. He would always call us 'stinky hippies,' it was really funny. I know he and Shannon had conversations. That was a wild tour."

Although taking a break in the middle of recording a debut album is hardly the norm, Thorn figures it actually helped. "That was also a really good thing for the band, 'cause we had the pre-tour recordings, went out and toured for six weeks, and played every single night. So we were even that much better when we got back. I felt like we were really firing on all pistons at that point." And firing on all pistons they were. Listening back today, 'Blind Melon' is definitely one of the more "pure" sounding rock records of the early '90s—modeled more after Lynyrd Skynyrd and the Allman Brothers, rather than the usual suspects that all the grunge and industrial bands were studying at the time. While most of the tunes were finalized after the band had worked on them together, two standouts were penned entirely by lone members prior to their formation—Hoon's acoustic "song of hope," "Change" (a composition he'd played at his tryout), and a quirky tune that Smith had penned about the constantly depressed state of a former girlfriend, "No Rain."

When 'Blind Melon' was finally released on September 22, 1992, the G n' R-linked buzz that surrounded the band a year previously had largely died down. Thorn: "I think we were all under the false assumption that our record was going to come out and be a giant hit. And then reality sorta struck us—we realized, 'Wow, this is really hard work.' We were having a lot of fun, 'cause we were playing and seeing the country, but I think we were a bit stressed out. We didn't realize that you actually had to work a record. Thank God we had a record company like Capitol, who knew it was going to be a slow build, and they were more than prepared to keep us on the road for a really long time." Smith has similar memories from this time period. "We named one of our t-shirts 'Crammed in a Van Tour.' We knew we were making an impact, 'cause we'd come around to the same city the second time, and the crowd had doubled or tripled, and the word was getting out about the band. That was probably the most romantic period of my musical career."

It was during this time that the band hooked up with "Smells Like Teen Spirit" video director, Samuel Bayer, to shoot a clip for the upbeat ditty that always received a raucous reception at their shows, "No Rain." By combining shots of the band playing in a breezy field and of their album cover coming to life (the infamous "bee girl"), the feel-good video catapulted the band to the top of the charts in the U.S. during the summer of '93. While their "rock n' roll dreams" were finally coming true, trouble was brewing.

"Songwriting issues came up, which was a bummer," admits Smith. "It's really hard to talk about, 'cause you're so young at the time, and it came down to writer splits. It was really fueled by Shannon and I duking it out, 'cause he wanted to split up the songwriting, and I at heart did not want to split up the songwriting. But Shannon had written a pretty hefty portion of the songs at that point, and so had I. So I got kinda dragged into a situation where I had to fight for my own splits. And one of the songs I had written all of was 'No Rain.' That's the song that became successful, and I think that bred some kinda resentment. It's a shame, 'cause there's bands that do it the way we should have done it—which is everything gets split evenly. There's none of that unspoken for resentment and grievances towards each other that I think we had. I got really lucky. In my mind, 'Change' should have been the hit." In the end however, everything worked out, as Stevens explains, "We got all that sorted out. It was sorta a brutal battle, but we got it sorted out in a way that everybody was happy with it. We all compromised, and I was really proud of that."

Perhaps taking their cue from previous rock outfits that stay on the road for an extended period to cash in on their success, Blind Melon remained on the road for a solid year and a half. Looking back now, Smith feels the scheduling should have been set up more wisely. "The pitfalls of keeping the band on the road—idle hands are the devil's workshop, and Shannon took that proverb to heart. He'd made a mess of himself on the road after a certain point, and we should have gotten off the road sooner. Hindsight is 20/20. We should have been in the States when 'No Rain' was getting played on the radio, but we were in Europe touring with Lenny Kravitz for two months. It was just small mistakes that brought down a flying ship. I remember fighting for that at the time, but these great tours kept coming up, and the managers were convincing members that we should take advantage of this, and from a business standpoint, you trust them. But from a longevity standpoint, I don't think it was the right thing to do."

The grind of the road merged with the group's sudden success proved to be a dangerous cocktail, as Hoon indulged in his drug of choice, cocaine. But this was nothing new, according to Stevens. "Shannon's drug use…that was from day one. That wasn't a new thing. I mean, he went through phases; he was always game for whatever. I think he had a lot of problems back when he was living in Indiana, and he got out. Coke was the problem—heroin was never the problem or anything like that. So anyway, we tried to deal with it—got him into treatment a few times and things like that. We did an intervention one time and he didn't show up for it! Pretty classic." It appeared as though Kurt Cobain's suicide in April of 1994 had served as a wake up call for Hoon, who took his first serious stab at sobriety around this time—lasting only a few months, however.

Finally off the road, the Melon men opted to retreat to new hometowns (Thorn: Seattle, Smith, Stevens, and Graham: New Orleans, while Hoon moved back to Indiana), as they regained their focus, and cooked up some new tunes. But before recording sessions could commence for their sophomore effort, Blind Melon was offered a spot on the mammoth Woodstock '94 bill, which they accepted. Thorn's memories remain clear ten years later—"I was really overwhelmed. You have those shows where you feel like you're really in control, you know what's happening, and you can 'feel it'—you're taking it all in as you're playing. And for some reason, Woodstock was so overwhelming, I almost kinda felt 'shut down.' There are two main memories—flying in on a helicopter, the first helicopter I've ever flown on, and you'd see, as far as you can see, people. I'll never forget being backstage and seeing Peter Max, the famous artist, standing right behind Joe Cocker, who was opening the show. He goes on, and sings 'Feeling Alright,' and just being, 'Oh my God, we have to follow this? The guy at the original Woodstock just played, give me a break!' I remember Shannon showing up in a dress, and just going, 'You're fucking nuts, what are you doing?' But that's what was great about him, he was never going to give you the same old shit—you didn't know what you were going to get from him. That's why he was such a great performer. I remember him just going for it, giving 100%."

With Woodstock out of the way, Blind Melon's attention turned to sessions for their all-important second album. Selecting producer Andy Wallace due to the variety of acts he'd worked with previously (Nirvana, Slayer, Jeff Buckley, etc.), the quintet opted to record in New Orleans, Louisiana—a town which always seemed to get to Hoon. Smith: "That was total mayhem. At the time, I had just come out of my 'pot haze,' but the band wasn't finished with that kind of stuff. So there was a lot of cocaine, ecstasy, heroin, marijuana…whatever you wanted. It was at the studio all the time—it was a mansion. Daniel Lanois' mansion called Kingsway. And it was fucking crazy man. We didn't go into the studio until two or four o'clock in the afternoon, and nobody left until the sun was coming up. It was just a total vampire existence, laced with drugs, alcohol, and fucking craziness. People were there that I had no idea why they were there. And looking back, it's amazing that we got a record done at all. But again, still, our chemistry was that we had our shit together—everybody in the band could play, and we had this crazy, unspoken for telepathy. And we finished songs so fast. We got together two months before the record, threw together everyone's ideas, had 26 pieces of music, and recorded 16 for the record. It was so fucking fast—bands don't do that these days, it's so over-calculated."

With such madness going on around and within the band, it would be understandable if the resulting album, 'Soup,' was a complete mess. Turns out, it was anything but. Arguably one of the '90s great lost rock albums, it certainly did catch the average Blind Melon admirer off guard upon first listen—gone were the loose funky jams, and most obviously, no sunny sing-alongs a la "No Rain." In its place were songs about child murderer Susan Smith ("Car Seat"), serial killer Ed Gein ("Skinned"), the effects of heroin ("2x4"), a suicide jumper ("St. Andrews Fall"), and a barroom brawl ("Lemonade"), among other "pleasant" subjects. But after a few spins, 'Soup' showed how much the group had grown musically, and how they had put together an album that improved immeasurably with each successive listen.

Critics weren't as patient with the album, as they savagely panned it—suspiciously branding the group a "one hit wonder" before 'Soup' was released (Stevens: "Shannon pissed off so many journalists that they were all taking it out on him"). But as Smith points out, the band was ready for the slings and arrows. "When people become really successful, people just can't wait to see you fail. We were prepared for that—that's why we made the record we did, to be quite honest. If we tried to follow up that first Blind Melon record with some more happy shiny songs, y'know, chicken fried grooves, that would have been a dismal failure, in a sophomore slump kinda way. But when you come out with an art record, that's pushing the envelope and sounds completely original, it's hard to argue with that."

Another tune on the album, "New Life," saw Hoon contemplating whether the impending birth of his daughter would sober him up once and for all. It appeared as though fatherhood would finally straighten out the singer's party hearty ways—fresh out of another stint in rehab, Blind Melon set out for a tour of European festivals right around the time of 'Soup's' release, on August 15, 1995. The next month, Blind Melon embarked on their first full-on U.S. tour in well over a year. Despite being upset with the album's poor reviews and wanting to be back home with his newborn, Hoon returned to the road—clean and sober, at least initially. Thorn: "I remember going from Seattle down the coast, and Lisa [Hoon's girlfriend] and the baby were there on the bus. It was great, it kinda felt like, cool, this is the next 'phase' of Blind Melon. I remember playing really well, kinda loving it. Then we got to L.A., and some boneheads turned Shannon on to drugs."

From there, things worsened, especially when the band's management put a caretaker on tour to watch Hoon and limit his drug intake. "This guy came on tour with us," remembers Stevens. "This big, huge guy, and his job was to keep drug people away from Shannon. And the guy flips on the headlights of the bus, as we were in the parking lot of the hotel to drive out of L.A., and Shannon walks into the headlights and buys drugs right in front of him! That was the big 'fuck you.' Shannon was a scrappy guy." When it became clear that the drug counselor wasn't doing his job (Thorn: "Shannon's in the back of the bus doing drugs, and the guy's up front, taking up room in the bus. We were like, 'Why is this guy here? If he's not actually doing his job, this is stupid.'"), the band decided to send him packing, with the idea that Hoon's latest binge would soon end, and things would return back to normal.

But drug use had now spread to other members of the band. Starting to affect their performance, Smith considered taking drastic measures. "It was a secret I had between me and my now-wife, that I may just slip off in the middle of the night, get a plane ticket and go home. 'Cause this is fucking stupid. I was really frustrated. And I think part of that was because I didn't use cocaine. I never have. So when you see your friends start crumbling around you from that kind of substance abuse, you're out on the road and you're trying to make the best of this 'people waiting on you to fail,' you're giving them a lot of reasons to follow through with that emotion. And lo and behold, we did because of the cocaine use. It was really hard on me, personally. We could've done better than that."

After an especially sloppy performance in Houston, Texas on October 20th (Thorn: "I felt that Shannon was high before he went on, and it just felt like a terrible show"), the band boarded their tour bus, looking forward to getting things back on track for their next show, in their adopted hometown of New Orleans. Little did the group know, that this would be the last hours they would spend as a band together. With Hoon staying up all night doing cocaine, the bus pulled into a New Orleans hotel the next morning. While the rest of the band checked into their rooms, Hoon opted to roam the city streets, before climbing into one of the bunks on the bus. He never woke up, dead of a cocaine overdose at the age of 28.

In the wake of his death, many cast blame on the group and its management, saying that Hoon shouldn't have been back on the road so shortly after completing a rehab assignment. But Stevens is quick to point out that Hoon's hometown of Lafayette wasn't the best place for him. "He had a lot of connections there. We caught a lot of flack later on, but I always told people, 'Look, this guy is showing up to rehearsal twenty pounds underweight.' And we hadn't even been around him. Then when we got out on tour, he was clean for a while, in the beginning. This was one of these instances where it was a two-day situation that got him to where he is today, after being clean for a while."

The surviving members pondered the idea of continuing on with a different singer, but eventually agreed that Hoon was simply irreplaceable, and decided to go their separate ways. Nowadays, most of the chaps are involved in other projects—Stevens is collaborating with former Spacehog front man Royston Langdon in the New York City-based outfit, Sparticle, Smith and Thorn are now producers in Hollywood, where they opened their own recording studio, Wishbone, while Graham seems to have retired from the music biz all together—living in North Carolina and spending his days painting. With one posthumously issued outtakes set already issued, 1996 'Nico,' it appears as though Thorn will be assembling an all new collection of previously unheard Blind Melon tracks, as well as a possible live album, in the near future.

Looking back nearly a decade since Hoon's death, Smith recollects something that the singer said to him shortly before his passing. "The last meaningful conversation I had with him, I think it was after he got out of rehab. We were talking about how things were going to be better and different, and how he was sorry." For Shannon Hoon, those days sadly never came.

www.blindmelon.com

Classic Rock—October 2004, issue 71

Adrian Belew

Three's Company

He's played with some of rock's biggest names, but Adrian Belew is perhaps most at home going it alone. Ever prolific, this year Belew will issue three "solo" albums, the first starring members of Tool and Primus …

Throughout 2005, Adrian Belew will be making up for lost time with this solo career. It's been nearly eight years since Belew issued his last full length solo release, 1997's 'Op Zop Too Wah,' as the guitarist has been busy working with prog rock veterans King Crimson, as well as the power pop outfit the Bears. But this year, Belew is focusing primarily on solo work, as he will be releasing three separate albums—'Side One,' 'Side Two,' and 'Side Three.' "These are records that were done over the last four/five years," Belew recently explained, "While I was busy re-establishing King Crimson, and to a lesser extent, the Bears. Over that time, we did a lot of touring of King Crimson, several new records, a DVD—we did basically on a smaller scale, the same thing with the Bears. This left me a few weeks here, a few weeks there, where I'd be home between touring or something, and I'd be in my studio. I could try out new ideas, record new things. Gradually, I realized I was accumulating a lot of material for solo records."

And "accumulate" he did, working up a total of 30 tracks, including compositions that focused on drum-looping ("A lot of looping and very little vocal—a new area for me"), as well as rockers that utilize a "power trio" set up. Belew— "At first, I started doing the power trio stuff as I usually do—by myself playing all the instruments. That's my normal procedure for making a solo record—to try and do everything myself. But I realized I'd really like to hear a better drummer and bass player—someone more adventurous than myself." Belew couldn't have found two better-equipped players, as both Primus bassist Les Claypool and Tool drummer Danny Carey joined him. Due to conflicting schedules however, when Belew tours in support of these three albums, Claypool and Carey will be replaced with previously unknown, new recruits. The trio may get back together further on down the road though, to complete several leftover pieces of music. "I think what we would do with those tracks is we might decide at some point to do some kind of project in the future. That's what we talked about."

In addition to his solo albums, Belew has a few other projects on the horizon. First up is putting together material for King Crimson's next phase, which sees '80s era bassist Tony Levin return to the fold. "I feel that King Crimson will start a new direction—it's a little early to describe. But my hope is Pat [Mastelotto, drums] and Tony working together will bring the band into a different rock area, that we didn't have with any of the previous Crimson's." Belew plans to collaborate with Crimson founder Robert Fripp off-and-on throughout the year, and has already come up with some rough sketches. No song titles have been set, however. "They always have titles that don't make any sense. They're just something that happened at the moment. One is called 'Sub Octave Funk,' for example, which I'm sure has nothing to do with the way the song will end up. It just happened to be the name of the program that was on my guitar effects box [laughs]."

And Belew's other "New Year's Resolution" will be launching his very first instrument line, via Parker Guitars. "We have designed a new guitar—it's a customized Parker Fly—which will be my first signature guitar. 'The Adrian Belew Signature Guitar.' It has basically all the things that I've come to rely on in guitars. The reason why I didn't switch to Parker until now was because I couldn't let go of the MIDI abilities that I have, and the sustainer part of the guitar that I have. So we just put all those things on the Parker [laughs]." Having stuck by Fender Strats throughout his career, it was Parker's construction that won Belew over. "It's so revolutionary in the way that it's put together. You have a wooden guitar there, but it's coated in this sort of 'space age material.' I think it's a carvin glass polymer. And it's just this tiny little shell, that is kinda like an M&M coating. And because of that, it strengthens the stability of the guitar to such a degree, that that's why for example the neck on the Parker Fly is the thinnest, easiest neck to play on any guitar. It makes every other guitar seem like you're playing a baseball bat. And that was the thing that first attracted me about it—you play this guitar, and you just play better."

Another selling point for Belew was the instrument's spot-on intonation. "The neck on the guitar, for example, is fully intonated at all times. In other words, every note on the guitar neck is perfectly in tune—there are no dead spots, there's no intonation needed. Which is revolutionary in itself, I mean, when do you ever have a guitar that stays perfectly in tune? You can take this guitar anywhere, pull it out of the case, and it'll be exactly in tune." As for when the "Belew Signature Parker" will appear on the market, a set date has yet to be confirmed. "It's not quite finished yet, but I expect it to be finished soon. I think during the NAMM show in January, I'm going to go out there and we're going to see—it may be the time that we officially announce it. But my feeling is it will be for players like me. Sort of the Ferrari of guitars—it'll have everything that you'd want."

www.adrianbelew.net

Guitarist—March 2005, issue 261

The Raspberries

All The Way To Nowhere

John Lennon, Keith Moon, and Kurt Cobain were fans. They were an influence on Kiss, Cheap Trick, and even Mötley Crüe. So how come classic '70s power-pop band the Raspberries never quite made it? Eric Carmen and Wally Bryson look back on the band that could have caused a ripple.

Hard rockin' anthems, tender piano ballads, impeccable vocal multi-harmonies, snazzy outfits, a charismatic frontman. A fair description of the formula that Queen rode to the top of the charts, but also fitting for their U.S. counterpart, the Raspberries. While Queen conquered the world however, the Raspberries remained woefully overlooked, despite making fans out of such rock icons as John Lennon and Keith Moon.

Few songs from the early 70's summarized the "power pop" style as splendidly as the Raspberries' "Go All the Way." Three and a half-minutes of pure pop bliss, the song merged the best bits of early Beatles and the Who. While its title gave a not-so-subtle clue to its lyrical content, the song offered a unique spin—it was sung from the point of view of *the girl.* "I always thought if it saw daylight, one of two things would happen," explains singer/guitarist Eric Carmen. "Either it'll get banned because it's dirty—then maybe people will buy the album to check it out—or if it ever gets on the radio, I think it'll just be a hit based on the title alone." And get on the radio it did, resulting in a near U.S. chart topper. But for a myriad of reasons, the Raspberries were unable to use the single to catapult their career into the stratosphere.

Midway between New York and Chicago, Cleveland, Ohio is far from any ocean, and a recipient of brutally cold winters. By the 1970's, the city was hit hard when the once-thriving steel mill and automobile manufacturing industries had dried up. In other words, not the type of place you'd expect a "sunny" power pop group like the Raspberries to originate. But that's exactly where Carmen, guitarist Wally Bryson, bassist Dave Smalley, and drummer Jim Bonfanti called their home.

Smitten by the aforementioned British acts, Carmen had heard about a local band that was creating a stir during the late 1960's. "I was going to high school, and there was talk that there was this really great band, the Choir. I ventured out to see them, and they were awesome—Wally, Dave, and Jim were all members. They played all the chords right, they sang the harmony parts right. I looked up at that stage and said, 'Boy, if I could get into that band, we could really do some damage'." Carmen meanwhile, bid his time fronting his own outfit, Cyrus Erie, which also became a local favorite.

With the Choir and Cyrus Erie unable to expand their following outside Cleveland, both acts eventually split in 1970. Soon after, Carmen hatched a plan—similar to what punk bands would later adopt. "At that time, all the stuff that I grew up loving, which was three and a half-minute singles—well crafted pop songs with great melodies by the Beatles, the Hollies, the Who, and the Byrds—was going away. Replacing it on radio was Cream and Traffic. It wasn't the three-minute pop stuff that I loved. So Jim and I sat down and said, 'What's happening is not what we love, so let's start a band and make it the antithesis of everything that's going on now. Let's play three and a half-minute pop songs. No extended guitar solos, no boring drum solos.' None of this sort of self-indulgent stuff that all the bands were doing."

Originally comprised of Carmen, Bryson, Bonfanti, and bassist John Aleksic (their first choice, Smalley, was serving in Viet Nam at the time), the Raspberries set out to see how their "three-minute pop stuff" would go down. It went down a storm, but the band hit a dead end while trying to expand their local following. "You could hardly get out of Cleveland," recalls Bryson. "Nobody wanted to talk to you—they didn't think anybody had any real talent here. So for us and the James Gang, it was tough to 'get out of Dodge,' and hit the rest of the world."

With Aleksic ousted in 1971, the Raspberries played as a trio, with Carmen assuming bass duties. When Smalley returned, he was enlisted into the band—first as a rhythm guitarist, then as bassist. It wasn't long before a plan was hatched, and airplane tickets were purchased for New York. With a demo in hand, the group "ambushed" producer Jimmy Ienner in New York's Grand Central Station, imploring him to listen to their tunes right then and there. Ienner was impressed—soon becoming their producer, and helping the quartet sign with Capitol.

Entering New York's famed Record Plant Recording Studios (where the group would record all their albums), the Raspberries and Ienner got to work. But a problem soon developed—how to recreate their show's energy in the studio. Bryson- "[Engineers] wanted the guitar really clean, low volume. You can't really imitate what you're doing live, and you can't get any 'balls.' It was a big struggle to record and have it come out the way I heard in my head."

If that wasn't enough, Carmen was appalled when he heard the initial version of "Go All the Way." "When I brought the song into the band, I explained it by saying, 'It's sort of a concept song. Picture this, guys—the song opens and it's the Who playing 'Won't Get Fooled Again.' You hit the verse, and it's suddenly the Beach Boys playing 'Don't Worry Baby' with McCartney singing. And then when the chorus comes, the Left Banke come in and sing background. Then it goes back to the Who.' They were all looking at me like, 'What? *Are you nuts?!*' [When] we got into the studio, it just wasn't flying. I remember going to Jimmy Ienner, and begging him to leave it off the record, because the track was just laying there dead."

With the song that was once a bona fide hit almost deleted from the album, engineer Shelly Yakus attempted to revive the track—running it through a limiter. Carmen- "All of a sudden, I came in the studio, and they played this thing for me. It was like, 'Oh my God, there's my record'!" And just like that, the Raspberries had the song that would launch their career. A few months after the Raspberries' self-titled debut album hit the racks (complete with scented cover) in 1972, "Go All the Way" raced up the charts, peaking at #5 in the U.S. Elsewhere on the album though, there was little else that resembled the rockin' good time of their hit—comprised mostly of mid-tempo fare and ballads.

Another mishap occurred when the group was planning a cover photo for their follow-up effort, 'Fresh,' also issued in 1972. With all their favorite bands adopting an identifiable image, the Raspberries came up with an ill-advised fashion idea—matching white suits—that looked straight out of the closet of Saturday Night Fever's Tony Manero. Bryson- "I thought it was a total mistake. I would go along with it though—being the kid from Cleveland, I thought, '*If this is what we have to do.*' All my instincts were crying out against it." Additionally, Carmen disapproves of the cover shot. "Well, I always refer to that album cover as 'Madame Tussaud's Raspberries'—it's like four wax dummies."

Musically however, 'Fresh' was an improvement over the debut. The group began feeling more comfortable in the studio, resulting in their highest charting album, thanks to their second hit single, "I Wanna Be With You," one of their best ballads in "Let's Pretend," and the Beach Boys tribute, "Drivin'

Around." But it was around this time that Carmen became the group's chief songwriter, leaving Bryson out in the cold. "I was contemplating leaving at that time. I went from writing or co-writing [several] songs on the first album to writing one on the second album. So there were some arguments over songwriting credit. I ended up staying."

And it's a good thing Bryson stayed, because as evidenced by such gems as "Tonight" (a song Mötley Crüe would later cover), "Ecstasy," and "Hard to Get Over a Heartbreak," the group's third release, 1973's 'Side 3,' is arguably their finest. Carmen- "I think that 'Side 3' was the first time we began to sound on record the way we actually sound. But we began to have friction within the band about, 'Is this direction working?' Dave was moving off into a more country-ish direction, and I was not happy with that." Additionally, Carmen recalls that it didn't help that the group was handled by a revolving door of shady managers, who did not properly look after their best interests. "The frustration of doing what we were doing—having hit records and having no money, touring and playing crummy places—was starting to overwhelm us. It was starting to get tense."

Things only worsened when Capitol continued to push the group's image. Carmen—"We had always been musicians first and foremost. We wrote our own songs, we played our own instruments, we sang all the parts. When Capitol said, 'We're going to organize interviews for you,' I remember us all sitting in a big conference room at the Capitol Tower in Los Angeles, waiting for Rolling Stone, Creem, and Crawdaddy to come in. And in would walk Fave and 16 Magazine—'What's your favorite color? What do you like to do on a date?' And as a bunch of young guys who once again, didn't have management to say, 'This isn't what we were talking about,' we answered their questions. And the next thing you knew, we were all over 16 Magazine, and no self-respecting 17 or 18-year-old guy was going to say, 'Oh, those guys are cool, my little sister likes them.' Because of the marketing campaign of Capitol—who really didn't know what we were—they just blew off the whole album buying audience. And that was really the kiss of death for the band."

But the Raspberries' original line-up was able to hold it together a bit longer. And for a brief moment, everything fell into place, when they decided to gamble and headline New York's famed Carnegie Hall. Carmen—"I thought it was the best show that we ever played, by far. Everything came together for that show. We decided—wear whatever you want, but it's got to be black.

When we walked on stage, we realized that the backdrop at Carnegie Hall was completely white. And the effect of it all was like looking at a black and white movie, which was cooler than I ever could have anticipated. I thought, 'What would be the last thing that a New York audience would expect us to do?' I eventually came up with the idea that with all the Beatles comparisons, the last thing they would ever expect us to do would be to open with a Beatles song. So I figured out a way to play the intro of 'Ticket to Ride,' and segue it right into 'I Wanna Be With You.' It worked like a charm. Wally hit his Rickenbacker, those opening strings, and you literally could hear a gasp from the audience. They were just *stunned*. And then when we launched into 'I Wanna Be With You,' the place just roared, and we owned them from that minute on. Paul Stanley was in the audience, [and] the drummer from Blondie—he said it was one of the best rock shows he ever saw."

Frustratingly, what would have made an exceptional live album will never be. Bryson- "I had my TEAC four-track set up with Shelly Yakus ready to record it, and our manager hadn't paid the $150 fee, so they wouldn't let us turn it on. All set up and ready to roll. We said, 'We'll pay you now!' They said, 'No, you have to have the permit'."

Despite winning over New York, Smalley and Bonfanti realized that they were moving in a different direction, and jumped ship shortly thereafter. Carmen and Bryson opted to carry on with replacement members—bassist Scott McCarl and ex-Cyrus Erie drummer Michael McBride—although the decision was tough for Bryson. "They were buddies of mine from the Choir—it was a real difficult situation. I felt real torn. In the end, I decided to stay with 'the outfit,' and got to work with Scott McCarl, which was great, and my brother-in-law Michael. At the time, he was married to my younger sister."

Knowing that their fourth album was "make-or-break" for the band, Carmen and Bryson hunkered down with their new bandmates—crafting yet another pop masterpiece, 1974's 'Starting Over.' Highlights this time around included the Queen-like epic, "Overnight Sensation (Hit Record)" and "Play On," but as evidenced by such titles as "The Party's Over" and the title track, the group knew the writing was on the wall.

Once more recording at New York's Record Plant, the group got to meet one of their heroes, John Lennon, who was producing Harry Nilsson's 'Pussy Cats.' Carmen- "I knocked him down coming out of the bathroom at Record

Plant, that was my first meeting—not exactly how I planned it. [Lennon and Nilsson] were recording 'Loop de Loop,' and he had a bunch of school kids in there, clapping hands. He needed some people who could actually clap and keep time. So he came and got Michael and I. Which of course, we were out of our minds—*'He wants us to clap on his song!'* It was so cool. Later on, Jimmy Ienner had told me that one night when he was working on the mix of 'Overnight Sensation,' John had come by and said, 'Fabulous, love it'!"

It also turned out that the Record Plant housed a prized piece of Beatles memorabilia. "I'd heard the Beatles' Mellotron was upstairs. They showed me this room, and there is this big white Mellotron sitting there. I remember going over to this thing, putting my fingers on the keys, and the first thing that I found was the entire ending of 'Strawberry Fields Forever.' All the flutes and craziness—recorded on these different keys. I was standing there pushing these keys, and way down at the other end of the room was John sitting—just watching with a big smile on his face. He was wearing all black, he was very pale, and I remember looking at him and thinking, 'He looks like a black and white photograph of John Lennon'."

A few months later, the Raspberries got to meet another one of their heroes, when Keith Moon jumped onstage to jam during a performance at the Whiskey A-Go-Go. Bryson- "He came up, and I guess he had some drinks. But in about twenty seconds, the fog lifted, and he really played great. We played 'All Right Now'—it was a good time. I just thought, 'Wow, this means we made it—Keith Moon is jamming with us!' I was blown away."

But with little money in their pockets and 'Starting Over' soon becoming their lowest-charting album, tensions ran high. Following an ugly physical confrontation between Bryson and Carmen in a Chicago parking lot, Bryson exited. After playing the rest of the dates as a three piece, the Raspberries split in 1975.

In the ensuing years, Carmen launched a successful solo career (scoring mega-hits with "All By Myself" and "Hungry Eyes"), while Bryson and the duo of Smalley/Bonfanti appeared with other groups—Tattoo and Fotomaker (Bryson) and Dynamite (Smalley/Bonfanti). But the Raspberries' stature continued to grow, as they left an unmistakable imprint on such acts as Kiss and Cheap Trick, while "Go All the Way" was introduced to a new generation via Cameron Crowe's 'Almost Famous.' As a result, rumors of an original

Raspberries line-up reunion appeared throughout the years, but didn't come to fruition until last year, when Carmen-Bryson-Smalley-Bonfanti performed a handful of gigs at House of Blues venues in the U.S.

With the prospect of a full-fledged tour beckoning, the Raspberries appear to be blossoming once more. Bryson- "Glad to be buddies again and making music. And man, our fans are the best in the world; they just wouldn't let us die. They waited all these years, it's astounding. Our music lived on, and forced us to get back together."

www.raspberriesonline.com

Classic Rock—July 2005, issue 81

Tommy Bolin

Diamond Teaser

*Tommy Bolin played guitar with some of the biggest names of the early
'70s rock world—the James Gang, Billy Cobham, and Deep Purple.
With a fiery and technical style, Bolin helped bridge the gap between the
Jimi Hendrix and Eddie Van Halen "generations." He had the looks
and the talent, but also a deadly drug addiction. Classic Rock takes a
look at the tragic career of this guitar great, through band mates, friends,
and family.*

In the early '70s, you had your fair share of guitar heroes. But most stuck to
a single style, and in the wake of Jimi Hendrix's death, almost all hailed from
England. Sioux City, Iowa native Tommy Bolin stuck out like a sore thumb.
Best described as the "David Bowie of guitar," Bolin jumped from one style to
the next—making each one his own, and almost just as quickly discarding it
for the next detour.

Bolin's band mate in Deep Purple, Glenn Hughes, agrees with this
assessment. "Well he was different, wasn't he? Tommy came from a very South
American-flavored, Brazilian, reggae-ish twisted, Americana way of playing
guitar. It wasn't European. It was be-boppy, it was jazz, it was everything
Deep Purple weren't. Which I liked—having another guy in the band that
wasn't frightened to do that, or play on instinct. He was a genius."

Born on August 1, 1951 to working parents (his father Richard in a
packing plant, his mother Barbara in a grocery store, and he was the oldest of
three brothers, Johnnie and Rick), young Tommy discovered rock n' roll via
Elvis Presley. "My dad, although he never played nothing, was really behind
having all of us play an instrument," explains Tommy's brother, Johnnie.
"Tommy got his guitar when he was ten. So right from the very beginning, he
was taking lessons."

Although he did time with such obscure outfits as Denny & the Triumphs,
Patch of Blue, and the Velairs, Bolin became increasingly fed up with the
nowhere local music scene. Soon after, Bolin told his parents he was relocating
to the then-musical hotbed of Denver, Colorado. Johnnie: "My mom and
dad were behind him 100%. I mean, to let a kid go hitchhike to Denver at
15, it's not like they didn't care, but he said, 'That's what I really want to do.'

And my mom didn't like the fact that they kept throwing him out of school [because of his long hair]."

Shortly after landing in Denver, Bolin found some like-minded musicians via a chance meeting, recalls singer Jeff Cook. "I first met Tommy when I had a band called Crosstown Bus—we were rehearsing in the basement of a dress shop in downtown Denver. We were playing away, and kept hearing this rattling upstairs. There was a blinding snowstorm, it was the dead of winter, there was a kid with a guitar in his hand, and he said, 'Hey man, can I jam with you? I heard the music.' We wanted to blow him off because he was a couple of years younger than we were. But he was so persistent that we let him set up and play. Needless to say, we fired our guitar player the next day and Tommy joined."

It was during this period that Bolin and Cook paid their dues—soon forming a new outfit, American Standard. Cook- "We lived in Denver, so we would hop in a van with bald tires and drive up in the mountains, crossing ice covered patches to play in Aspen or Steamboat Springs for 75 bucks a night. That was a great chance to bond—our common struggle. The interesting thing about Tommy, he was very humble about his gift, and he never made any of us feel that we weren't as good as he was. In that environment, we were able to grow, and become better players and better people."

It was also around this time that Bolin met his longtime girlfriend, Karen Ulibarri. Johnnie- "He met her when he was 17 and she was 18. He met her right away—he was only out there like a year and a half. I don't know how they met—probably at a gig."

When Cook decided to relocate to England, Bolin looked elsewhere— hooking up with Zephyr, in 1968. But instead of showcasing their young guitarist's talents, the group's sound was largely based on singer Candy Givens' Janis Joplin-esque wailing. The group did give Bolin his first major label appearance however—1969's 'Zephyr' and 1971's 'Going Back to Colorado.' Bolin convinced the others to let a drummer friend from Sioux Falls, Bobby Berge, join up for their sophomore effort. Recorded in New York City at Electric Lady Studios, Berge recalls this period helped solidify Bolin's love for jazz. "[Zephyr was] living at the Chelsea Hotel for a couple of months. Hanging out in the Village at the time, the studio was beautiful, and working with Eddie Kramer. Used to go down to the Village all the time and hang out—Tommy and myself would go see Charlie Mingus, Mose Allison. It was great."

"Tommy had so much going musically. In his mind, he wanted to play jazz from the get-go, back in Sioux City. The thing that pops into my mind is—he's like 14 or 15, and he hardly knew me, but he took the time to send me a letter in Sioux Falls. All I remember was in the middle of the letter, in big letters, was 'I LOVE JAZZ.' He underlined it. He was into jazz from the get-go, and blues, funk, R n' B, and rock. That's what set him apart from everybody else—he could play it all."

But with Bolin no longer seeing eye-to-eye with the rest of Zephyr, he and Berge split—setting out to form a new group that incorporated rock with their love of jazz. Titled Energy, Bolin and Berge went through several musicians until finding a steady line-up, consisting of Bolin's old pal Jeff Cook on vocals, bassist Stanley Sheldon, and keyboardist Tom Stephenson. "I think it was an interesting time, because Boulder was a musical mecca," recalls Sheldon. "Joe Walsh had moved to town, Steve Stills was there. All these people were putting bands together—Three Dog Night. And Jim Guercio [Chicago's manager/ producer] had his studio up in the mountains, Caribou Ranch."

Despite the fertile local scene, Energy was met with indifference. Sheldon- "Nobody really understood what we were doing. We were playing in a lot of bars and playing this instrumental fusion music, which no one out there had heard before ever. So they liked it I think, but nobody knew quite what to make of what we were doing. They would just sit there kind of flabbergasted, with their mouths open. 'What the fuck are these guys doing?' Some people got it and some people didn't."

Energy continued to press on however, as they began backing many well-known artists who were passing through town, including John Lee Hooker, Chuck Berry, and Albert King. Sheldon- "Tommy and Albert King got on famously. Albert would be playing, and Tommy had this Echoplex gadget. They'd be trading fours, and Tommy'd just blast off this amazing thing with the electronic effect, and Albert would just grin and say, 'Boy, you got me that time, but you got that box'!"

Also, it was during this time that Bolin discovered glam rock, and began incorporating flashy visuals into the mix—a gold lamé suit made by his girlfriend Ulibarri, plus multi-colored hair and leopard platform boots. But more seriously, this is widely agreed to be the era when Bolin fell in hard with drugs. Sheldon— "The club owners back in Boulder used to pay us with coke. We'd do a gig for a week, and they'd give us like a quarter ounce. And then Tommy and I would go to everybody's house and portion it out to the players. Of course, our portions were enormous and everybody else's were considerably smaller [laughs]."

Sheldon recalls one particular episode, which sadly served as a sign of things to come for Bolin. "Tommy and I were always the romanticists, thinking heroin would be fun. I can remember we were up in Cheyenne, Wyoming, he had shot up, and he almost died right then. I stood there and watched him almost die—he went into convulsions. At that point, I knew that Tommy's system was a little more susceptible to these things. He was only 20 years old at that point."

It appeared as though Energy had finally caught the break they desperately sought, when a record executive from Columbia Records expressed interest in signing the band. A showcase was soon arranged. Cook—"We came out, and the first set, we were just smoking—really on top of our game. [Energy's manager] came back with the record guy and they were very excited about the set, and said, 'Hey, we love it—I think we can make a deal. We'll see you guys later.' And of course, in the dressing room after hearing we were going to get a record deal, between sets, we decided to celebrate, and we were drinking shots. Well, we celebrated more than a little bit [laughs]. We were all shit-faced by the time we got to the stage for the second set. But what we didn't know was that the guy stayed—he saw the good, the bad, and the ugly."

With the proposed record deal down the drain, Energy's days were numbered, when one day, Bolin received an unexpected visit. Sheldon- "I was in his apartment the day Billy Cobham knocked on Tommy's door, and invited him to play on the 'Spectrum' album. Tommy had this little apartment in Boulder where he lived with Karen, on Euclid Avenue. He'd met [Mahavishnu Orchestra drummer] Billy Cobham out in L.A. through Jan [Hammer]. So Mahavishnu was in town, and Tommy had obviously made some contact with him. The next thing I knew he was inviting Tommy to play on his new solo record."

To say Cobham's 'Spectrum' was an accomplishment in the jazz-rock world is an understatement, as it helped launch the fusion boom of the early-mid '70s. According to drummer Carmine Appice, Bolin's expert playing also inspired Jeff Beck on his future instrumental classics, 1975's 'Blow By Blow' and 1976's 'Wired.' "I was with Jeff with Beck Bogert & Appice, and we used to drive together. We would listen to Mahavishnu Orchestra and the

Billy Cobham album with Tommy on it. The whole vibe of that jazz-rock mixture, Jeff really liked it. We did a song called 'Jizz Whizz,' that came out on 'Beckology' that was supposed to be on our second album—sort of the bridge between Beck Bogert & Appice and 'Blow By Blow'."

Not only was 'Spectrum' an artistic success, but a commercial triumph as well, topping the U.S. jazz album charts, and reaching #26 on the pop album charts. While Cobham's drumming and Jan Hammer's keyboard/synth skills were extraordinary, it was Bolin's fluid playing—especially on the over-the-top jamfest, "Quadrant 4"—that had everyone talking. Soon, the James Gang came a-callin'.

Led by guitarist/singer Joe Walsh, the James Gang was the stateside answer to Cream—a hard rockin' outfit who had no problem filling the spaces with only three players. But when Walsh exited the group at the height of their popularity (after scoring hits with "Funk #49" and "Walk Away"), the rhythm section of bassist Dale Peters and drummer Jim Fox decided to soldier on—expanding to a quartet with singer Roy Kenner and guitarist Domenic Troiano. After a pair of spotty releases, Troiano left, and at the suggestion of their old pal Walsh, Bolin was welcomed aboard.

Peters recalls Tommy relocating to their home base of Cleveland, Ohio. "Tommy was great. He just seemed like the right guy, played the right way—a spectacular guitar player. Very nice guy. Tommy was actually relatively quiet, just the drug thing was hideous. He'd get up in the morning and take like a zillion aspirins. I mean, like 20, just to get going. When he was high, he was great—happy, showed up on time, played great. You could tell immediately when he couldn't find anything, because man, he was just miserable. Just a massively addictive personality."

Despite Bolin's chemical dependency, there's no denying the two James Gang albums he appears on, 1973's 'Bang' and 1974's 'Miami,' are among the group's finest, and rank among the most underrated rock releases of the decade. The group also let their newest member call the songwriting shots, as Bolin brought in quite a few songs that he co-wrote with new collaborator John Tesar, and old pal Cook. While hard rock remained the group's specialty, as evidenced by "Standing in the Rain" and "Do It," some of the strongest material was tranquil compositions—"Alexis" and "Spanish Lover" (both of which saw Bolin assume lead vocal duties).

Cook recalls this period providing Bolin with his "First taste of rock stardom, because then the groupies and all the hangers on were there. It was truly 'rock n' roll time.' I think that was really what he was drawn to." But soon, Bolin was feeling restricted. "He was elated at the beginning, because it represented financial freedom, which to him, represented freedom to express musically. I do believe that the James Gang thing became sort of prohibitive to him on a musical level. There were the formula songs and the formula performances, and the rigidity probably bored him to tears. I think that's why he became discontented with it, even though it was providing a lot of money and notoriety."

Johnnie Bolin tried talking some sense into his older brother, which fell on deaf ears. "I was at his house in Boulder when 'Miami' had just come out, and Chuck Morris came over, he had something to do with managing Tommy. And said, ''Miami' is #80 with a bullet.' And Tommy said, 'I don't care what it is, I'm quitting.' You can't quit; you just did the album and wrote all the songs. Plus he moved, he was starting to make some money, had a really nice house." But Tommy had already made up his mind—out with the James Gang, and onto his next musical venture.

But by spending so much time on the road and in the studio, Bolin and Ulibarri's relationship had many peaks and valleys, as Sheldon described it as "Volatile because of the nature of the business, y'know? They were apart a lot, and there was some infidelity involved. When they were together, they loved each other hard, and they fought each other hard [laughs]. I can remember they were sitting in the back of my future wife Judy's Volkswagen, and we were driving around L.A. And Karen was kicking the shit out of Tommy in the backseat, with her high heels! And her feet were coming up and hitting us. So I slam on the brakes, and Judy kicked Tommy out of the car. So he had to walk, and then we left and drove home."

Although his love life may have been turbulent, Bolin was still firing on all cylinders musically, as he was invited by another respected jazz-fusion drummer, Alphonse Mouzon, to play on his third solo effort, 1975's 'Mind Transplant.' Quite similar stylistically to Cobham's 'Spectrum,' it showed that Bolin had retained his love of jazz-rock, as his playing once more ignited such standouts as "Nitroglycerin." Mouzon- "Tommy was a very caring, sincere and funny guy. Tommy used to call me 'Fonzi' instead of Alphonse—always funny and making jokes. He was really happy and sincere—it all showed in his guitar playing. He didn't read music but it didn't matter because he had a special gift that allowed him to memorize melodies and chord changes immediately."

Relocating to California, Tommy finally received what he wanted all along—a solo recording deal. Johnnie- "That was kind of the era of Frampton—the solo male singers. The record company said, 'Why don't you be the singer?' And he's like, 'I don't really want to sing.' But they said, 'If you do, then you've got yourself a record deal, if you don't, you probably won't have one'." Tommy wisely decided to pull double duty as a lead singer and guitarist, and got his deal.

But just as his solo career was materializing, Bolin received another phone call out of the blue, asking if he'd be interested in trying out for Ritchie Blackmore's vacated position in Deep Purple. Purple bassist Glenn Hughes recalls that "[Ian] Paice was a big Billy Cobham fan. I think he came up with [Tommy's name]. He'd heard 'Spectrum,' came over my house and played it for me, and [David] Coverdale heard it. We were blown away. I've always been interested in newer, cutting edge artists, and I was also always into 'the look' as well. And Tommy looked bizarre."

Bolin agreed to a tryout, which Hughes remembers fondly. "The first day, we were rehearsing at Pirate Sound [in L.A.]. We only auditioned two people—[Humble Pie's] Clem Clempson and Tommy. Clem didn't get the gig, not because of his ability as a guitar player; I think it was because to fill Ritchie Blackmore's boots you have to be a character. Tommy on the other hand, when I walked in and saw him, I shouted across the room, 'Whatever happens, you're coming home with me!' We were just peas in the pod together. Tommy's a Leo; he's a very sweet man, very sensitive, and very funny. An artist, you know? I saw he had the Echoplex set up on a stand, and I saw his Hiwatt's, and I could just see the way he picked up the guitar he was going to get the job. I particularly wasn't looking for a Ritchie Blackmore clone. So I think getting him in, we weren't interested in jamming old Purple songs that day. We wanted to just forge ahead. And lo and behold, we started coming up with stuff immediately."

With two commitments now solidified, the guitarist worked simultaneously on his solo debut, 'Teaser,' and his Purple debut, 'Come Taste the Band,' both released in late 1975. Both sessions proved to be loose affairs. Hughes remembers Bolin working on tracks at his home beforehand ("Gettin' Tighter"), but that Purple waited until they were in the studio to pen the rest of the material. "In Musicland in Germany, we were still sort of writing the record when we got there. 'This Time Around' was actually written in the studio in Munich. 'Ode to G' was Tommy's instrumental that we added on to 'This Time Around'—it was written separately, but we sort of forged it together. I guess if Tommy and I had our own druthers, we would have drifted off into our own camp—definitely a 'Hughes-Bolin camp' going on."

The 'Teaser' sessions resembled a big party, as Bolin invited countless musicians to stop by and lend a hand—Phil Collins, Jeff Porcaro, and Jan Hammer, among others. The result was arguably the best album Bolin ever appeared on, thanks to such "shoulda been" classics as the swaggering title track, as well as a pair of beautiful-yet-haunting compositions—"Dreamer" (which included an uncredited appearance by Hughes) and the album closer, "Lotus."

Also in 1975, Bolin found time to appear on the self-titled debut by Canadian Led Zep clones, Moxy. Johnnie—"He did that because they paid him in coke. That's all he remembered about it. He played good though—Tommy did the solos."

Up next for Bolin was an intense Purple tour schedule. During dates in Japan though, Bolin's new band mates discovered his dangerous drug habit. Hughes- "Japan was a miss because he was given some morphine, and he fell asleep on his hand, twisted—rupturing some tendons, torn or whatever. He put them to sleep. So when he woke up, we had to get him into therapy with his hands in Japan. The 'Live in Japan' record—his right hand was dead, so he couldn't play."

"We did not know that Tommy had opiate problems—downers. I found out from Karen Ulibarri that Tommy had a slight heroin problem in the James Gang, or maybe even before. Throughout his time with Purple, there were times on the Starship, our private plane, where I would look across at Tommy, and he would nod out. His face would become ridden with scratch marks. We thought it was cute—because we didn't know about the effects of heroin or opiates. We didn't enable it, because we didn't know he was doing it. Tommy would do blow with us or drink Vodka and grapefruit—that was his drink. We were very naïve and vulnerable to the fact that we didn't know that Tommy was on opiates or heroin. He wasn't on them all the time, but I can tell you that if he had the chance to get a sleeping pill, he would take it. I remember back in the day, all of Deep Purple would have our sleeping pills from the Harley Street doctors. And I think I gave Tommy most of mine, because I was never really a 'pill guy'."

While the Bolin/Purple line-up managed to improve during their stateside trek of early 1976, by the time they hit the U.K. in March, it was becoming painfully evident that the group was over. Hughes- "The shouts for Blackmore were overwhelming. And Tommy just could not deal with that. A young man growing musically, mentally, or spiritually couldn't deal with that aspect. He basically gave everybody the finger, and he played below par." Shortly thereafter, Deep Purple split.

With Bolin unable to properly tour in support of 'Teaser' due to his Purple commitments, the album never received the attention it so rightfully deserved. Soon after, Bolin entered the studio to work on a follow-up. While Bolin's sophomore solo effort, 'Private Eyes,' expectedly contained more top guitar work, it appeared as though Bolin was now attempting to go after a slightly more mature rock sound, as tracks such as "Bustin' Out for Rosey" and "Someday We'll Bring Our Love Home" brought to mind Steely Dan and Peter Frampton. But still, there was plenty of hard rock to go around, especially the near ten-minute track, "Post Toastee," a tale about a drug addict on the ropes.

But when Carmine Appice stopped by Los Angeles' SIR rehearsal studios to check out his old friend's new band, it became obvious that "Post Toastee" had become an autobiographical tale for Bolin. "He was out of his tree. I know he was taking Quaaludes, cocaine, drinking—taking whatever they gave him. Anything they gave him, he'd take it. So I remember going up to him, and saying, 'Hey Tommy, what's up man? You've got to stop doing this stuff; you're going to kill yourself. You're never straight anymore.' [Mimics Tommy's voice] 'Ah Carmine, I'm fine. I'm alright, I'll be good.' I said, 'Yeah, well you better watch it bro.' And then I [pulled aside] one of the band members. I said, 'You guys got to keep an eye on him, because he's not looking good.' They said, 'Yeah, we know'."

Appice's former bandmate in Vanilla Fudge, keyboardist Mark Stein, had recently joined Bolin's band, and also worried about the guitarist. "He was very open about [drugs], it wasn't like he did it in a closet. It was just a fact, it was a known thing. It just got worse and worse. It's hard for me to talk about it, because I can just see him in that kind of state right now. I used to talk to him all the time about it. Again, it got to the point where he just couldn't overcome that. A lot of people tried to talk to him, but to no avail."

Things got so bad that Stein decided to leave the band mid-tour. "I left the band because I was having a hard time with Tommy. Trying to get him to be a little bit more 'normal minded,' for lake of a better word. I felt he was going down a negative path, and I didn't feel like there was anything that I could do, so I thought it would be best for me to bow out. Also, I think I was at odds with some of the management and some of the other things that were surrounding him at the time as well. I just made a decision that it was time for me to leave."

During the summer of 1976, Tommy had invited his brother Johnnie to play drums in his band, and one of his first gigs was at the enormous Mile High Stadium in Denver, as part of a festival that also included Steve Miller and Peter Frampton. Ex-Energy bassist Stanley Sheldon was in Frampton's band, which was riding an enormous wave of success with 'Frampton Comes Alive.' Sheldon was surprised by Bolin's reaction after the pair met backstage. "Tommy was crying. I remember that he was just so upset that he wasn't the headliner—I think it was really getting to him at that point. I mean, he was happy for me, but he was just a little frustrated, and definitely way too high."

Towards the end of the summer, bassist Jimmy Haslip became the latest recruit of the Bolin band. An avid vegetarian and yoga enthusiast, Haslip could see Bolin was becoming increasingly destructive, and offered some help. "We were trying to get Tommy into that kind of a regimen, and see if we could curve his appetite for other things that were going on in his life. And on some levels, we were successful. Things were kind of moving in that direction for a while, and then we took a little tour break. When we got back together, we noticed that Tommy had fallen back into his old ways."

Although Deep Purple had been over for months by this point, Hughes and Bolin's friendship continued, as the pair took in an advance showing of Led Zeppelin's concert film, 'The Song Remains the Same,' in Los Angeles during September. Hughes had also struck up a friendship with Ulibarri, and when Hughes realized drugs had replaced Ulibarri in Bolin's life, a fight ensued. "I actually had an argument with him—the last time I saw him, we actually rolled around the floor of the Beverly Hilton Hotel. I was mad at him for leaving her. He didn't want her to see any more of his behavior on drugs. There was a rumor going around that he was on the needle." Soon after, Hughes and Ulibarri became an item themselves—marrying a year later.

With 1976 almost at a close, the plan for Bolin was to finish the tour in support of 'Private Eyes'—with a string of shows opening for Jeff Beck—before getting to work on his next release, supposedly a more R n' B-based affair, to be titled 'I Got To Dance.' But Bolin's lifestyle finally caught up with him in the early hours of December 4, 1976.

The Bolin band had just performed a strong set at the Jai Alai Auditorium in Miami, Florida. Afterwards, Haslip left Bolin backstage, offering some advice. "I told him to be careful." Haslip's words would prove to be eerily prophetic, as he retraces secondhand the events of that fateful night. "When I left, I heard that there was an entourage of people that ended up in Tommy's [hotel] room, and there was some partying going on. And that's when from what I understand, that there was a major problem. Tommy passed out, and basically, his body was being deprived of oxygen for some reason. He was turning blue."

"Supposedly, right away somebody wanted to call 911, and this guy who was sent out to be Tommy's babysitter put a halt to that, and said 'I'll take care of him.' I guess on a certain level, you can think about it and you figure, well, the guy's an ex-Marine drill sergeant, or whatever he was. He probably had skills in saving people's lives—the skills that a paramedic might know. Y'know, you bring in an ambulance with paramedics, that's going to bring a lot of publicity. So you can think of it on that end, that maybe he was trying to protect Tommy from any kind of strange publicity like that, and try to revive him on his own. They supposedly threw him in the tub, and started pouring cold water over him, to try to bring him back into consciousness. From what I understood—his color came back and he was breathing fairly normally. Then they got him into bed and he started turning blue again. And I think at that point in time, they did call 911. But by then it was too late, and when the paramedics got there, they could not bring Tommy back." Tommy Bolin was dead from a heroin overdose, at the age of 25.

Since Tommy's death, a sizeable cult following has developed, thanks in part of such organizations as the Deep Purple Appreciation Society and the Tommy Bolin Archives (the latter of which has issued concert and demo recordings since the mid-'90s). Additionally, annual Tommy Bolin Tribute shows are organized by Johnnie, a double disc Bolin box set, 'The Ultimate,' was issued by Geffen in 1989, and Mötley Crüe's cover of "Teaser" has appeared on several compilations over the years. As a result, interest continues to surround Tommy's music, as evidenced by 'Private Eyes' finally receiving gold certification in the U.S. in October 2000. Currently, Johnnie is working with producer Greg Hampton to issue newly discovered, pro-recorded outtakes from the Teaser sessions [UPDATE—the tunes were released as 2006's 'Whips and Roses I' and 'Whips and Roses II'].

Looking back today, Hughes suggests that had the guitarist lived, he would have certainly blurred the musical boundaries further. "Tommy Bolin today? I don't know if he'd have been playing an electric guitar—he would have definitely gone on further than most. Tommy would have been really avant-garde. Probably wouldn't have gone mainstream—Tommy would have been your 'Jeff Buckley' of the axe. He shined brightly; and he was *way* ahead of his time. He was my brother and I miss him tremendously."

Bonus Bit #1: In Praise Of "Alexis"

The greatest classic rock tune you never heard

Although Tommy Bolin's discography is littered with songs that in a perfect world, would have been hits, one in particular stands out—"Alexis." A gorgeous tune about lost young love set in the south of the U.S., it features one of Tommy's best vocal performances (his first ever on record), while the music slowly builds before erupting in a smoldering solo. The song made its official debut on the James Gang's 'Bang,' but it was written and demoed earlier in Colorado. "I think it's one of the best songs he ever did," praises co-writer Jeff Cook. "It had sensitivity, strong lyric imagery, and the music fit the mood of the song very well." Stanley Sheldon recalls that Energy did in fact "Record a version of that, early on in Boulder. Tommy, I, and [drummer] Joe Vitale cut that track. It was a really good version—it never got to vinyl, but our version I liked a lot better. I've never heard that one released, but it should be, because it was a nice version. That was the first time [Tommy] started singing, we recorded it, and we didn't know who was going to sing it, so he said, 'I'll sing it.' Johnnie Bolin recalls the song's initial recording. "I was at the studio when he first did 'Alexis.' It was a 16-track in Boulder, and he turned the lights off. He was kind of unsure of himself as a singer.

He sang all the time, but he didn't think he was a good enough singer to be a singer." Interestingly, years later, the song's lyrics came true for Cook. "I wrote the lyrics to that. The song was just a piece of fiction. When I wrote the song, I'd never been to Atlanta, I'd never been to New Orleans, and the lyrics were all just imagination. But what's very interesting, is that whole song came true in my life. Ten years later, I ended up moving to Atlanta, meeting a woman younger than myself, marrying her, and having a daughter—so we named her Alexis. And her whole family was actually from New Orleans. So the song actually came true." It remains a wonder why this standout track was never issued as a single, as it had "hit" written all over it. Cook- "I live in the constant hope that someday, somebody will cover that song. Because I still believe it could be a hit song."

Bonus Bit #2: The Top Teasers

The best of Bolin

1. Tommy Bolin— 'Teaser' (1975, Nemperor/Epic): Tommy finally gets his chance to show what he can do on his own, and boy does he deliver. A potpourri of musical styles is showcased—hard rock, instrumental jams, jazz, reggae, ballads—and Tommy's songwriting is at its peak. This one has it all, folks.

2. James Gang— 'Bang' (1973, ATCO): Many left the James Gang for dead after Joe Walsh's initial replacement didn't work out, but Tommy got the band back on track. Not as musically diverse as Tommy's solo outings, but a solid, woefully overlooked rock classic.

3. Deep Purple— 'Come Taste the Band' (1975, Warner Bros.): How do you possibly fill Ritchie Blackmore's shoes? By cranking your Echoplex up to ten, of course. Savagely panned at the time of its original release, Deep Purple's last studio effort of the '70s has aged quite well. Well worth a second listen.

4. Billy Cobham—'Spectrum' (1973, Atlantic): Jeff Beck must have taken note of this fusion classic, since it served as the blueprint for his classic 'Blow By Blow' and 'Wired' sets. Played a large part in Bolin landing his gig with Purple two years later. Bolin's wild solo in "Quadrant 4" is a precursor to Eddie Van Halen's "Eruption."

5. Tommy Bolin— 'From the Archives, Vol. 1' (1996, Rhino): Tommy left behind a plethora of demos and unreleased tunes, and 20 years after his death, Rhino issued a surprisingly strong collection of this material. Along with 'Teaser,' probably the most musically diverse Bolin release.

www.tbolin.com
www.tommybolin.biz

Classic Rock—November 2005, issue 86

Jethro Tull

A Prog Piss Take?

Ian Anderson reflects on Jethro Tull in the '70s, and why their classic prog rock epic, 'Thick As A Brick,' was among other things, a "spoof," a "satire," and a "piss take."

The late '60s saw the birth of Blackpool's own Jethro Tull, who apart from the presence of a quirky front man who played flute and hopped about on one leg, initially didn't sound much different than the rest of the blues rock pack. But once the '70s got underway, Tull transformed into an entirely different beast, as explained by leader Ian Anderson.

"At the very beginning of the '70s, we were—I suppose like many others, including the then-defunct Cream and the rampant Led Zeppelin—thought of primarily as a 'riff band.' Although there were obvious elements of folk, classical, jazz, and world music, in some of what we did. But a lot of it was riff-based—repeating motifs that were typical of that evolution, from pop and rock music to the 'thing' that became progressive rock music. But epitomized by bands like Cream, and developed in the more heavy metal sense by Black Sabbath and Led Zeppelin."

"Led Zeppelin was probably the biggest and most potent musical force at the time. We were, I suppose, in a similar vein, but not quite as grand or aggressive—or quite as 'sex, drugs, and rock n' roll' as Led Zeppelin were. We were a kind of slightly more esoteric band than perhaps the 'Zeppelins' were. American blues was the big moving force. That was what we were always looking for—a new riff, an exciting phrase."

"But as the '70s progressed, and particularly as bands like Yes, Genesis, and the early Emerson Lake and Palmer came to the fold, the bombastic and overblown side of rock music became known as progressive rock. And concept albums were the rage. We diverted in 1972, to the 'Spinal Tap version' of the concept album—a deliberate send-up, a spoof of that genre. Something that was meant to be larger than life, and a little surreal and ridiculous, in what was then the age of Monty Python. So that kind of overblown, slightly satirical side was where we fooled around for a couple of years, in '72 and '73."

As exemplified by selections from their first two albums (namely "A Song For Jeffrey" from 1968's 'This Was' and "A New Day Yesterday" from 1969's

'Stand Up'), Anderson is spot-on by describing Tull as an initial blues-based band. But soon after the dawn of the '70s, it seemed like Anderson and his ever-changing band mates—guitarist Martin Barre proved to be the only other constant member—made a conscious decision towards a more challenging and varied approach—especially on 1970's 'Benefit' and 1971's 'Aqualung.'

Anderson is quick however to point out that this wasn't a deliberate move. "It wasn't an idea, it was just a natural development from longer songs into something more continuous. But the Moody Blues were one of the first bands to do something that was recognized as a 'concept album.' It was I think in the wake of the Moody Blues, that many of the more musically adventurous bands, like Yes and ELP, went down that road. But it was, from the beginning, that approach to music did have its critics. People did see it as overblown, overly ambitious, bombastic. So it was a fitting opportunity to fool around with it in a tongue in cheek way. And I think 'Thick As A Brick' played it both ways."

Ask any '70s era prog rock fan what some of the landmark albums of the era were, and Jethro Tull's over-the-top 1972 tour de force, 'Thick As A Brick' (and to a lesser degree, 1973's 'A Passion Play'), is sure to be at the top of the list. But what many prog heads don't realize is that Ian Anderson and his Tull bandmates were actually poking fun at the genre. "We were being overtly spoof and satire oriented in the way that we did it. I guess we had it both ways—in as much as people enjoyed it for its adventurous, complex, and large-scale nature. I think we got lucky with that one—it worked both as a concept album and a piece of music—but its saving grace was that it was a piss take. And its performance on stage, and everything about the way we did it, seemed I thought pretty obvious. But looking back on it, 50% of the people didn't get the joke—they thought it was an entirely serious and grandiose work."

"But it was just a bit of fun, for the most part—as was evidenced in the lyrics and the album cover, it was I think a pretty clear pointer that we were having a bit of fun with the concept album genre. It was taken seriously, and half-seriously, by the same people that like to *believe* in Spinal Tap. The same people that like to believe in Iron Maiden, Status Quo, Judas Priest, and Black Sabbath—believe in this stuff that is sort of real. As opposed to some pantomime rock creation designed to simply glorify the often inane and quite silly side of rock music. People go along with the joke. I say the joke—of course I'm not making necessarily references to Black Sabbath, Judas Priest or whoever just being a joke, but there's a sense of humor of what they do. And I know that—I'm not great pals with [them], but have been around some of those bands, and I know they have a sense of humor about what they do."

After their dalliance with the "concept album," Tull returned (for the most part) back to basics for the rest of their '70s studio sets, with varying results—1974's 'War Child,' 1975's 'Minstrel in the Gallery,' 1976's 'Too Old to Rock N' Roll,' 1977's 'Songs from the Wood,' 1978's 'Heavy Horses,' and 1979's 'Stormwatch.' Anderson recalls that this era "Developed for Jethro Tull in a variety of ways—the folk music side came into the music. Classical and folk music were influences that continued to bare upon our music in the mid to late '70s, and less of the American forms—jazz and blues. So I suppose we were more European in our affiliations in the latter part of the '70s, particularly."

Additionally, the '70s saw several rock artists leave an impression on Anderson. "In American music, probably only Frank Zappa and Captain Beefheart. But then moving into the late '70s, there were good pop rock bands, like Foreigner—Lou Gramm I think exemplified the real age of maturity for American rock tenors. I think he was a great voice, and they had those anthemic kind of songs that Bon Jovi can only dream about. So some great pop rock music came out of that period."

As a live band in the '70s, Tull was one of the world's top concert draws, as the group played their largest gigs ever—in the UK and US—during the decade. But both do not hold fond memories for Anderson. The Isle of Wight Festival in 1970 was supposed to be the UK's answer to Woodstock, with a strong/varied line-up of artists assembled—Jimi Hendrix, ELP, Joni Mitchell, Sly and the Family Stone, and Jethro Tull, among countless others. But the festival reflected little of the peace and love that surrounded the aforementioned Woodstock.

"It felt like a social experience. I have to say, I was never one for the 'hippie thing,' and the rather laidback...and [in] the UK rather louche, sort of druggie, arty behavior. I think it was a little different to how it was in the US. So we just kind of got on with it and did our bit. It was not a good gig, it was not a bad gig, it was just a little frenetic and a little tense. Things were going around both backstage and front of house, in the sort of 'unpleasant department,' that made it a little unpleasant for everybody. But it was out of control, and the organizers were struggling to keep the thing from degenerating into something quite horrible."

By 1976, Tull had reached such a pinnacle that they headlined the mammoth Shea Stadium in Flushing, New York, over Robin Trower and Rory Gallagher. And while the "dark side" of the Isle of Wight wasn't present this time around, Anderson and company quickly realized that a stadium used for baseball and (then) US football games was not the best venue for a live music performance.

"You couldn't hear yourself because of the sound of traffic in the air—it was next to LaGuardia Airport, and so the music was completely shattered by the sound of 707's and 727's circling overhead. The absurd nature of playing in a football field with the audience miles away, and the fact that it was generally a sports event, not a concert. I remember someone pouring something from high up in the stands, as we were waiting to come down the tunnel to go onto the stage. Something wet was poured over me from high up above, and the smell of it seemed distinctly like the smell of male urine, rather than a benign watery American beer. It may well have been watery American beer, but it had been filtered through somebody's intestinal tract on the way. It was actually quite unpleasant, and I was quite glad to get out of there, I have to say. Not a memorable series of moments, for any of the right reasons. It was not something that I would remember with fondness. It just echoes of how absurd it was for music acts to play there."

Anderson also voiced his displeasure about another renowned New York venue, Carnegie Hall, which the band originally played in 1970 (briefly documented on the 1972 compilation, 'Living in the Past,' and more substantially on 1993's '25th Anniversary Boxed Set'), and again recently. "Not a pleasant experience playing in a place that sounds so bad, where you're not allowed to use your own equipment. You have to use the house sound and light systems, which are appalling, in a venue which is really just a box. It sounds actually quite horrid. And operated and run by union-ized, overpaid, under-working, and generally rather unhelpful people, who don't want rock music in their hallowed hall."

"Other concerts people remember positively, but it doesn't necessarily work in the same way for the performer on stage. I do not equate having a good show overall with people jumping and down, screaming and shouting, and visibly having a good time in the audience. That's a side event for me, I mean; I'm just caught up in my own world on stage. I don't really necessarily get terribly moved by the over reaction of people in the audience. If anything, I prefer them to under react. I prefer there to be that sense of restraint, and that sense of tension, which I find very stimulating. When people get their jollies too quickly and too vociferously, then I suspect that they're getting too easy a ride to whatever it is they're looking for."

Looking back on what is commonly referred to as the "Me Decade," Ian Anderson recalls an outlandish and turbulent time. "Probably the strange naiveté of the late '60s, and the hippie ideals began to crumble—really around the time of the Isle of Wight Festival. The first part of the '70s, I remember as really being filled with a lot of disillusionment, on the part of some young people growing up then, and the beginning of a lot of violence and unpleasantness at concerts. Provoked mainly by the audience—but sometimes aided and abetted by the police, who were overly confrontational if they saw their 'children' behaving badly. It was a kind of mixture of emotions, but above all, a period of change, from that relatively short-lived hippie ideal to something a little more dark and unpleasant. I think the true colors of certain individuals came out."

www.jethrotull.com

Classic Rock—1970s Special, issue 1

The 1970 Isle of Wight Festival

"We Want the World, and We Want it Now"—
The 1970 Isle of Wight Festival

They thought it was going to be several days of peace, love, and music—
just like Woodstock had been a year earlier. They thought wrong.
Marred by poor planning and audience unrest, the 1970 Isle of Wight
Festival turned out to be a precursor of sorts to what was to follow in the
coming decade. Several members of bands that played the festival, as well
as director Murray Lerner (who filmed most of the acts), look back on
the good, the bad, and the ugly.

You could make a valid argument that the '60s were all about trying to change the world, and that the '70s were all about the individual. Perhaps Jim Morrison summed it up best while performing with the Doors at the 1970 Isle of Wight Festival—"We want the world, and we want it now!"

"First of all, a huge crowd—potentially dangerous, but never became that way," recalls film maker Murray Lerner about the festival. "A lot of hassle between the songs, but then when the songs came, things quieted down. And some great classic rock performances, like the Who, Hendrix, and the Doors. Joni Mitchell was more in the folk tradition, but she was great, and Miles Davis, of course."

Heckling the performers, crowds breaking down fences and getting in for free, anarchists disrupting the proceedings, a fire on top of the stage, and festival organizers being in well over their head were just some of the "highlights" of the 1970 Isle of Wight Festival. As a result, there wouldn't be another Isle of Wight Festival for another 32 years.

The inaugural Isle of Wight Festival occurred in 1968, supposedly when the Isle of Wight Swimming Pool Association needed to raise money. The idea of holding a pop festival sounded like a splendid idea, and a one hundred acre field, Hayles Field (dubbed "Hells Field"), was secured as the site. Held over two days, 10,000 attendees were treated to sets by such artists as the Move, Tyrannosaurus Rex, Jefferson Airplane, and Arthur Brown, among others.

The '68 festival was such a success that its founders/organizers, the Foulk brothers (Ray, Ron, and Bill) and Rikki Farr, set their sights on putting together another festival. And this time, they planned big. Able to convince

Bob Dylan to come out of his "exile" to play his first show in a dog's age, the 1969 Isle of Wight Festival was held at Forelands Farm, Wootton, and attracted 100,000 music fans.

And this time, the crowd was treated to three days of music—including the Who, the Moody Blues, and the Band (both on their own and backing Dylan), while spectators included various members of the Rolling Stones, the Beatles, and Pink Floyd, as well as Elton John.

With the festival growing by leaps and bounds between its first two years, there was no way anyone could have predicted the amount of people that would turn up for the 1970 edition. Now stretched over five days, the festival featured some of the world's biggest music names—Jimi Hendrix, the Doors, and the Who, to name but a few.

Sensing that the audience would be even larger than the previous years, a new festival site was scouted. And the organizers thought they'd found a keeper at Churchill's Farm in Calbourne. But when they were unable to secure it (allegedly because a member of the city council expected a "cut" of the earnings), it was determined that the 1970 Isle of Wight Festival would be held at Afton Farm. Only one small problem—it was overlooked by Afton Down, a hill that created a perfect view of the stage. Despite knowing that there would be a large number of non-paying patrons camping out on the hill rather than paying for entry, the Festival went ahead.

Director Murray Lerner was no stranger to filming music festivals, as he had directed the Academy Award nominated 1967 film, 'Festival!,' which chronicled the highlights from several years of the Newport Folk Festival in the US—which included Bob Dylan's first ever "electric" performance. By 1970, Lerner was ready to document another music festival on film, and hooked up with the Isle of Wight.

"It was bigger than Woodstock, it had 600,000 people," explains Lerner. Dylan was there the year before—he put it on the map. They had 150,000 people at that time. But because he had been there, it got a lot of attention, and became a big deal. You might actually call the film 'Bob Dylan Once Sang Here' [laughs]. I'm serious, because the fringe element—the kids that said they didn't have money to sleep anywhere or do anything—that was called desolation row, after his song 'Desolation Row.' [It] became the byword of the fringe element, which was not such a fringe element—it was hundreds of thousands of people. Huge. You see it in the aerials if you saw the film."

But almost immediately after he began filming, Lerner discovered an unexpected "vibe" surrounding the 1970 festival. "I think that whole movement began to break apart. It started with the Newport stuff, and then became commercialized, and the kids got upset about the commercialization and the money part that was going on in terms of co-opting the music. So there was a lot of 'back-and-forth.' And then they were radicalized by…I guess a certain element went to radicalize these kids. To get these kids to think about what's wrong with society essentially. When you get that many people, and one guy starts 'Let's get in for nothing,' there's a ripple effect. So they all want to get in—smashing the fences."

Lerner also recalls "A lot of trouble in terms of the crowd. There were no fatalities, unlike some other places. Then there was the potential fire which we show [in the film], but it was just a guy was told two weeks earlier to schedule fireworks. And without thinking, he just shot them off, and everyone thought, 'OK, the stage is being attacked by flame' [laughs]. I thought that was 'it'."

As with most multi-day long festivals, the first two days—26 August and 27 August (a Wednesday and a Thursday)—featured mostly newer artists, as a sort of warm up to the bigger acts that were to follow. Included were performances by such then up-and-comers as Supertramp and Terry Reid. Lerner remembers the first days featuring artists that were embraced, and also rejected, by the still-assembling crowd.

"David Bromberg received a phenomenal reception from the audience. It was funny because he thought that they were booing him. They weren't— they were cheering him. When he got off the stage, he said, 'I'm a star!' You would've thought that Bromberg was going to be the biggest star in the world that night. I think he had four encores."

Unfortunately, a then-unknown Kris Kristofferson didn't fare nearly as well. "He had a lot of difficulties with the audience. I think just because his voice was lower than most were used to, and there was a lot of catcalls. He said, 'I guess we'll finish, providing we're not shot.' Then he walked off the stage without taking a bow or anything. But on the other hand, it kind of set the stage for his fame. Because a guy who was really important at the festival became his manager, and built him up right after that. He became not only a singing star, but a movie star."

When Friday, 28 August rolled around, the festival was truly gaining steam, and quickly reaching it's peak attendance figure, said to be 600,000.

One of the first true standout performances of the '70 Festival came on this day—Chicago. Although they later became known as power balladeers in the '80s, Chicago early on was much more rock-based (led by the late/great guitarist Terry Kath), with a blazing horn section that made them stand out from the pack. Chicago's sax player, Walter Parazaider, recalls the events leading up to their set.

"They had us in a holding area on another island, with cottages and everything, which was just spectacular. The weather was great. Isle of Wight was our first experience at [playing festivals]. And you talk about people being really young—eyes as big as silver dollars, and taking everything in. From the campers backstage—the people that were the modern day gypsies. My wife and I were just walking around, taking in the whole backstage area—that was a show within itself. I just remember walking by different people that were from Austria, Germany, or whatever. I thought of the old 'Dracula' or 'Wolfman' movies, where there was a gypsy cart. I remember sitting with a bunch of people, and realizing they were gypsies. There were areas back there where you could warm up."

Parazaider also remembers being overwhelmed by the event. "The whole spectacle of it was amazing. It was massive. And when you get that amount of people—just a whisper from a crowd like that is a roar. It's an unbelievable thing. And if you don't keep within yourself, you could just as easily throw your horn in the crowd and run around like a lunatic just freaking out from it."

But Parazaider and his band mates needn't have worried, as they were warmly received by the crowd. "The crowd was very receptive, and it was very receptive from the start. We wondered, but that first album [1969's 'Chicago Transit Authority'] had 'I'm A Man' on it—a cover of a Spencer Davis tune—and it had gone over quite well in England. They knew the material and we were quite well received."

"It was one of the highlights of our career—it was a knockout. To play in front of 600,000 people—at that point in our career, we were nuts. We were just sky high from the whole experience before we even hit the stage, and had to really keep our feet on the ground, and pay attention to our business, which was the music. We all sort of hung together, I don't want to say spiritually, but we were all close in the original band. On stage, we just sort of hung together to keep ourselves together to survive a maelstrom—like 600,000 people yelling. To compare that to any other shows, at that time, it was the epitome of anything we had done."

Later the same day, the crowd was treated to further sets by Procol Harum and the Voices of East Harlem, before the day ended in the wee hours of the morning, with a set by hard blues rockers Cactus. Cactus' drummer, Carmine Appice, recalls that the festival's main attraction for many, Jimi Hendrix, had turned up early to hang out. "The thing that I remember the most is the fact that we were hanging out a lot backstage with Hendrix. It had sort of a 'tent' kind of vibe—everybody had little areas where they hung out. Hendrix was hanging out with us—he and Jim McCarty [Cactus' guitarist] were real close. And we knew Hendrix for a long time—I knew Jimi since '65, before he was even 'Jimi Hendrix'."

"I remember a lot of jamming going on, with two guitars and banging on tabletops. It's too long ago to remember conversations. At these festivals, there was always a lot of drugs. We used to drink a sip of wine backstage, and you didn't know—sometimes it would have mescaline in it or something weird. Everybody's pot smoking. It was a pretty fun backstage area. That's the thing I remember most about it. It wasn't like the best of circumstances, as far as the backstage areas. From what I remember, it was some sort of tent area."

Appice remembers that the weather had taken a turn for the worse during their set. "It was cold—it was rainy. I think it was damp and foggy. Horrible. I don't remember it as being a tremendous show. I think the Isle of Wight was a bit of a disaster. And that was the drag of being a headliner of those kind of festivals, because that used to happen to us with Vanilla Fudge when he headlined some festivals. By the time you go on, it's like the wee hours of the morning, and your audience is going away. I mean, you look at Hendrix playing Woodstock—he had nobody there. It became such a legendary performance, but nobody was there, which is pretty funny. He played to an empty house, whereas Santana played when the place was packed. It was the same kind of thing here, but I don't think they had a lot of people. I might be wrong, but it didn't stand out—the performance—in my head."

Appice also recalls the growing unrest among audience members led to an indifferent reaction. "I remember something about that. But maybe that would account on why it didn't leave an impression as far as the audience—maybe the audience response wasn't great for everybody, because they were all pissed off. Sometimes that happens."

Saturday, the 29th would feature the most acts during a single day, as twelve wildly musically varied performers took the stage. But perhaps it was *too* varied—most of the attendee's were ready to rock along to the likes of Hendrix, the Who, and the Doors. When folk singer/guitarist Joni Mitchell hit the stage early, trouble soon started. A clearly 'out of it' gentleman hopped up on stage uninvited, which led to the crowd voicing its disapproval when he was forcibly removed from the stage.

Lerner: "There was a famous scene where the crowd was yelling and yelling, and keeping her from singing. One guy came on the stage to try and interrupt her. She decided to face down the crowd, and was playing the piano, vamping, and almost crying. Said to the crowd, 'We've put our lives into this stuff—you're acting like tourists.' That changed the whole tenor of it. That was a very dramatic scene. Some people were afraid—she decided not to be afraid, she told me. She called the crowd 'The Beast' and she decided to face them down. Because she had had problems with other places, and had given in. But she decided in this case not to give in."

"I would say it was always on tenterhooks—was the crowd going to rush the stage? If they did, that would be the end. I was always worried about that, but they never did. It was really frightening when she was on. It's hard to imagine when you have those many people in front of you, I can tell you that. I was always worried, because I didn't understand what 'a crowd' was until that festival. Then I realized there was nothing you can do—if the crowd moves, than it's the end. You saw it in the Cincinnati thing [when fans were crushed to death trying to enter a Who concert in 1979]."

Although Lerner pointed out that Mitchell had earned the crowd's respect by the end of her set, the crowd's reaction prevented what would have been undoubtedly been a festival highlight. According to the 1995 book 'The Visual Documentary' by John Robertson, Neil Young was going to duet with Mitchell, but changed his mind after witnessing the friction—leaving the festival before the end of Mitchell's set.

Since the crowd was on edge, it didn't seem like the wisest idea to put Tiny Tim on next—a gentleman best known in the US for his TV talk show appearances, and for strumming the ukulele/singing in an impenetrable falsetto. But Lerner was in for a big surprise. "Tiny Tim the audience went wild for! Because it was like a campy reaction. You would have thought that he was the biggest star in the world." Although his band didn't play until the following evening, Jethro Tull's Ian Anderson also remembers Tiny Tim at the Isle of Wight—but for other reasons. "I will always remember Tiny Tim, who seemed an innocuous fellow, in a rather James Brown/Chuck Berry kind of vein, refusing to go onstage until he had the money in cash in a briefcase, at his feet. Not exactly in that with the spirit of the age."

With Tiny Tim's set completed and the crowd "back on track," Miles Davis stepped up to the mic. In the midst of his groundbreaking jazz-fusion period (which would see the release of two all-time classics, 1969's 'Bitches Brew' and 1970's 'A Tribute to Jack Johnson'), the famous trumpeter/band leader had the crowd in the palm of his hand, remembers Lerner. "Miles Davis was a surprise and really unusual. A really great performance. I liked his electric period, so I thought this was great. It was a revelation. It had pieces of 'Bitches Brew' in it and stuff like that, but it was an amalgamation of different things. I was amazed that he was there, and the crowd really liked it. It was fantastic—he just went on and played, waved his hand at that audience, and walked off. And that was it [laughs]. He played for approximately 38 minutes straight, without stopping. I wondered whether it was going to be accepted by the audience, or whether I would like it."

After Ten Years After had laid some more blues rock on the enormous throng, the second-ever performance by prog rockers Emerson Lake and Palmer unfolded. ELP's singer/bassist, Greg Lake, recalls the vastness of the crowd. "The enduring memory is the actual physical sight of that many people. It was the first time in my entire life I'd seen that many people all together at one time. I supposed before that time, the only other time you'd see that many people gathered together, would have been a war. It was the first time in peace time that that many people had assembled in one place—peacefully—to listen to music. At least that I had seen. So it was a staggering sight to look at. It was also the second show of ELP. So that was kind of bizarre. The night before we had played to something like a thousand people, and then the next day, it was 600,000. So it was as shock."

Lake also remembers the festival not exactly reflecting the "peace and love" vibe of the times. "The whole nature of those festivals—Woodstock and the Isle of Wight—there was a kind random chaos taking place. In a way, it was all meant to be relaxed and 'peace, love, and have a nice day,' but there kind of was a tension about the whole thing. Because of the vastness of it, there was this tension going on all the time. And of course, you had some very important entertainers on the bill. It was a highly charged event—sort of cosseted in this 'hippie/anything goes' cloak. It was a strange sort of dichotomy of elements, really. And that was more or less my memory. The actual playing of the show was over very fast, and one concert tends to feel much like another one. You do the best you can, and most of it is out of your control—other than the playing, really."

The crowd's response to ELP was very receptive, according to Lake. "It was a shock to the system, and we were very different from all the other acts on the bill. I think mainly because the music that we were playing was largely European-influenced, as opposed to most of the other music on the festival, was really, in one way or another, American-influenced. So there was a difference in that point of view."

Lake and company also managed to dodge a possibly disastrous situation, when a stage prop went awry. "The one thing we did decide to do for a bit of a spectacle, we decided to fire these 19th century cannons, at the end of 'Pictures at an Exhibition'—to sort of emulate 'The 1812 Overture.' It was just a bit of a stunt really, and what happened was unbeknownst to us in the band, the road crew had doubled the charge in the cannons. We had tested them the day before for safety, with the appropriate charge in. But they had somehow decided overnight that it would be cleverer to double it. So when it came time to fire these things, we had it on a footswitch. Keith [Emerson, keyboards] and I both pressed the footswitch at the same time, and all I can remember was seeing this solid iron huge cannon leave the ground! It just took off. It blew a couple of people off the stage, and it was of course a silly thing to do, because it could have been potentially extremely dangerous. But luckily enough, there was obviously no cannonball in it, thank God! So the charge just blew out, but it was so powerful that it lifted the thing off the stage. That was the one shock of the performance."

Similar to Santana's performance at Woodstock, it was ELP's show-stealing performance at the Isle of Wight that catapulted their career. Lake: "After that festival, the very next day, ELP was the front page of every newspaper. It was indeed one of those 'star overnight' situations."

One of the more intriguing performances would be up next—the Doors. Then in the midst of singer Jim Morrison's trial in Miami, Florida (for supposedly exposing himself during a performance), the band was granted permission to briefly leave the US to perform at the Isle of Wight. According to Lerner, the Doors weren't going to change their approach for anybody.

"The thing about it that was interesting to me was Jim Morrison, who I knew, said, 'I don't think you're going to get an image because our lights are so low—but we're not going to change it.' I said, 'I'll get an image.' Which I did, I got some beautiful images by looking into the light, and making it surrealistic and abstract. It was just hypnotic, because of that way of doing it. I liked it a lot—the performance—it was low key. [Morrison] said, 'We want the world and we want it now.' I forgot what song that's from, but he was screaming during that."

"They had to leave right after the performance—they were on trial in Miami. They were let out just for that performance, because of money, so they had to leave right away. They were in a low-key mood. But I was really hypnotized by the way I photographed it and the way by looking into the light, going in and out of focus. I know that a fan magazine of the Doors said it was a fantastic performance. The crowd was quiet—big and they seemed to like it. There was no yelling during it, that I could hear. Plus, they were very tired, the audience."

If the crowd was momentarily hypnotized by the Doors, they were about to be walloped back to their senses by the Who. Then still plugging their classic 'Tommy' set, the Who handed in a stellar performance—considered one of the finest of their entire career.

Lerner: "They consider that one of their best performances. The Who performance was really fantastic—a great, theatrical presentation—with huge spotlights behind them that dazzled you. But also, 'Young Man Blues' and the new song, 'Water,' I thought was really fantastic. The ending of 'Tommy' was really incredible. And 'Naked Eye' was great—'Naked Eye' they had the lights on behind them also. 'Water' also was a new song at the time, and they said it was about Woodstock. In my interview with Pete [from the 2004 Who DVD, 'Live at the Isle of Wight Festival 1970'], I got into the philosophical aspect of a song like 'Water.' It's kind of interesting, because 'Water' has a lot to do with—I'm being highfalutin—salvation and the philosophy of his guru [Meher Baba]. I said, 'Was 'Water' spiritual?' And he said, 'Yes.' But I said, 'The rest of the song is 'And somebody's daughter'.' So he said, 'I wrote that for Roger' [laughs]! So there's that aspect of his relationship with Roger."

"And of course, Keith Moon was fantastic—playing around and having fun. He was in good shape while he was playing. I don't know what happened afterwards [laughs]. As Pete says in this interview, often [Moon] was revved up, and then when he got off the stage, he would collapse or throw up. But he took a lot of stuff to get himself in 'good shape'—energetic shape, let's put it that way [laughs]."

If the promoters were attempting to follow through with the claims of the 1970 Isle of Wight Festival being the UK version of Woodstock, it was on this evening that it became quiet apparent, as three 'Woodstock veterans' closed the evening—the Who, folk/pop songstress Melanie, and multi-member funkateers, Sly and the Family Stone.

Sly and company were one of the world's top acts by this point—mixing social commentary with songs that appealed to both rock and dance fans. Family Stone sax player, Jerry Martini, recalls a not-so-smooth arrival. "I remember we had to fly in on a little two engine private jet. It was really windy and shaky—especially going back from there. Some girl was screaming at the top of her lungs. Because they didn't just have the band members, they had other people [too]—they were just shuttling us back and forth."

"I remember the beautiful cobblestone streets, and we stayed at a hotel that had a night club there. It was just really neat. I remember the concert was really happening. However, we did White City Stadium in London at the same time—the Isle of Wight was on a series of concerts that we did. We did White City Stadium in London [and] Frankfurt, Germany—the Ferman Island [Festival] was the last one. It was exciting for us. We did well."

Martini also remembers that the crowd was receptive. "It was good. I don't remember any bad things at all. I just remember us playing our concert, going over well, and having a great time at the night club that they had there. Jam packed—it was probably the only nightclub they had at the time. I remember leaving that with a good feeling."

While Sly and the Family Stone's performance at the Isle of Wight went off without a hitch, Martini admits that it wasn't quite as magical a performance as a certain previous performance. "I don't think it was as good as Woodstock for us. Woodstock did the most for us, but it was way up there." And while other acts experienced problems at the Isle of Wight, Martini says it was nothing compared to another show the band was about to play.

"We did well at every concert, except Fenham Island on the Baltic Sea, which we didn't even play, because it was total chaos there. It was raining and storming, and there was a German gang there, they were shooting guns off—it was a nightmare. Jimi played though, but they were going nuts. It was rumored that the promoter got shot, because there was a German gang shooting off automatic weapons. I remember crawling on my hands and knees on the mobile they had there for us—glass was breaking everywhere. It was kind of scary."

Sunday, the 30th would be the final full day of performances—featuring the gentleman who many considered to be the headliner of the whole 1970 Isle of Wight Festival, Mr. Jimi Hendrix. In the morning, an ill-advised attempt was made to clear out the enormous audience for Jethro Tull's soundcheck, to ensure that those without a 'five day pass' would pay the fee for the day's festivities. According to Lerner, the scene soon turned ugly.

"[Tull's] soundcheck was very dramatic in the sense that they tried to empty the arena during the soundcheck—a famous scene. Of course, they couldn't. People had one day tickets as well as overall tickets, so they figured, people would just stay and not pay. The attempt to empty the arena was really funny—it was impossible. Then they said, 'They're not going to do a soundcheck unless you leave, then [Tull's] manager Terry Ellis said, 'Don't tell them that, because we don't care if they're here.' Kind of a nice scene—very dramatic."

"They tried all sorts of things to try to get rid of the people but they couldn't. They were all very tired—they'd been up all night. They were saying stupid things, and they thought the radicals were French, who were giving them a hassle. So the announcer that worked for the festival said, 'Hey, does anyone here speak French?' So out of nowhere, this girl came. And of course, spoke French very crudely, so the whole crowd was snickering. Then she really got into being part of the administration, and said, 'If you haven't paid, you've got to leave.' She said, 'I'll know what we'll do—those people who have tickets, burn your tickets, and then we'll know you have a ticket.' She said, 'Let's see these fires.' It was stupid. You're talking about 100,000 people, they weren't going to leave easily." Soon, the audience was throwing debris at the stage.

Around this time, a van of young hopefuls pulled up the site of the festival—in hopes of being granted permission to play an impromptu set. It was agreed that they could indeed—but outside the festival. That band was space rockers Hawkwind. Hawkwind leader Dave Brock still remembers the day well. "We all decided we would head off to the Isle of Wight, it's one of those sort of 'iconic' sort of festivals and go and play there outside. Which is what we did! The festival itself was quite a nice spot actually. What you've got to remember is the Isle of Wight has some lovely chalk cliffs. But the actual festival itself had all of these big corrugated sheets—it was like a prison camp. Once you're inside the festival, you're in this corrugated prison camp. We of course didn't want to go in there, we just thought, 'OK, we'll set up our gear and play outside.' Outside the festival there was this big sort of 'Canvas City,' which was a gigantic sort of inflatable tent, which was blown up—it has a generator running it, blows the air up, and the whole thing gradually inflates up. Someone came along and said, 'Hey, would you like to play inside.' And we said, 'Yeah, we'd love to.' So we actually played inside this inflatable sort of tent. The generator ran out, and [the tent] started sinking down!"

Brock also recalls drugs being passed freely amongst the crowd. "We all took loads of LSD of course. Our lead guitarist, Huey [Huw Lloyd Langton], freaked out very badly, because he'd been spiked up on some orange juice, that was in the front of our yellow van. Unfortunately, I had some as well. The worst thing was, when I went back to the van, someone said, 'Don't go in the van, because I think Huey is having a bad time.' I said, 'Why is that?' And he said, 'Oh, he drank somebody's orange juice—it was on the dashboard, it's spiked with LSD.' I went, 'Oh no!' And suddenly, I had this great rush come over me—I was all tingly and peculiar. It was very strange LSD, actually. I had this lady with me, who took me away up to the cliff tops for a walk, to try and calm me down."

Additionally, Brock recalls bedlam going on outside the gates of the festival, and also a close brush with one of rock's all-time great guitarists. "There were a lot of anarchists-going's on's. They were all into saying that when the festival has made enough money, then the fences should be down, and all the people outside should be allowed in. And of course, they started ripping the fences down. There was a lot of bad scenes—people threatening each other and all that. There were I supposed about 10,000 people outside the festival."

"When I was telling you about this 'Canvas City' deflating, Jimi Hendrix actually came in there, funny enough, to see what was going on. Because he sort of kept tabs on what was going on, and we had our saxophonist who had his face half painted silver. I think in the Hendrix set, he actually dedicated one of the numbers to 'the guy down in the front with a silver face,' which is Nik [Turner], our saxophonist at the time. Nik eventually got around to talking to him and asked him if he'd have a jam with us in this big canvas structure. But by the time he got there, it was deflating and people were all standing with their hands up trying to support the thing—it was about eight foot high."

Back inside the festival, an early standout performance of the day was the Paul Rodgers/Paul Kossoff-led Free—who was supporting their classic 'Fire and Water' release, and monster hit "All Right Now." Lerner: "To me, they were a revelation. I had never heard them before. I thought they were fantastic—their energy and their sensibility. And 'All Right Now' to me was really a thrilling song—it was very unusual, I didn't know what it was a blend of. It wasn't hard rock, yet it was rock."

Soon after Free's set, another performer impressed Lerner—the Moody Blues. "I think it was at twilight, and the lighting was unusual. I liked the singing, which was a little different—it was more melodic than most of the other groups. Especially 'Nights in White Satin.' I guess they were progressive rock, but speaking as a person who didn't know that much about it at the time of the festival, Emerson Lake and Palmer was progressive rock—very different than the Moody Blues. I liked the sensibility they revealed when they sided with the crowd, essentially. They were sympathetic to the crowd—that I remember quite well, and the beauty of the light at the time they performed."

Hawkwind's Brock recalls making it into the main area, in hopes of catching the Moody Blues' set. "I saw the Moody Blues there actually. Everything ran late there. After the fences came down, we actually went inside there to see some of the bands. I had that really strong acid during the day, and by that time, I'd been given a Mandrax—a sleeping tablet to calm me down. I think I feel asleep, which was a bit of a shame, because I was quite looking forward to seeing them!"

Hendrix's performance was now growing near and anticipation was building—there was only one more performer to go, Jethro Tull. Tull leader Ian Anderson has not-so-fond memories of the Isle of Wight, despite handing in a very strong performance. "Things were going around both backstage and front of house, in the sort of 'unpleasant department,' that made it a little unpleasant for everybody. But it was out of control, and the organizers were struggling to keep the thing from degenerating into something quite horrible.

There were some unpleasant degrees of rioting, violence, and bad behavior—more than one group of people who were intent on wrecking the festival. It was perhaps a testimony to the local police and generally the welcoming residents of the Isle of Wight, that the thing happened at all. It could have gotten really nasty. And for a while, around the time that we were taking the stage—it was looking a little tense around that period of time." The tenseness soon subsided however, and Tull handed in one of the festival's best sets.

Interestingly, it was Tull's refusal to play Woodstock, that set up their Isle of Wight appearance. "We were invited to play Woodstock and we didn't, mainly because I didn't want to spend my weekend among a bunch of unwashed hippies. And I didn't really think it was a good thing for us to do from a career point of view. I think that may well have been proven right, because it was both the big moment and the last moment of our peers Ten Years After, who had been born of the same music stable—in early Chrysalis Records and management side of things. Well, some other acts on there that did go on and survive pretty well, namely Joe Cocker and the Who. It was also too much of a defining moment for a brand new band. It would have been the beginning and the end for us, as it was for Ten Years After. So I think we were best off not doing that one. And the Isle of Wight Festival seemed like a bit of tamed fun, compared to Woodstock. As it turned out, I think it was a defining moment in that change from the hippie ideals to the rather dark and more pragmatic side of music."

It also turns out that Tull went on, knowing that getting paid for their services was going to be a chore. "Not only from the point of view of the audience, who were learning a few lessons, but also as was evident backstage amongst the behavior of some of the bands and musicians. We on the other hand knew we were unlikely to get paid, and determined fairly early on that his was something that we really just had to go through and try and keep a modicum of a smile on our faces. And get through with as least drama as possible. So we just kind of got on with it and did our bit. It was not a good gig, it was not a bad gig—it was just a little frenetic and a little tense."

With Tull's set completed and Hendrix's gear set and ready to go, the MC made a most-welcomed announcement. "Let's have a welcome for Billy Cox on bass, Mitch Mitchell on drums, and the man with the guitar, Jimi Hendrix." Finally, the performer that many of the 600,000 had come to see was about to launch into a near two hour-long set, which included old favorites, as well as previews from his next proposed album, 'First Rays of the New Rising Sun.' But as evidenced by Hendrix's performance on the 2002 DVD, 'Blue Wild Angel: Jimi Hendrix Live at the Isle of Wight,' something was wrong with one of the greatest guitarists of all time. Hendrix appeared dazed throughout, while almost every song included a meandering guitar improv and a flubbed vocal line. Additionally, Hendrix appeared more concerned with constantly consulting with roadies then concentrating on the performance at hand.

As Pete Townshend reminisced in the 2001 DVD, '30 Years of Maximum R&B Live'—"What made me work so hard was seeing the condition that Jimi Hendrix was in. He was in such tragically bad condition physically. And I remember thanking God as I walked on the stage that I was healthy." Sly and the Family Stone's Jerry Martini agrees with Townshend's assessment. "His pants were falling down, [while] he was standing on stage. And I felt bad for him, because everybody in Sly and the Family Stone, including Sly, were really big fans of Jimi's. Everybody was concerned about Jimi's health. But at the time, everybody was afraid to talk to Sly or to Jimi about any problems, y'know? Usually, they have management and their representatives do that."

Murray Lerner admits that Townshend may have known more about what was going on behind the scenes than the director, since he was out front, filming the proceedings. "[Townshend] knew Hendrix better than I did. Yeah, he looked tired, but he really played well, I thought. You'd have to judge for yourself. I didn't think he was in bad shape, I just thought he was tired. He did great renditions of 'Red House' and 'Machine Gun,' which I think is as good as anything he's ever done. I mean, there's a lot of different discussions about that concert and Hendrix. He didn't give the usual wild, waving around [performance], which I like. I think it wasn't just tiredness, but I think that he was starting to feel that he was through with all that other stuff—of putting on a show—and was more into playing his music. And other people have said that also, that he was looking forward to being that way, and starting to emphasis the music more than the theatrics."

Still, Lerner enjoyed Hendrix's performance, nonetheless. "He was pretty funny sometimes. He really just improvised, and before he went on, he said, 'How does 'God Save the Queen' go?' And then he played 'God Save the Queen.' He said, 'Everyone stand up for your country and your beliefs,' and as an aside, he said, 'And if you don't, fuck you.' Then of course, 'Machine Gun' is always great, but in this case, it was like, 'Here's a song for the skinheads in Birmingham,' and for this and that. And then he says, 'Oh yeah, and Viet Nam, I almost forgot about that,' which of course, is not true—it's ironic. 'Machine Gun' was great, it goes on for about 17 minutes." Sadly, this would prove to be one of Jimi Hendrix's last ever performances. He would die just over two weeks later, at the age of 27.

Although many assume that Hendrix closed the 1970 Isle of Wight Festival, as he did a year earlier at Woodstock, this is a false assumption—Joan Baez and Leonard Cohen played in the wee hours, and Richie Havens closed the whole thing at daybreak.

Lerner recalls the last two performers of the festival. "I remember [Cohen's set] was late at night. He said some very nice things about the radical movement of the time, saying, 'We're a small nation, but we're going to grow. We need our own land, we don't have it yet.' I remember he had a lot of beautiful women singing with him—I was jealous. He had that kind of attraction I think—the suffering poet [laughs]."

"I don't consider [Havens] the last, because he played at dawn. For me, the last was Leonard Cohen. I think [Havens] wasn't on the stage—he was walking around singing off the stage. Singing at sunrise. It was very moving." With the end of Havens' set, the remainder of the dwindling crowd made its way for the exit—undoubtedly bleary eyed, hungry, and unwashed. Although catastrophe seemed to hover over the festival throughout its duration, it never came to a head.

There would obviously be other UK festivals in the wake of the turbulent 1970 Isle of Wight Festivals, but it was now clear that all future gatherings could not get by merely on the 'peace and love' ethos of the '60s. Rock festivals now spelt big business—with adequate facilities for the audience, proper security, and contracts that ensured that the artists receive their full monetary sums for performing.

Ian Anderson for one, was glad to see the "change of the guard," so to speak. "I have to say, I was never one for the kind 'hippie thing,' and the rather laidback, and the UK rather louche, sort of druggie, arty behavior. I think it was a little different to how it was in the USA. But nonetheless, the sort of hippie thing as epitomized by some of those British pop and rock bands—like

Mick Jagger for example, was I supposed someone who readily slipped into that hippie, druggie, laidback thing. It was something that I always found quite distasteful. I didn't grow up with that kind of approach to life, and I didn't readily sort of linger within that kind of social embrace. It was interesting—at the Isle of Wight, that really started to crumble."

Bonus Bit #1: Jimi Hendrix: A Legend And A Friend

Sly and the Family Stone's Jerry Martini and Chicago's
Walter Parazaider remember Hendrix.

Although Jimi Hendrix has gained a mythic stature since his death, two of the performers at the 1970 Isle of Wight Festival remember him as a mere mortal, and a good friend. Jerry Martini: "Jimi was really good friends with the members of our band—a really nice guy. He didn't have that 'star attitude' like, 'Screw you, I'm better than you.' He was just a real gentleman. I saw him [shortly] before he died at the hotel at the Isle of Wight. It was a shame—well, everybody was getting high back then, but Jimi, he just over did it."

Walter Parazaider: "Hendrix had taken us out on the road. We were playing the Whiskey A-Go-Go in Hollywood—we got done playing, I was putting my saxes away, and all of a sudden, a guy tapped me on the shoulder, and it was Hendrix! In a very calm manner, he said, 'You three horn players are like one set of lungs, and your guitar player [the late Terry Kath] is better than me. I'd like to take you out on the road as my opening act.' I don't think I had ever met as kind a human being—somebody who really wasn't ego'd out or full of himself that he didn't give a shit about other people. He was just a good human being, and he saw something in us that we didn't even see. He was generous enough to give us a shot at doing something. I said, 'How could we ever repay you for this, for how good you've been to us?' And he said, 'Pass it on.' Jimi was very articulate, but a very soulful guy. Yes, he was spiritual, and that guitar, he could make it talk. We'd sit on a plane and talk about different things. I'd say, 'Sometimes you seem real bummed out. How come you are?' And he said, 'You're going to know about this even more than me. You're going to have a lot of hit records, and you're going to have to play them night after night for people. I have hit records, and I have to play them night after night.' And I said, 'Is that such a bad thing?' And he said, 'You'll see how it'll be down the road.' I said, 'What would you rather do?' He said,

'I'd rather take my guitar and I'd rather take my old lady, and play every Southside bar anywhere in the world'."

Both musicians also recall an invitation from Hendrix to join him in the studio, signaling that he was eager to work horns into his sound. Parazaider: "He said, 'I'd like to take the horns in the studio and do an album with you'." Martini: "Every time I saw him, he'd ask me, 'Come on down to the studio man, come on down to the studio.' Which I never really went, because Sly didn't want us to record with anybody else but our band at the time. He wanted us to have more of a mystique. And I know that Jimi was really interested in getting [bassist] Larry Graham in the studio. It didn't really happen, but they had talked about it—because of Larry's innovative bass styling."

Bonus Bit #2: The Isle of Wight on DVD

Wondering where to find the aforementioned performances on DVD?
Wonder no more…

With nearly all of the performers filmed by Murray Lerner, a few of the acts have issued their own DVD's, while others can be found as part of a compilation. To view what many consider to be the best performance of the entire festival, check out the Who's 2004 release, 'Live at the Isle of Wight Festival 1970.' Long considered the greatest live rock band of all time, this release confirms it once and for all, as the cameras capture arguably the group's best gig ever. The only complaint is that several key 'Tommy' tracks are omitted, including "Amazing Journey/Sparks." Jethro Tull's 2005 release, 'Nothing Is Easy: Live at the Isle of Wight 1970,' is also highly recommended, as the group hands in (according to Lerner), "a kinky, quirky performance." Heavy on the early obscurities however, and light on the renowned classics. The 2002 Jimi Hendrix release, 'Blue Wild Angel,' is a true-to-form live document of the guitarist's set, warts and all, while the 2004 Miles Davis release, 'Miles Electric: A Different Kind of Blue,' features some great jazz-fusion playing. Lerner also finally released his 'Isle of Wight movie' in 1997 ("I was a bad salesman," he jokes), 'Message to Love: The Isle of Wight Festival,' which collects performance highlights and behind-the-scenes footage. According to Lerner, more Wight-related DVD releases are forthcoming—an ELP release is set for early 2006, and an agreement was met to release Joni Mitchell's set on towards the end of 2006. Additionally, Lerner is currently in discussions to release a DVD of the Doors' performance. Unfortunately, we will never see Chicago or Sly and the Family Stone's performances on DVD—both acts declined to be filmed.

www.isleofwightfestival.com

Classic Rock—The Great Rock Festivals Special Issue, 2008

William Shatner

Keep On Trekking

Once more, William Shatner boldly goes...into a recording studio. Greg Prato sets his microphone to "stun."

Whenever a new William Shatner musical recording appears from a galaxy far, far away, it's time for Trekkies and fans of anything-but-ordinary music to rejoice. The former captain of the U.S.S. Enterprise recently took the time out—well, more like nine minutes—to look back on his past and present musical cosmic voyages. Prepare for lightspeed...

"What's your expectation? Shall I start talking?" Out of the jillions of phone interviews this interviewer conducted over the years, here I was, momentarily baffled at such a straightforward—yet unexpected—question. But this question was not coming from any run-of-the-mill interviewee. No, no, no. This was coming from the incomparable Mr. William Shatner. A modern day renaissance man if you will, Shatner will forever be best known as James T. Kirk of 'Star Trek' fame. But in the ensuing years, Shatner (or as his assistant refers to him, Bill) has stuck his fingers in as many pies as possible—author, actor, TV commercial pitchman, and even singer. In fact, to this day, his cult classic album, 'The Transformed Man,' continues to pick up fans due to Shatner's so-dramatic-it's-comedic-genius vocal delivery.

But getting back to the initial question that Shatner lobbed my way...what exactly was my expectation with this interview? Did I expect it to teach me the true meaning of life? Help cure society's ills? Turn me into a "Transformed Man" as well? I decide to keep mum and let the chips fall where they may. Like an old pro, Bill took hold of the reins, and decided to discuss his latest musical endeavor first.

While not as "brilliant" as the aforementioned 'Transformed Man' or his other musical forays (which we'll get to in a little bit, don't worry), this year's 'Exodus: An Oratorio,' sees Bill get downright Biblical on us, putting passages from the Bible and the Haggadah to a swirling symphonic accompaniment. Despite not featuring a single drop of rock n' roll on it, the CD shows Shatner in his preferred element—as the center of attention, pontificating in front of a live audience.

"The CD is called 'Exodus.' It's an edited version of a Biblical chapter, and it has original music written to it by David Itkin. 350 voices sing the chorale and it has a 72-piece orchestra—if everybody bought the record who worked on the record, it would be a best seller! It's a really good oratorio—I think something very interesting happens between the audience and the actor, and that can be heard on the recording. It's a very palpable feeling from the audience, as they hear what we had to do and at the end, you hear them explode into applause. It's really a meaningful record for me. It was done in Arkansas with the Arkansas symphony, and it was a personal pleasure to have worked with them. It was an original—a world premiere. So we didn't know how exactly it was going to be taken. The audience's reaction—which was wonderful—was a surprise. A good surprise, and an enviable surprise."

OK. With 'Exodus' out of the way, it was time to start getting to the real nitty gritty. Back in the late '60s, when 'Star Trek' was still on its original run on TV and "William Shatner" had just started to become a household name, Bill was offered the chance to record a musical album, and in several instances, classic poetry was connected to then-current pop hits (including Bob Dylan's "Mr. Tambourine Man" and the Beatles' "Lucy in the Sky with Diamonds").

Depending on whom you speak to, the resulting album, 1968's 'The Transformed Man,' is either a fascinating Andy Kaufman-esque is-he-serious-or-is-he-joking? tour de force, or one of the most indulgent and bombastic recordings ever committed to tape. In fact, in 2003, viewers of the digital TV channel Music Choice were asked to vote in a poll to determine "The Worst Beatles Cover of All Time." Beating out some very stiff competition (including such stinkers as Bananarama's "Help!" and the unforgettable Pinky and Perky's "All My Loving"), Shatner took the top prize with his rendition of "Lucy in the Sky with Diamonds."

But in the album's linear notes (penned at the time of its original release), Shatner could barely contain his excitement at his heady accomplishment upon first listen, as he gushed, "Now I've had some great thrills in my career, starring on Broadway for the first time in 'The World of Susie Wong,' playing in my first motion picture, 'The Brothers Karamazov,' going on stage for the first time in Shakespeare's 'Henry the Fifth,' but the thrill I got from hearing this album all the way through was deeper and more satisfying than anything I had ever experienced. The three of us [referring to the album's producer, Don Ralke, engineer Stan Ross, and himself] sat there alone in the studio transfixed until 2:00am. I had a 5:30am call at 'Star Trek' that morning. But I walked out of the studio on air and soared through the rest of the day. I was really in orbit!"

Bill was willing to give some insight into the story behind this wondrous audio asteroid, exactly 40 years after it first came crashing down from orbit. "'Transformed Man' was a concept album. My thought was to relate literature and the literature of the day—which was essentially songs. So original music was written to the literature, and then I spoke the songs as a piece of poetry, as I did with the literature. The whole thing had a theme to it. Sometimes, the songs correlated in philosophy with the literature, and sometimes, it opposed it. It was an interesting concept—not totally successful—but there were elements of it that I thought were very good. As a result of having done that record, Joe Jackson and Henry Rollins, for example, had heard it, and years later, when I was allowed to do another record, wanted to be part of the second record—because of 'The Transformed Man'."

Does Shatner have any standout memories of the sessions? "I don't remember, it's been some years. But the literature I think was Cyrano de Bergerac's speech, which ends [with] 'I may climb perhaps to no great heights, but I will climb alone,' segued into a drug song, 'Lucy in the Sky with Diamonds.' I was correlating a man who was going to make it on his own, with a man who needed drugs to help him." But Mr. Shatner suddenly becomes a bit distant when asked what is his take on a select number of earthlings who consider 'The Transformed Man' a stone cold classic. "I don't know—I'm going to leave that to people like yourself." Fair enough.

Despite 'Transformed Man' not exactly doing battle with Herb Alpert a top the album charts at the time of its release, Mr. Shatner wasn't ready to turn his back on music. In the ensuing years, he would sing (actually, more specifically, *speak*) several songs on such U.S. TV shows as 'Dinah!' (Harry Chapin's "Taxi") and 'The Mike Douglas Show' (Frank Sinatra's "It Was A Very Good Year"). But come 1978, at something called 'The Science Fiction Film Awards,' Bill—who was also the host of this televised event—decided to take on the Elton John/Bernie Taupin classic, "Rocket Man" (a performance which was even introduced on-stage by Taupin). The result? Another so-bad-it's-outstanding classic, which sees Bill dragging on a cigarette, while a total of *three* William Shatners ultimately appearing on screen—all taking turns with the lyrics. Unfortunately, Bill takes a pass on a deep analyzation behind his stunning "Rocket Man" interpretation (which can be viewed—along with the aforementioned Chapin and Sinatra covers—in all its awe-inspiring glory on YouTube). "The 'Rocket Man' performance was for fun, and was not supposed to go anywhere but stay in that small arena. Somehow, it's been used again and again. We all have fun with it."

Throughout the '80s and much of the '90s, Shatner's musical career tragically took a backseat to appearances on such TV programs as 'T.J. Hooker,' revisiting the Captain Kirk character in several 'Star Trek' movies, and penning 'Star Trek' books. However, come 1998, Shatner was ready to whip his vocal chops back into shape—upon an introduction to singer/pianist (and Shatner fan) Ben Folds. "Ben Folds wrote me and wanted to work with me. I agreed to. He wrote a song for me, called 'White Oleander' (later re-titled 'In Love'), for his album, 'Fear of Pop.' That song became popular, I did that song in concert with him here in Los Angeles, which resulted in a record company called Shout Factory! asking me to do another record."

With Folds at he helm, work on Shatner's first full-length musical recording since 'The Transformed Man' was ready to roll. With guest appearances by the likes of Joe Jackson and Henry Rollins (and Folds himself—who co-wrote most of the songs on the record, and also produced it), the resulting album, 2004's 'Has Been,' showed that the world's first-ever rapper hadn't lost his golden touch.

"I recorded that in Nashville, and I had an extreme experience. It was really life changing. The album is a very personal statement. Joe Jackson agreed to sing the one song I didn't write, 'Common People' [originally done by Pulp]. There I was, doing rock n' roll with Joe Jackson, who's a great artist. It was an extraordinary moment. And then Henry Rollins came aboard, and we did a rhythmic song ["I Can't Get Behind That"] that Ben hired percussion people to accompany us, and then he laid tracks down himself on different percussion instruments. It was an exercise in rhythm. Among the other artists on the album is Brad Paisley, who wrote a song ['Real']…come to think of it, that's another song I didn't write. The album has been received universally great reviews, and it's something I point to with great pride."

The recording also led to several bonds being formed, and William was gracious enough to give us a peek into his circle of musician friends. "I enjoyed spending time with [Jackson]—he's a real character and a wonderful artist.

He's a very interesting man. Eating Chinese food with him—he ordered my meal. Henry Rollins has become a buddy. He's on tour almost his whole life. But when he's not tour, he comes back to Los Angeles, and I see him with some frequency then. Ben Folds is a genius. A good friend of mine now. In your lifetime, you're lucky to work with somebody you think of as a genius. And Ben Folds—in my opinion—is a musical genius." That said, are there any plans for another Folds/Shatner musical meeting of the minds? "I don't know."

Suddenly, Mr. Shatner gives an unexpected two-minute warning that the sands of time are about to run out on this conversation. However, he does have the time to plug his new book, 'Up Till Now,' co-penned with David Fisher, and out on Sidgwick & Jackson in the U.K. (and Thomas Dunne in the U.S.). "The book, 'Up Till Now'—let me get onto that because I'm going to have to get off the phone—is an autobiography. Again, getting great reviews. I point with pride at the book. It's a very personal statement, it's filled with laughter, and I also think it's touching as well. I think your reading audience will enjoy reading that book."

But let's get back to the subject of rock for a second. Bill, do you have a favorite rock album you could recommend to readers? "I wish I could be very cool and suggest one that isn't a Beatles album or something. I don't feel qualified to tell somebody to own a particular album."

OK, but..."I must go now—a pleasure to talk with you." And just like that, my conversation with a man so fearless that he once saved the world from a Tribble infestation, endured the wrath of Khan, and didn't think twice about going toe-to-toe with Henry Rollins in a vocal booth, is officially over. To answer your earlier question Mr. Shatner, yes, my expectations for this interview were certainly met.

www.williamshatner.com

Record Collector—November 2008, issue 355

Jimi Hendrix

Freedom!

*Woodstock remembered by Hendrix's bassman in Gypsy Sun
& Rainbows, Billy Cox...*

What do you remember about the whole Woodstock experience?

It was great. We rehearsed, had a house in Woodstock for maybe 30 days, and then the Woodstock Festival finally came up. We worked, practiced and rehearsed very diligently for that. And the day finally came when we did that, and it was kind of a relief off our minds. We really did it as a group. One cannot separate the music from the festival itself, for they both were magical. The people and the entertainers co-existed in the spirit of oneness. I consider myself blessed to have played at the party of the millennium. The jury is still out on [the DVD 'Live at Woodstock'], I have not heard it, did not have anything to do with the production. But I know that I was a part of on stage, and that was good music. At Woodstock, Jerry Velez, Juma Edwards [also known as Juma Sultan], Larry Lee, Mitch Mitchell, Jimi Hendrix, and Billy Cox were on stage close to two hours. The group was tight because we were well rehearsed, and we were all on the same vibe. "Jam Back at the House" showcases a cohesiveness of the group. At Woodstock, Jimi and I knew we were witnessing his "Sky Church concept." Sky Church was a vision that Jimi had shared with me when we first reunited in New York. Right here, I'm going to give you a little musical trivia—I'm the only bandmate that can say he played with the Jimi Hendrix Experience, Band of Gypsies, and at Woodstock, it was Gypsy, Sun and Rainbows. The music Gypsy, Sun and Rainbows made at Woodstock is standing right now the test of time.

What was Jimi's impression of Woodstock?

He thought we did real well. In fact, he was so into it, if you listen closely to "The Star Spangled Banner," you will see that I stayed on him. We had a vibe of our own, and I knew that I had to lock in with him mentally. And when he started "The Star Spangled Banner," that impromptu thing, you hear the first four, five, or six notes; I'm in there with him. Then I said, "Wait a minute, we didn't rehearse this, and it doesn't sound too good with me playing." I backed away, and he continued and made a classic out of that.

What do you remember about hearing his version for the first time?

It was great—it was him releasing himself. His freedom had finally been unleashed.

How would you describe the vibe at Woodstock and the audience?

Great—we went and played with the attitude of, "Look at all those people, everybody's doing something different." It's like watching television; we'll go with the vibe. So the energy from them came to us, and we threw it right back at them.

How do you feel Jimi's performance at Woodstock compares to his other famous live shows (Monterey, New Years '70, etc.)?

It's right in the cut. He was very good—excellent.

What do you think Jimi's attitude to playing live was at the time?

In the earlier times, when he was with Noel and Mitch, the songs were very simple songs—"Foxy Lady" [hums riff], "Purple Haze" [hums riff]. The songs were very simple in their formation and in their production. And then, he was growing musically, and all artists do grow. The body grows—new cells come every day. So all artists continue to grow in same way, form, or fashion—whether they're a painter, a musician, whatever. So he was growing. The simplicity of the "Foxy Ladys" and the "Purple Hazes" now went into some pretty intricate things, like "Jam Back at the House" and then later the "Freedoms," the "Dolly Daggers," and "In from the Storm." And you don't have the time to do a lot of pyrotechnics; you've got to play.

Why didn't the Gypsy Sun and Rainbows line-up ever do an album?

There were a lot of, I'll say "entities," that never wanted that group to go any further. They felt that they started off with concept of Mitch and Noel, let's continue that. This was just a whim from Jimi, get it over with, and let's go back to the original concept. But you can't go back home.

But Jimi did want to take 'Gypsy Sun and Rainbows' into the studio to make an album though?

Yeah, he wanted to do some other things. It was stopped cold.

How would you compare playing with Gypsy Sun and Rainbows to Band of Gypsies?

It was just a different thing. We had a different drummer, went in a different direction, did some different things. Like people ask me, "Do you like playing with Buddy Miles or do you like playing with Mitch Mitchell?" I like playing with good musicians who know their act. So Buddy's good, Mitch is good. I have no problems with them. We had six musicians on stage at Woodstock, and we had three on stage at the Fillmore East, so there's a difference there.

Talk a bit about the Cort Freedom bass.

They asked me to do a bass. All musicians want to do something different for instruments if they had the opportunity. So I came up with the concept 15, 20 years ago. I put it down in some file cabinets and left it there. I was approached, and I said, "Oh, I've got some stuff." Sent the drawings in, they said, "OK, we did about three or four basses." Prototype, prototype, prototype, and then finally, "Ah, this is the one." I like it, I play it every I play. If nobody else likes it, that's too bad—but I'm enjoying it.

What are some memories of being in the military with Jimi (in the early 60's)?

I first met him; we formed a group there. I felt intuitively he was unique. We became friends, and that friendship lasted a lifetime.

How would you describe Jimi as a person when you first met him, and when he became a rock star?

When I met him, he was ten years younger—when you grow, you mature. He was a little more mature.

*Was it true Jimi invited you to go with him to England when he first
went over in 1966, to play in his band?*

Yes. He called me and said, "Hey Billy, this guy's going to send me over to
Europe to make me a star." He was in New York, and he said, "I've told him
about you, you can go too." I said, "Well Jimi, I don't even have any fare to
get to New York. Number two, I'm renting an amp. Number three, I've got
three strings on my bass"—the fourth was tied in a square knot. And he said,
"Well that's OK—I'll make it and we'll get together. I'll send for you." And
that was it.

What was your last conversation with Jimi?

"Hey man, we're going back in the studio Friday, OK? Be there."

www.jimihendrix.com

Guitarist—September 2005, issue 26

Artists' Favorite Queen Songs

[As Part of 'One Vision: Freddie 60th Tribute' Article]

Jesse Hughes [Eagles of Death Metal]

"Another One Bites the Dust"

"'Another One Bites the Dust' because it's a downright-dirty-disco-fuck-song if ever there was one. It's nasty. Queen is one of those unique bands that is made up of truly gifted musicians—the minds of composers. And being able to take all that ability and channel it and control it, is best evidenced and best exemplified with this song. It's a simple vocal line—it's very compact. It's basically drums, bass, guitar, vocal, and that's it—it's not a thousand tracks. It's compartmentalized perfectly. When Brian May's guitar comes in, it's just a tight riff—no one can hold a candle to it. Combined with a simple, driving drum beat, that I dare say, has not one single fill, and a non-alternating bass pattern. Simplicity in its purest form. Honey, clearly, I am a true child of Freddie Mercury—I'm like his 'straight nephew,' as my friends like to say. Sam Elliot showed me 'cowboy style,' Magnum P.I. showed me a little swagger, but Freddie Mercury—he didn't like have a moustache, *he owned it*. It's a necessary and crucial component to who he is as a performer and a person."

Mike Patton [Faith No More]

"Bicycle Race"

"I think that Queen record 'Jazz' had some weird shit on it. I happened upon, I can't even tell you where I got this—there is this weird…it's almost like we used to trade demo tapes in the olden days of bands. But there's this kind of circle of engineers and recording enthusiasts, that collect Pro Tools sessions. Lots of big name artists from years past. I happened upon some Queen ones from that record, and the way this shit was recorded to me was *really fascinating*. We're talking about 16-tracks, with all of those vocal harmonies—I was astounded at how economical they had recorded this stuff. If you listen to how dense it is, it sounds more dense, more deep, more rich than these Pro Tools systems that you can record 96 fucking tracks on. So that I would say really impressed me—not to mention the music—but really, how the fuck did they do it?"

Carmine Appice [Vanilla Fudge]

"Bohemian Rhapsody"

"I guess 'Bohemian Rhapsody' is really one of my favorites. Vocally, it's just amazing. I just saw Queen on this tour they just did [with Paul Rodgers]—it was really great how they did that. They used a big video screen, and they used a video of Freddie singing the intro, and then the band played to him, without a click, which was pretty cool. And then Paul Rodgers came out and did the hard rock part of it. But for me, the vocals were so amazing—that was the epitome of what Queen was all about right there. I knew all those guys, I was real close with Roger and Brian. Brian invited me down to the studio when they did ['A Night at the Opera'] in 5.1 surround sound mixing. And he says, 'Just sit in the middle!' I sat in the middle, and I heard all this stuff going on around me, it was really great."

Todd Rundgren

"Death on Two Legs"

"The first Queen song that really turned me on was 'Death on Two Legs.' Even though everyone will say 'Bismillah let me go.' That particular one had all of the elements that became 'signature Queen elements'—the big stacked up vocals, the fiery guitar thing. But it also had a bit of production pizzazz. It just generally had a very quirky arrangement, with a lot of stops and starts, and syncopated hits in it. That was what made it arresting to me. I bought the album because of that song."

Charlie Benante [Anthrax]

"Get Down Make Love"

"One word comes to mind about this song—SEX! This wasn't an ordinary song. The verses were spastic and the chorus was big and catchy—and then there is the middle section that sounds like a noise orgasm. I love the way Queen sound, they always had 'their sound.' I don't know what it was that set them apart from the rest, when you heard Queen, you know who it was. Freddie was such an amazing singer, he could incorporate anything and make it sound like Queen. I have many more Queen favorites—this one is in my top five. Nine Inch Nails did a killer cover of this."

Eddie Kramer

"Good Company"

"When I was working on the Brian May pedal [Digitech's 'Brian May Red Special' pedal], I was fortunate to listen to all their multi-track tapes. It was very interesting hearing his tonal quality. There are so many fantastic tracks. There's a song, and it's multi-layered track, and [May's guitar] sounds like a clarinet, a trumpet. It's just spectacular. It's sort of old-time vaudeville-ish. It's wonderful. I never really appreciated it until I was able to listen to the multi-tracks and see how he did it. It just recently has become one of my most favorite tracks. And I say that Brian May is a bloody genius."

Curt Kirkwood [Meat Puppets]

"I'm in Love with My Car"

"I really love that song. The drummer wrote it—I love it when drummers write. The first time I heard 'I'm in Love with My Car' is just like a lot of Queen stuff—their arrangements are unique and fascinating. Their band impetus and approach is fascinating. What a lush, evocative arrangement…of something completely stupid. One of the best bands ever—everybody knows it. The musicians in the band are just wonderful. Freddie Mercury…after Elvis, probably one of the best frontmen ever. I mean, just flat-out, there's nothing you can even say about it."

Paul Stanley [Kiss]

"Liar"

"The first song I heard was 'Liar.' You only get one chance to make a first impression, and that was the song that made it for me. Obviously, they grew into something I think very different, but I remember hearing that, and as far as the personality and the sonics of it, was very impressive to me. Later on, it became something else which was equally impressive for other reasons—the diversity and the ability of everybody in that band to write a #1 song is pretty much unmatched—except by the greats."

Mike Portnoy [Dream Theater]

"Tenement Funster/Flick Of The Wrist/Lily Of The Valley"

"My immediate reaction is to pick something like 'Death On Two Legs' or 'The Prophet's Song,' which are two of my very favorites…but I think I'll have to go with a more obscure favorite. This mini-operetta off of 'Sheer Heart Attack' was a sign of bigger musical pieces and direction to come. A mini-trilogy of three different songs put together—a la side two of 'Abbey Road'—combining different styles ranging from Roger Taylor's rocker edginess to Freddie Mercury's theatrical romantic."

Mick Thompson [Slipknot]

"Under Pressure"

"I always thought ['Under Pressure'] was an awesome fucking song—it was all over the place. There's a lot in the way of dynamics—there's some building towards the end and it really breaks open and jams. And it's very moody. What I don't like about it is if you're ever playing it, and someone under the age of say, probably 28, hears it, they automatically think 'Vanilla Ice.' And I get almost violent [laughs]. I'm like, 'Hey now, don't [insult] the good name of Queen and David Bowie like that!' That bass line is so immediately identifiable, that when rappers steal shit, they tend to take stuff that's absolutely a major hook that will stick in your head. And if you hear that song, you will have that song in your head for quite a while afterwards. There's just so many aspects of brilliant songwriting in that song. I can't really think of much it doesn't encompass in that one composition."

www.queenonline.com

Classic Rock—October 2006, issue 98

The Stories Behind the Songs

"The Spirit of Radio" Rush

Prompted by rock radio becoming too structured by the dawn of the '80s, Rush wrote a tribute to yesteryear's free-form stations—and got their first UK hit single.

Over the years, countless established rock bands have attempted to either update or streamline their sound. But this certainly isn't as easy as it sounds. Some acts do manage to navigate through their "sonic makeover" intact, while others fail miserably, and at the behest of disgruntled fans, return back to their roots. Rush is one of the few bands that managed to successfully pull this off. Perhaps it was because they did not use the hope of crossover chart success as a main motivating factor—instead, it occurred naturally, and also, reflected their listening tastes at the time (the Police, Talking Heads, etc.). This change can be traced directly back to the Canadian trio's classic 1980 release, 'Permanent Waves,' and more succinctly, it's opening track, "The Spirit of Radio."

Up until this point, Rush was best known for penning sprawling epics, often with sci-fi lyrics. Rush guitarist Alex Lifeson remembers a conscious decision among he and his band mates—bassist/singer Geddy Lee and drummer Neil Peart—to depart from this style, both from a compositional and lyrical standpoint. "I think that was a time when we made a concerted effort to move away from the long thematic songs, especially the full side songs—albums like 'Hemispheres'—into something shorter. Although there are a couple of long tracks on that record—'Natural Science' is pretty long."

The group also decided to record their first release of the '80s at a studio close to home. "The first time at Le Studio. We had a great time there. It was in such a great part of Quebec, up north, a really great studio—very cozy." When asked about any specific memories of recording "Radio," Lifeson recalls an unorthodox approach. "I'm sure we did it in the control room, because that's how we worked. On a stool, sitting behind Paul Northfield, who engineered the record, with Terry [Brown] there—giving Paul a kick in the back of his chair every so often, when he drifted away [laughs]."

Peart handled the lyric writing on Rush's 1980 release, as with all Rush albums from 1974's 'Fly By Night' onward (save for the rare exception), but

Lifeson offers some insight about the song's lyrical meaning. "That song was really a statement of where radio was going, where it had been. Y'know, growing up in the early '70s, FM radio was such a free forum for music. You'd have DJ's that would play stuff for an hour. They'd just talk about the songs; there were no commercials or anything. Being so free form, really a platform for expanding music at the time. And then it was moving more towards a format, and away from that freedom. Becoming more regulated, more about selling airtime. It just speaks about that really."

Lifeson also points out where the song's title originated. "I think that was a common motto for radio stations at the time. Like, you'd hear [speaks in a DJ voice], 'The Edge, 102!' There was a station here in Toronto, CFNY, that used that as their call motto. But it wasn't really specifically about them—it was more about the idea." Also included in the song is a "tip of the cap" to Simon and Garfunkel's "The Sound of Silence"—"The words of the prophets are written on the subway walls, and tenement halls/And whispered in the sounds of silence" became "The words of the profits are written on the studio wall, concert hall/Echoes with the sounds of salesmen." "Just a play on words—Neil being a little clever," explains Lifeson.

Fitting in with the song's lyrical meaning, Lifeson had a clear vision of what he wanted the opening guitar riff to sound like. "I just wanted to give it something that gave it a sense of static—radio waves bouncing around, very electric. We had that sequence going underneath, and it was just really to try and get something that was sitting on top of it, that gave it that movement."

"The Spirit of Radio" also saw Rush touch upon reggae during a brief breakdown section, no doubt due to their appreciation of the then-burgeoning Police. But with Rush scaling back and some of the leading new wave bands branching out—once-completely different musical worlds had now come to the same intersection. As Geddy Lee stated in a 1980 interview from Rush's recent DVD, 'R30,' "All the real interesting new wave bands seem to be developing and progressing into more interesting styles. I wouldn't say that Talking Heads, for instance, are minimalistic at all. Quite subtly complex."

While Neil Peart pointed out in the same interview, "The new Boomtown Rats album too [1979's 'The Fine Art of Surfacing']—the production and music is very progressive. Very complicated arrangements and all kinds of subtle effects in it. It's just the same thing we were doing a few years ago. It's just a different period."

Although always thought of as an "album band," Rush scored their first sizeable UK hit single, when "The Spirit of Radio" peaked at #13 in the charts. Lifeson: "We're always surprised when we have a hit anywhere. We've never really been a 'radio band.' But ironically, it made sense. I think it's a fairly catchy song. It's got some good pace to it, got a good chorus—I think that's a very catchy musical moment—the guitar riff and the sequencer underneath it."

The song quickly became a concert highpoint, often used as a set-opener on ensuing tours. What does Lifeson attribute to its on-going popularity? "I think it does have a lot going for it—in terms of construction and the way it plays out. The verses have a particular feel to them, that is classic in a way. The choice of notes and chords. It is fun to play it. I still really enjoy playing it. Even the most current version of it is still pretty rewarding to do. It's probably one of the band's most popular."

www.rush.com

Classic Rock—June 2006, issue 93

"I Want You To Want Me" Cheap Trick

How did a song written as a joke and dismissed by the band as "stupid" become a huge hit and Cheap Trick's defining moment?

With the break-up of such bands as Big Star and the Raspberries, power pop seemed to be growing extinct by the middle of the '70s, as prog-rock and disco ruled the radio stations and record racks worldwide. But with punk rock bringing short-but-sweet song structures back en vogue, a new crop of power pop outfits emerged, such as Rockford, Illinois' finest, Cheap Trick. And it would be a song they'd been working up since their bar daze, "I Want You To Want Me," that put them over the top. However, it would have to wait until album number four.

According to Cheap Trick bassist Tom Petersson, the song was originally penned as a lark by guitarist Rick Nielsen. "My recollection is that he just did that song as a bit of a joke, because at the time when we had done that song, there was a lot of pop music on the radio. ABBA, and all sorts of things—disco. He thought, 'I'm just going to do an over-the-top pop song, I just want to do one that's so silly—total pop—and then we'll do a heavy version of it.' He didn't know what was going to happen with it. The idea was to have it like a heavy metal pop song. Cheap Trick doing ABBA—except a very heavy version."

Nielsen explains his unique perspective of penning the song. "I just pictured myself in a big, overstuffed chair, and my dad turned on the TV, there were like three stations. I wanted to watch Gabby Hayes—he was a cowboy—I always wanted what wasn't there, so I think that's what's got me inquisitive throughout my whole life. When you wanted Gabby, Gabby's not there, when you want your dad, your dad is not there. It was the easiest lyric I could think of, and I wish I were that stupid more often. It's like Van Morrison—some of this old songs, it didn't matter what the lyrics meant. It's how they sounded."

Interestingly, the song that has become synonymous with power pop went through a transformation. During sessions for their self-titled 1977 debut with producer Jack Douglas, Cheap Trick laid down an almost punk/garage reading of the track (Petersson- "It was more like the Yardbirds"). But the version was ultimately shelved—later popping up on the album's 1998 CD reissue. With Tom Werman at the helm for the group's sophomore effort later that same year, 'In Color,' Cheap Trick revisited the track—as a barely recognizable lounge-y version, that completely neutered its infectiousness.

Petersson- "It turned out that the studio version was produced not the way we would have done it. And we've never done it since like that anyway—with a little 'Shakey's Pizza Parlor piano' and twinky little sounds. It was like, 'Ugh'."

With Cheap Trick building a fanbase by steady touring in the U.S., word came back that they were already superstars in Japan by the release of their third studio effort, 1978's 'Heaven Tonight.' Dates were soon booked in the land of the rising sun, a sold-out performance at the cavernous Budokan was recorded, and voila, Cheap Trick finally had their definitive version of "I Want You To Want Me."

Interestingly, the song didn't stand out from the pack the night it was recorded on stage. Petersson- "That in particular, it was no more of a hit than anything else. We had for some reason had several hit singles over there, so they were just going bonkers no matter what we did. It wasn't that they were sitting there politely applauding, and then all of a sudden 'I Want You To Want Me' came on and they went wild. They were just going wild no matter what." Nielsen voices Petersson's sentiment. "It was just as bad as all the other songs that were out at the time. It's hum-able and it's listenable. Dick...I'll give it a ten!"

Petersson also sets the record straight regarding a popular rumor, that the zealous Japanese audience was so vocal that the group couldn't hear themselves on stage. "No, we could hear ourselves—we were loud."

With 1979's 'At Budokan' racking up impressive sales initially as a high-priced Japanese-only import, the bigwigs at Epic got wise and issued the album domestically. A smart move, as the album was a blockbuster hit—spurred on by the monster success of the live "I Want You To Want Me" single.

Petersson- "That was surprising—we didn't have any idea. What we think are going to be hits, we kind of go both ways—we think everything should be a hit, or we don't really expect it. So it's always something [that] is a surprise I've found—like that live record. And it shouldn't be a surprise, because that's how we were signed to a record label—people saw us live, and that was a strong suit of ours. When we did 'I Want You To Want Me' on the second album, it sounded nothing like us, and it wasn't successful. So it turned out that the live thing worked."

The "live thing" certainly did work for Cheap Trick. The album eventually racked up sales of three million stateside, made them an arena headliner, and led to an expanded version of 'At Budokan' being issued in 1998, 'At Budokan: The Complete Concert.'

Ever since, "I Want You To Want Me" has been in Cheap Trick's set each and every night. Does performing the song ever get old for the band? Not so, according to Nielsen. "We play to a different audience every night, so it's not like you're playing it to somebody who's heard it every night like we have. It makes people clap, smile, and have fun. Gee, if we were certain bands, we wouldn't do it, but we're Cheap Trick—it's good to get applause."

Bonus Bit #1: Cheap Trick Do Disco?

How the Band Almost Took the Disco Plunge

The late '70s/early '80s saw a plethora of rock veterans briefly crossover to the dance/disco charts, specifically the Rolling Stones ("Miss You"), Kiss ("I Was Made for Lovin' You"), and Queen ("Another One Bites the Dust"). It turns out that Cheap Trick was not immune to the temptation of penning a disco tune, which they did around the same time "IWYTWM" was originally written. But unlike the other acts, Cheap Trick was concerned about getting pigeonholed. Petersson- "We had done a song called 'Disco Paradise'—'Yeah, we're going to do this disco song as a joke'—and it became one of the most popular live songs. People to this day—'Oh, you've got to do 'Disco Paradise'!' We knew better than to release that thing [laughs]. It would have been a huge hit and we'd have been screwed." As a result, "Disco Paradise" has never seen the light of day.

Bonus Bit #2

Despite Cheap Trick's unhappiness with the 'In Color' rendition of "IWYTWM," the lesser-known studio version has its admirers. Nielsen- "We did a radio show with Steve Jones from the Sex Pistols, 'Jonesy's Jukebox.' I said, 'We've been re-doing the 'In Color' album ever since we finished it basically, because I never liked how it was sonically.' And he says, 'That's my favorite version!' You never know..."

www.cheaptrick.com

Classic Rock—August 2006, issue 95

"Walk This Way" Run-DMC/Aerosmith

Joe Perry thought Run-DMC were smoking crack. They weren't. They were resurrecting Aerosmith's career, and inventing rap-rock. It was 1986—times, they were a-changing...

The beginning of the now-classic video for Run-DMC's version of "Walk This Way" begins with the Hollis, Queens rap trio (M.C.'s Run and DMC, plus D.J. Jam Master Jay) trying to drown out the noise from a band rehearsing next door—Aerosmith's Steven Tyler and Joe Perry. What occurs is each faction cranking up the volume, until Tyler smashes a hole in the wall with his bandana-strewn mic stand. Eventually, a "duet" between both camps ensues. This could also certainly serve as a metaphor for how separated the rock and rap camps were at the time.

By the mid-80s, Aerosmith was a shadow of its former self. After an unfocused reunion album [1985's 'Done with Mirrors'] failed to recapture the

group's earlier glories—coupled with its members ongoing drug problems—
it seemed like Aerosmith's chart-dominating days were over. On the other
hand, Run-DMC was a band on the rise—their first two albums (1984's
'Run-DMC' and 1985's 'King of Rock') helped put rap on the map, and as
evidenced by the title track of 'King of Rock' and "Rock Box," the seeds for a
rap-rock hybrid were already planted.

But it didn't truly come together until sessions began for Run-DMC's
third album, 'Raising Hell,' in early 1986. One day while in the studio, D.J.
Jam Master Jay and DMC resuscitated a sample from their early days.

"Before rap records were made, we used to have to find beats to rap over,
and 'Walk This Way' was one of our favorite beats," recalls DMC (real name—
Darryl McDaniels). "There's something about 'Walk This Way'—when the
D.J. threw that on, the beat was so cool, the way those guitars came in [sings
main riff]. And then the D.J. would cut it back to the beginning of the beat."

"But we had never heard the lyrics, because we never let the record play.
We were in the studio one day looping the beat, and [producer] Rick Rubin
walks in. He's like, 'Yo, do you know what that is?' And me and Jay were like,
'Yeah, that's 'Toys in the Attic.' We didn't know the group was Aerosmith—we
just went off with what was on the cover. He was like, 'No, this is Aerosmith,
'Walk This Way'—he was giving us the 411 on Aerosmith."

When Rubin suggested that Run-DMC re-do the entire song, DMC
remembers the producer was met with resistance. "Me and Run were like,
'You're taking this rock-rap shit too far—you're going to ruin us. That's going
to be fake, nobody in hip-hop is going to like it.' But they persuaded me and
Jay to sit down and listen to the lyrics, so we put the needle on the record.
When Steven Tyler opened his mouth [sings opening lyrics], we got on the
phone—'Y'all motherfuckers, we're going to be ruined!' We had this big
argument."

What Run-DMC didn't know was that Rubin had already secured Perry
and Tyler to drop by Magic Ventures Studios in N.Y.C. "We went into the
studio and laid down a weak version—because we didn't want to do the
record—and then left. About eight hours later, we get a call to come back to
the studio. We walk in, and Joe Perry is playing his riff over, Steven Tyler is
in the booth doing the lyrics over. Me and Run knew we had to step our game
up. Jay was like, 'Yo, don't think of the record as 'Steven Tyler and Joe Perry's
record,' think of those lyrics as 'Run-DMC' lyrics.' So we went in the booth

and we did the switch-off. That went so good that Steven said, 'Yo, let me get in with y'all'."

In the 1997 book 'Walk This Way: The Autobiography of Aerosmith' (by Aerosmith with Stephen Davis), Aerosmith's then-manager, Tim Collins, admits not knowing what rap was when Rubin first inquired about setting up the session—but agreed when offered $8,000 for a day's worth of studio work. Perry added, "I didn't know what was gonna happen when I walked into the studio. I thought they'd show us some ideas on how to rearrange the song, but all they had was a drum track."

DMC remembers his first impressions of the Aero-duo. "Joe Perry didn't say one word, and Steven was very friendly. But Joe, it's not that he was rude, he just didn't say nothing. 'Hey Joe, what's up?' He'd nod at you, go over and play the guitar, finish his riff. 'Are you ready to play?' He'd shake his head yes. But Steve was just very friendly and inquisitive, like, 'Wow, do the D.J. thing Jay—show me how to D.J.' He was like a little kid—excited and enthused."

Also in the aforementioned 'Walk This Way' autobiography, Tyler reflected on the sessions. "Run and D and Jay were huddled in a corner, really intent on something. I go, 'Joe, what are they doing?' 'Probably smoking crack,' he says. Later we went over to the corner. They'd been eating lunch from McDonald's."

As soon as Run-DMC began playing their version of "Walk This Way," DMC knew they were on to something. "Everybody flipped out. Me and Run were so puzzled, because the reaction was overwhelming. We didn't think it was going to be a big hit, but people were loving it." Soon after, the aforementioned video clip was filmed, which MTV aired incessantly throughout the summer of 1986.

Still, DMC admits being surprised by the single's success, and how it was embraced by both rock and rap fans. "We didn't think people were going to like it as much the other stuff we did." Nevertheless, 'Raising Hell' was a smash, peaking at #6 on the U.S. album chart, while "Walk This Way" peaked at #4 on the singles chart. However, it was Aerosmith that may have benefited greater from the single's success—they soon after kicked their addictions, and embarked on a second round of hit albums/singles.

Looking back on "Walk This Way" today, DMC can see what the song single-handedly accomplished. "People tell me that it's the greatest rap record ever made, and the greatest video. VH-1 did the 'Top 50 Videos of All-

Time'—we were #1. What it did wasn't just really about Run-DMC, it was about bringing generations of music together, which is what music is supposed to do—evolution and unity."

Bonus Bit: *DMC Discovers Classic Rock*

Although long-credited as being part of one of hip-hop's groundbreaking groups, DMC has a soft spot for classic rock. "I'm a big lover of classic rock—all I listen to is classic rock. For the first time in my life, I listened to Pink Floyd's 'Dark Side of the Moon'—it changed my whole perspective of music. Then I listened to Neil Young, Crosby Stills Nash & Young, Procol Harum, Led Zeppelin, the Beatles, Bob Seger—the list goes on and on. The best music on the face of the earth, besides hip-hop, is classic rock. What I like about classic rock is they don't just talk about one thing—they talk about the world we live in. Like if there was a war in Viet Nam, they wrote about it—they didn't care if people thought it was right or wrong. They were a voice for the people. Everything else in the world will pass away, and classic rock will be for eternity."

www.rundmcmusic.com
www.me-dmc.com
www.aerosmith.com

Classic Rock—Summer 2006, issue 96

"Reelin' in the Years" Steely Dan

Walter Becker looks back on the early Steely Dan classic that deals with diamonds, geniuses, trips to Hollywood, and the importance of the almighty guitar solo.

Certainly one standout contribution that the 1970's gave to rock was the emergence of "twin guitar harmonies." The Allman Brothers, Lynyrd Skynyrd, and especially, Thin Lizzy, all popularized the use of two guitarists coming up with melodic lines that worked in conjunction with each other. But the song that probably introduced the use of this approach to the mainstream was Steely Dan's 1973 hit single, "Reelin' in the Years," with its simple yet highly memorable guitar harmonies in the middle of the song (courtesy of guitarists Jeff "Skunk" Baxter and Denny Dias)—not to mention extended solos by session man Elliott Randall, which are often considered to be among rock's all-time best.

But it wasn't the aforementioned guitarists that ruled the band. Songwriters Walter Becker and Donald Fagen (who also handled bass/backing vocals and keyboards/lead vocals, respectively) were the true driving forces of the group. The duo first met during the late '60s, while attending Bard College in New York, and was soon playing together in local bands, and eventually, writing songs for others. Shortly after the dawn of the '70s, the duo relocated to Los Angeles, and signed on with ABC Records. Thus, Steely Dan was born.

Compared to future Steely recordings that would take increasingly longer amounts of time to complete, Walter Becker recalls what made the recording of their debut album, 1972's 'Can't Buy A Thrill,' different than subsequent albums...and similar. "It went much quicker. But it was infused with as much anxiety and doubt as any of them!" The album would spawn several Steely classics (such as "Do It Again" and "Dirty Work"), but it was "Reelin' in the Years" that came together easiest, recalls Becker. "I remember that we had the chorus. We wrote the chorus and we had the musical idea for the verse, and we just ended up with that quasi-talking rhythm thing in the verse. It was very easy to write. It's quite a simple song. And then we rehearsed it instrumentally with our band up at the as-yet-unoccupied wing of the ABC Records building on Beverly Boulevard. We had never actually done any vocals until we got into the studio, so we got in the studio, cut the track pretty quickly—minus vocals and minus solo."

In addition to the song's memorable guitar work, Becker credits his songwriting partner for why the hard rockin' song turned out so well. "Donald stacked up all those big beautiful choruses that he does, and that worked really well. His range at the time was that he could really build a big chorus and make it very strong, resonant-sounding." But certainly, when many think of "Reelin' in the Years," it's the outstanding guitar work that makes the song. "For one reason or another, we decided to get Elliott Randall—who we knew from New York—and we were hoping to entice into our core circle of musicians, to play the solo on it. It's a pretty great guitar solo. My jaw was hanging open all day long. I haven't played with Elliott or seen Elliott in a long time, but he was a really unique player—and still is—in terms of how well prepared he was to play different kinds of things that most guitar players had not learned at that time. But basically being a very bluesy player."

And while Steely Dan would take an extended hiatus from live work and focus solely on the studio after the tour supporting their third release, 1974's 'Pretzel Logic,' Becker recalls "Reelin' in the Years" winning over audiences at the time more times than not during their early tours. "When we were playing live in the old days, the reactions we got were very variable, because we were almost always opening for people. But that song probably went over better than most of the other ones in the set."

However, when Becker and Fagen re-launched Steely Dan as a touring band in 1993, "Reelin' in the Years" was absent more times than not on consequent tours. "We may have played it a few times, but not that often. There's a good chance of it coming back on this coming tour. I'd say the Australians weren't too happy that we weren't playing it [Steely Dan wrapped up an Australian tour last September]. They figured, 'What the fuck? These guys finally come down here, and they're not going to play 'Reelin' in the Years'?' To which our reply was, 'Yes, that is correct!' It's hard to…the band that we have lends itself particularly to some of the more harmonically complex things. And it's more fun to play most of those things. Those really major-sounding pop/rock songs don't quite come across as well as you think they would, coming between 'Aja' and 'Babylon Sisters' or something like that. They seem kind of like somebody brought the Weavers on stage for a minute!"

But looking back on "Reelin' in the Years" today, it's a song that Becker remains proud of. "It's certainly one of the more successful records. As a song, it's not the deepest thing we ever wrote, but it is catchy. And if you're going to be a songwriter, there's something fascinating about the idea of writing a hit. Completely apart from what a hit buys you in terms of money or success—you want to be able to find things that just immediately penetrate into someone's consciousness in a certain way, and stick with them. That the guy wants to play the same record five times a day for the first couple of days. I would say it was one of those."

Bonus Bit: Alumni of the Dan

While Becker and Fagen have kept the Steely Dan banner flying high throughout the years (despite a hiatus that lasted much of the '80s), ever wonder what happened to the rest of the players on "Reelin' in the Years"? Well, Jeff "Skunk" Baxter became a member of the Doobie Brothers and also a much in-demand session player, while currently working as a defense consultant, and chairs a Congressional Advisory Board on missile defense (no lie!). Denny Dias appeared on all of Steely Dan's subsequent '70s albums, and currently works as a computer programmer, while Elliott Randall continued on a as a session guitarist, and also works as a consultant on streaming Internet content. Drummer Jim Hodder also worked as a session man, before sadly drowning in his swimming pool in 1990.

www.steelydan.com
www.walterbecker.com

Previously Unpublished

Every Home Should Have One

King Crimson 'Discipline'

An undervalued or forgotten gem you may have overlooked.

By the dawn of the '80's, punk had shaken rock music to its foundations—so much so that even one-time prog-rockers were streamlining their sound/approach. King Crimson was one such band, as evidenced by 1981's exceptional 'Discipline.' When leader/guitarist Robert Fripp decided to form a "new Crimson," overindulgences were trimmed—replaced by a sound heavy on rhythm and experimentation. A chance meeting would shape the rest of the line-up.

"I met Robert Fripp one night in New York, a club called the Bottom Line," remembers singer/guitarist Adrian Belew. "I was playing with David Bowie at the time—1979/1980—and [we] went to see Steve Reich. When the lights came up, Robert was at the table next to us. So I went over, and he wrote his hotel number on my arm! We had coffee, and got to know each other."

Belew then got the nod to open shows for Fripp's other band, League of Gentlemen, which led to a phone call. "In 1980, I started with the Talking Heads, and as [they] arrived in England, I got a call from Robert, saying, 'I'm starting a new band with [drummer] Bill Bruford and myself—would you like to be a part of it?' So I jumped at that chance."

New York auditions landed studio-vet bassist Tony Levin, which solidified the new Crimson. "I don't think any of us knew we were creating something so unusual. But now that I look back, it's easy to see—every one of us had new technology. I was the first to have a guitar synthesizer, and Robert was probably the second. Tony had the Chapman Stick, which no one had used before, and Bill was fooling with electronic drums. So you had these four monkeys in a cage together with new toys—something was bound to happen."

Something did indeed happen, as 'Discipline' sounded like nothing before it—featuring funky workouts ("Elephant Talk"), ambient soundscapes ("Sheltering Sky"), tranquil moments ("Matte Kudasai"), and freakouts ("Thela Hun Ginjeet," "Indiscipline"). But before entering the studio,

Crimson decided to fine-tune their new compositions. "We played around Europe, and we had so little music that we couldn't play encores! We only had a couple of older tunes, and all the new stuff we were writing. But we finished the tour—made it through without being killed by any audiences, went into the studio in London, and made the record."

An interesting occurrence developed during sessions for "Thela Hun Ginjeet," which Belew remembers vividly. "John Lennon had been killed, and he was my hero. So I tried to write a lyric about being molested with a gun on the streets of a city. I tried to think of phrases, as though it was an interview on the street after the occurrence. We were in a part of London that was a dangerous area, but I didn't know that. So I had a tape recorder, and Robert said, 'If you want to get realistic sounds, why don't you walk around on the street and say your lines?' I walked down one of the streets, and there was illegal gambling going on. It was done by a group of Rastafarian guys—pretty tough looking—and [they'd] gathered around me. They thought I was an undercover policeman—I had short hair at the time. They were about to kill me; I don't know how I talked my way out of it. At one point, the 'leader' grabbed my tape recorder, and played back what I had just been saying, 'He had a gun!' [laughs] And the guy freaked out—'What gun?!' They finally let me go, I'm not sure why, I went back to the studio, and I was so shook up. I ran into the control room, and was telling Robert the story. Meanwhile, he had whispered to the engineer to record it, and that's what you hear on the record."

Although 'Discipline' wasn't a chart-topper, it did re-establish Crimson, and touched a legion of up-and-coming musicians. "It certainly wasn't a record that your average person would know, but it had an affect on Primus, Tool, Trent Reznor, and so many people. That record affected the way they saw music. So for me, that's even better than saying, 'We had a big hit record.'"

www.king-crimson.com
www.adrianbelew.net

Classic Rock—November 2004, issue 72

Joni Mitchell 'Court and Spark'

Greg Lake

Greg Lake of ELP on Joni Mitchell's sixth classic studio album in a row, that was "made with passion, love, and real care."

"I find it very hard [to select a single album]. What do you say—is 'Electric Ladyland' better than 'Sgt. Pepper'? There's so many albums that I would say would qualify as my favorite record, and all for different reasons…Joni Mitchell's 'Court and Spark.' It just is so terribly difficult. My mother has this saying, that 'scum floats to the top,' and I think that in the end, most of the great albums that got made, got noticed."

"There are things that are perhaps more quirky—'Court and Spark'—an extremely beautiful record, but I wouldn't say it got overlooked. But it wasn't as big as 'Sgt. Pepper' or 'Dark Side of the Moon'."

"When I listen to 'Court and Spark,' [it is] a work of art. The musicality, the beauty, the poetry. The combination of harmony, rhythm, meaning, culture—so much a blend of so many good things artistically. It is that that endears me. Made with passion, love, and real care. It was really the beauty, the meaning, and the songs."

"It was a long way from the thought of the artists about how they were going to be video-d [laughs]. So many albums, especially these days, are based on their ability to be marketed. That is what I lament about the modern music market to the age that I grew up. During the age I came through in rock n' roll, you could identify every single group within three seconds of playing any album by them. Now I can sit and listen to an entire record, get to the end of it, and I don't even know who I've listened to, because they're based on so many similar clichés."

"They're all great, aren't they? 'Court and Spark,' 'Help Me,' 'Free Man in Paris,' 'Same Situation'—now there's a beautiful song. I like them all, actually. The work is rather like 'Sgt. Pepper'—they're all great. That's one of the things about a truly great album, is it is an 'album.' Tremendous record."

"These are the things that to some extent people ask, 'What influenced you?' Well of course, everything influences you. But things that bite deep, are sometimes the strangest things, and not really relevant. Somebody [could] say, 'Where's Joni Mitchell's music in Greg Lake's career?' You'd say, 'I don't know, really.' It's hard to find any Joni Mitchell in ELP. But in truth, that was quite a big influence—her musicality really, it was a high bar to jump. You have to be very good to play Joni Mitchell's songs."

"I was extremely young [when Lake first heard 'Court and Spark'], and it was an overwhelming thing. It was a quantum leap in everything. Quantum leap in production, in songwriting."

"Absolutely bulletproof. It hasn't dated and it won't date. It's classic, because the album wasn't based on fashion and vogue. That goes right back to what I was saying, about it being a work of art."

www.greglake.com

Classic Rock—March 2006, issue 90

Tour Bus Survival

Glenn Hughes

Music: "I listen really to a lot of acoustic, jazzy, late night, wind-down music. I mean, I'm at a point in my life where when I come off stage, I don't want to hear anything that's intense. I just want to wind down, so it's always going to be more 'light night music' for me. Whatever trips my fancy—it's mostly American artists. I must say, I don't really listen to a lot of music, in the last five years. Because my brain will not allow me to do anything but write music, and I don't want to be influenced too much about what's currently going on. That's why I don't listen to a lot of rock music, because I don't want to be influenced by somebody out there—I might be stealing somebody else's chops, which I don't do.

DVDs: "Chad [Smith, Red Hot Chili Peppers' drummer] keeps sending me his stuff to look at. Lots of Chili Peppers stuff, 'cause I'm ensconced with my friend, so I get to look at a lot of their footage. The last DVD I saw would be 'A Hard Days Night' by the Beatles. Please put that Glenn is an avid '60s freak as far as movies—I love to go back and watch old things like 'The Avengers,' 'The Saint,' '60s shows like that. Chad sent over to me 'The Office,' that's what I've been watching that lately."

Books: "'The Five People You Meet In Heaven' [by Mitch Albom]—brilliant. I'm into meta-physical and spiritual books, I'm not a New Age-r, but I'm into life in general."

Essential tour bus rule: "Y'know, when I travel, I travel in a car, I have a driver, and my band and the crew go on a bus. I go on a bus from time to time when I get a bit lonely. There's no smoking, and no making 'number two' on the bus! Basically, keeping a tidy bus, and the most important thing for me is there's no smoking."

Tour bus anecdote: "Obviously, people get left behind. It's the age-old story—'Where's Colin tonight?' or 'Where's Roger?', y'know? Once a week, one of these geezers are either stuck in some toilet somewhere, and running down the highway with their pants down! It's kind of amusing really—I'm glad it wasn't me. Something always happens. Remember this now—I'm the only guy that doesn't drink, so that alone, when you're traveling with a bunch of crazy Europeans, it's kind of like I've got to show some sort of example, so I try to wear earplugs a lot on the bus."

www.glennhughes.com

Classic Rock—June 2005, issue 80

Show Review

The Raspberries

B.B. King Blues Club & Grill
New York City—July 24, 2005

"They said it would never happen. They were wrong." A fitting message displayed on a projection screen just before the Raspberries' final show of a two-night stand in New York City. It's been well over 30 years since the original Raspberries line-up graced a NYC stage (Carnegie Hall in 1973), and Eric Carmen and company didn't blow it—handing in a strong n' stellar performance.

Keeping the audience on their toes with a few pre-recorded bars of "I Wanna Be With You"—before the *real* Raspberries kicked in—the mostly middle-aged crowd witnessed a perfectly paced, near-two hour set. All three front members led their own respective songs—Carmen ("Ecstasy," "Let's Pretend," a fantastic "Overnight Sensation"), guitarist Wally Bryson ("Party's Over"), and bassist David Smalley ("Goin' Nowhere Tonight"), while Jim Bonfanti's hard-hitting drumming recalled Keith Moon.

Usually the presence of additional musical "helpers" spells blahness, but a third guitarist, a multi-instrumentalist, and a female singer only bolstered the sound—especially the impeccable vocal multi-harmonies. The sole complaint was an overabundance of covers ("Please Mr. Postman," "Twist and Shout," etc.), which coulda/shoulda been replaced with more Raspberries classics—especially since fans had been waiting so long for this "live opportunity."

But by the time that a rousing romp of "Go All the Way" closed the set, it was perfectly clear—the Raspberries are still kings of the power pop domain.

www.raspberriesonline.com

Classic Rock—September 2005, issue 84

Heavy Metal

Features

Anthrax

Persistence of Time

Hailed as the masters of the "crunch riff" by the likes of Glassjaw, System of a Down, and even Slipknot, Metal Hammer took a long overdue look at Anthrax's 20 year career, through the highs and lows.

Circa the late '80s, Anthrax was the perfect model of a metal band sticking to their guns, and the mainstream moving to them, rather than merely catering to current fashions or tastes. It was all paying off nicely, as they were in the midst of a string of hit albums and sold out tours. From the outside looking in, it appeared as though Anthrax was gearing up to be one of the leading metal bands of the '90s, ruling the charts and arenas worldwide. But while the band was happy with the way the new decade began (especially with the arrival of new singer John Bush), the Anthrax train would soon almost completely derail. Switching from Island Records to Metallica's longtime home, Elektra, should've pushed the group to the next level, career wise.

But the switch did quite the opposite, founding guitarist Scott Ian recently filled us in. "Warners decided to clean house at Elektra, and the people who signed us, from the CEO on down, were gone. [Our manager] went in to meet the new chairperson, Sylvia Rhone, and the first thing she said was, 'I would have never signed this band, what do you want to do with this next record?' So right off the bat, it was basically 'We're not going to do anything for you. We're going to spend the minimal amount of money we have to contractually.'" As a result, 1995's 'Stomp 442,' nose-dived quickly after release. "To this day, people still don't know about that record, which is a fucking shame. Somehow, it wound up selling 150,000 copies on the basis of just Anthrax fans. From '83 up until '93, ten years of our career getting to that point that we really felt on the verge of, 'Alright, we're really going to break the door down and have this huge success.' And Elektra just decided, 'Oh no, sorry. You're career is over now.' At that point in time, '95/'96, heavy metal was at just such a bad state in the States that for that to happen to us at that point, it was the worst time ever."

OK, one misstep is no matter, especially to a veteran group like Anthrax. But what were the chances of stepping into another horrific record company situation for a second consecutive time? With Ignition/Tommy Boy backing them, 1998's 'Volume 8,' appeared to be the album that would put Anthrax's career back on track. Meet drummer Charlie Benante. "About a month into the record, the label lost their finance and backing. It was like a big balloon got the air let out of it—nothing could be done. So that album was a waste. And after that, there was some serious shit going on in the band."

The "serious shit" Benante mentions was a 1999 reunion album by the Anthrax side band, S.O.D. (aka Stormtroopers of Death), 'Bigger Than the Devil,' which managed to only add to tension between the band members. "At that time, Scott started to 'escape.' He got back into this S.O.D. thing, and I didn't want to do that. But he had some things in mind and contacted his people, Billy [Milano, singer] and stuff, and it was being done without me knowing it. That S.O.D. record would've been done with or without me. So I felt, from a fan's perspective, I should do this. So we did this record, and before I knew it, they were talking about tours, and I was like '*What?*' So I was totally put in a situation that I was not prepared for. To me, the greatest thing about S.O.D. was the mystique. There was this first record that was considered this classic record. I didn't want to go and fuck that with another record. Other people in the band could sense my unhappiness, and it didn't make for good company. That's when I started re-thinking things. I had other things coming in, offers to do this and that, but I went with my heart and stuck with the Anthrax thing."

Instead of jumping right back into the ring and fighting their way back, the longest stretch without an all-new Anthrax studio album followed, lasting from 1999 through 2002. Bassist Frankie Bello- "We couldn't get out of our contract. It was just bankers and lawyers getting together. We were going to take a break anyway, 'cause we went through a lot of shit."

It hasn't always been such an uphill battle for the group however. Hailing from New York City, Anthrax first came into being during 1981, when Queens-based Ian sought to form a band modeled after the New Wave of British Heavy Metal acts flooding import sections of U.S. record shops. The only problem was, gigs were scarce. Scott- "There really wasn't a metal scene, original band-wise—no one else really at that time was playing their own songs. The only way to get gigs was if you were a cover band, doing a Van Halen cover show. The covers we did was stuff off the first two Maiden records, 'British Steel,' old Sabbath, and Motörhead. So the covers we were doing weren't going to get us any gigs, we'd have to do it on our own. We'd rent Church basements, bring in a P.A., and sell tickets ourselves."

Joined by a rotating cast early on, Ian found an ally in Bronx native Benante. "I was into [the N.W.O.B.H.M.] and punk, so I had this thought of bridging it all together—kinda like Motörhead did." When a mutual friend told Benante a drum vacancy existed in Ian's band, a meeting was arranged. "Scott came over my house with Danny Lilker (Anthrax's original bassist), and I remember the first thing I said was "Don't ask me to play (Accept's) 'Fast As A Shark,' because it was the fastest thing at the time, with triple kick and everything. And as soon as I said that, the both of them said, 'Can you play 'Fast As A Shark?'' That was the beginning."

With the group up and running with a somewhat permanent line-up (joining Ian, Benante, and Lilker was a high school friend of Ian's, vocalist Neil Turbin, plus lead guitarist Dan Spitz), the group signed on with manager Johnny Z, who landed the group some prime gigs. Scott- "Soon after that he started giving us shows, with Manowar and people like that. And then of course, Metallica came to New York, and then we started playing shows with Metallica all around the area. Then the next thing you know, Johnny starts Megaforce Records, signs us, Metallica, and Raven, and that was it."

Anthrax issued their Megaforce debut, 'Fistful of Metal,' in 1984, but line-up changes beckoned. Turbin was turning tyrannical, and ordered Lilker out. With touring commitments set, the group obliged, and welcomed ex-guitar tech/Charlie's nephew/Bronx native Bello on board ("Literally, the day the first record came out was the day I joined the band"). However, the ensuing tour proved that Turbin would have to leave too. Scott- "We just couldn't live with the guy, it was a constant power struggle. We tried to work things out and make things more equal, but it was the 'lead singer disease.'" Immediately after a NYC homecoming gig with Metallica and Raven, Turbin was given the boot. Although singer-less, Anthrax congregated in Ithaca, New York, to begin recording sessions on what would become their first release for Island Records, 'Spreading the Disease.' With time dragging on and no singers fitting in, talk began of Ian and Bello splitting vocals, before producer Carl Canedy had a suggestion. Charlie- "Carl knew this singer, he played in some bands up there. [He] came into the studio to audition, and had a real fondness for 70's rock—Zeppelin and Journey. And we wanted a *singer* in the band, we didn't want somebody who was going to scream or growl, because we wanted to distance ourselves from the others." Soon after, Joey Belladonna became Anthrax's vocalist.

Ian made great use of his downtime during the 'Spreading' sessions, penning songs that would lead to the formation a hardcore sideband, S.O.D. "I used to draw these stupid cartoons of this character, Sgt. D. I would hang these politically incorrect cartoons around the studio, with things like 'Speak English or Die' or 'Kill Yourself,' which then became songs. That's when I called Danny Lilker and said, 'Hey man, would you like to work together again?' Danny took the bus the next day and we wrote the next ten songs. I already knew I wanted Billy Milano to be the singer, he had the right look and attitude—he would be able to come across as this character, Sgt. D., and really breath life into it. We recorded 'Speak English or Die' in three days [with Charlie handling drums]. Definitely the most spontaneous thing I've ever been a part of." The little side project soon took on a life of its own—serving as an important bridge between heavy metal and hardcore, a style now commonplace in rock music.

It was also around this time that "moshing" became widespread at Anthrax shows, and eventually, most metal shows. Scott- "I used to go to CBGB's Sunday hardcore matinee. I just loved getting to see cool bands—Agnostic Front, Cro-Mags, Murphy's Law, Crumbsuckers. I got involved in that scene, and loved slam dancing. When Anthrax started doing shows for 'Spreading,' there was a show at the old Ritz—I had invited all my friends from hardcore bands and guys at CBGB's, and they started a mosh pit. The metal kids had never seen anything like it before, it hadn't happened at a metal show in New York. Then that crossover started to happen—that whole scene just started to blur together."

The word on Anthrax began to spread worldwide, resulting in the group's first gigs in the U.K. during the spring of 1986. Touring as part of the Metal Hammer Roadshow with Overkill and Agent Steel, the dates concluded with a memorable gig at the Hammersmith Palais in London (Scott- "They didn't expect us to do even 600 kids and we wound up selling it out—1,700 people. That was the start of our love affair with the British"). Soon after, work began on what would become one thrash metal's all-time crowning achievements,

'Among the Living.' Hooking up with legendary producer Eddie 'Hendrix, Zeppelin, Kiss' Kramer, the sessions didn't exactly go smoothly. Scott- "Eddie was very headstrong. We hired him because we loved the albums he'd made in the '70s—very 'in your face' and dry. And he wanted to make 'Pyromania'— this huge, overproduced record. I remember him yelling at me, 'Is your opinion God?!' And I was like, 'Y'know what Eddie, right now my opinion is God because this is our fucking album. This isn't *Eddie Kramer*—Among the Living, it's *Anthrax*—Among the Living!'"

The sessions also accidentally gave birth to "rap metal," in the form of a throwaway song. Frankie- "'I'm the Man' wasn't supposed to do what it did. It's literally just me, Charlie, and Scott in the studio laughing our asses off." Charlie also remembers that a certain other group was supposed to appear on the track, "It was going to be a collaboration with the Beastie Boys. Our schedules couldn't meet, and we ended up doing it ourselves. That was a complete and total fluke, it was a b-side of the 'I Am the Law' single. It was released in England, and there was a demand for it in America, so we decided to put it out as an EP. And *BOOM,* it was just ridiculous."

Anthrax also became one of the first thrash metal bands to wear other clothing besides leather jackets and jeans—as they began sporting "jams" (long shorts)—a look that eventually would become *too* associated with the band. Charlie- "All part of ourselves, that's all it was. We originally had no image, than our off-stage look became our on-stage look. It was something that we all kinda got caught up in. The novelty wears off and sometimes you have to take a step back and say 'What's going on here?' and evaluate the whole thing."

1988 would be one of the busiest times for the band, as they spent the entire year opening for longtime idols Kiss, Maiden, and Ozzy. Their busy schedule ultimately hindered the group's fourth full-length, 'State of Euphoria.' Charlie- "The 'State of Euphoria' lesson, I'll call it that. That taught me never to rush anything. I told everybody, 'Guys, *never again.* I don't want to be rushed.' So with 'Persistence of Time,' we took things more slowly and creatively, it was a turning point for the band."

Many considered 'Persistence' the true follow-up to 'Among,' still one of their strongest—and darkest—releases. Once more, the sessions spawned another rap-metal experiment, courtesy of Ian. "I said, 'Look, I have this idea—it's basically 'Bring the Noise' from Public Enemy, we should cover it.' So we worked it out right there on the spot. Then it was a case of getting a hold of Chuck D. Someone at Def Jam got us Chuck, and he was like, "Bring the Noise?' We already did 'Bring the Noise!'" So I explained *we're* covering *you* guys, we wrote our own music with the idea of you guys rapping over this track. And he's like, 'Alright, let me think about it. I gotta talk to Rick Rubin.' Two days later, he calls and says, 'I spoke to Rick and he thinks it's redundant.' And I'm like, 'Dude! Let me send you the tape, you have to hear this!' And he's like, 'Alright, send it.' The next day he calls and says, 'This is fucking slamming, when can we do this?'"

A video was shot, which led to a full-blown tour with Public Enemy. Frank- "We just wanted to break every barrier down, because everybody was telling us, 'It can't be done, there's going to be race riots.' And we said 'People aren't like that,' they weren't giving them proper credit." In addition to the "Noise" video and the 'Attack of the Killer B's' compilation during the summer of '91, Anthrax united with Slayer and Megadeth for a tour of U.S. arenas, dubbed 'Clash of the Titans.' The shows were successful, but Charlie especially remembers the tour's opening band—"Alice in Chains...I remember feeling so bad for them, 'cause the audience was fucking ruthless—they didn't like them. It sucked 'cause we loved them." Frank even remembers instances when Layne Staley would go into the audience to brawl with hecklers.

While the Anthrax machine appeared unstoppable, the early '90s saw the exit of both Belladonna (Scott- "Creatively, we'd done everything we could possibly do with Joey") and Spitz (Charlie- "He lost faith in everything—he wasn't playing guitar, just...nothing"). While several temp guitarists (Paul Crook and Rob Caggiano, and on record, Dimebag Darrell) have subsequently appeared, ex-Armored Saint front man/Los Angeles native John Bush joined full-time, which led to a creative rebirth for the group. Charlie- "We felt fucking energized and charged up. I had a flow of music coming out, because it was just like writing for the first time again. I had this other voice I was hearing in my head." Bush remembers this era fondly—"The first show was in Tijuana, Mexico. It was awesome—totally crazy, a bunch of maniacs from Mexico and San Diego, packed. That was my 'trial by fire,' so to speak. I've always felt totally welcomed in the world of Anthrax." To add to the craziness of this era, Anthrax had inked a new deal with Elektra Records, which initially, proved to be a fine fit, as 'Sound of White Noise' was their highest charting U.S. release yet, debuting in the Billboard top ten.

But immediately thereafter, Anthrax embarked on their aforementioned "wilderness period," during which time only 1995's 'Stomp 442' and 1998's 'Volume 8: The Threat Is Real' appeared, as well as a hits set in 1999, 'Return of the Killer A's: Best of Anthrax.' The latter release saw the group welcome back Belladonna to duet with Bush on a newly recorded track, a remake of the Temptations' "Ball of Confusion." Talk of a tour that would've included both Bush and Belladonna soon got underway, and even though dates were booked, it ultimately failed to go down (with each camp blaming it on monetary reasons).

The group was then left with plenty of time to reflect on their recent woes. Something that wasn't necessarily a bad thing, felt Frank. "It was good, 'cause the hunger built and we made this great new record." Ah yes, the new record. 'We've Come for You All' (for new label Sanctuary) is a record which proves the veteran metal group still has plenty of fire in their belly. While Bush is content with the album ("Right now I think the record is awesome from top to bottom, one of the strongest we've ever made, but I can only give a fair evaluation of a record about a year later"), Benante feels very strongly about it. "This record is a labor of love. A lot of hard work went into it. It's just one of those records that makes you happy when you hear it, from an artist's point of view. Some of it was done after 9/11, and a lot of anger went into it. To me, it's a therapeutic type of record." Ian even goes a step further with his admiration of the recording, "As far as I'm concerned, it's the best thing we've ever done."

While Anthrax was clawing their way back, a funny thing happened—many of today's top rock bands became vocal of the group's influence. Scott-"Two of the guys in Linkin Park told me the first show they ever went to was Anthrax/Public Enemy, and that's how they knew they wanted to have a band. Tom Morello has told me that we were really influential on what [Rage] did. Bands like the Deftones. Dave [Baksh] from Sum 41. Corey Taylor has said that if it wasn't for Anthrax there would be no Slipknot. He said those exact words on stage to a crowd, which is pretty flattering when you hear someone from such a great band. They obviously took all their influences and turned it into something fucking spectacular. It's really good to see that." Charlie-"I've heard it from different people—System of a Down, Sum 41, Dimmu Borgir. Some of the newer bands, like Shadows Fall. Sometimes members of bands will say, 'Dude, you have no idea what that record meant to me.' And I'll look at them like 'Really?' Makes you feel old! But it's a good thing. Sometimes you don't hear it in their music, but it's in there—especially like Sum 41. I don't really hear it, but sometimes I'm like, 'Oh, OK.'"

So there ya have it folks, the Anthrax tale…loaded with ups and downs, but all about survival and perseverance.

Bonus Bit #1: We Love the 'Thrax

Jim Root: Slipknot

First Anthrax song you heard (& how old were you at the time?)

"I can't remember for sure, but I think it was 'Madhouse' or 'A.I.R.'. Whatever it was it was off 'Spreading the Disease.' I didn't hear 'Fistful of Metal' 'til later, I was probably around 15 years old."

Fave Anthrax song

"Well, that's tough, they've got different songs for different moods…maybe 'Black Lodge'…ask me later, and I'll give you a different answer."

Fave Anthrax album

"Fuck…I don't know, 'Among the Living' is a classic."

Neil Turbin, Joey Belladonna, or John Bush—

"All three…the albums wouldn't have been the same without each ones contribution…"

I'm The Man or Bring The Noise—

"Bring The Noise."

Best Anthrax memory—

"Playing a show with them in Boston."

Joe Fazzio: Superjoint Ritual

First Anthrax song you heard (& how old were you at the time?)—

"I was 13 when I heard 'Metal Thrashing Mad' off of 'Fistful of Metal'…and it blew my mind. Scott Ian's guitar sound was the heaviest guitar sound I ever heard."

Fave Anthrax song—

"Metal Thrashing Mad."

Fave Anthrax album—
'Spreading the Disease.'

Neil Turbin, Joey Belladonna, or John Bush—
"John Bush."

I'm The Man or Bring The Noise—
"Neither."

Best Anthrax memory—
"Scaring the heck out of people with Scott and Charlie in New Orleans at the House of Shock."

Bonus Bit #2: Cliff Burton Remembered

Next September 27th marks the 18-year anniversary of Metallica bassist Cliff Burton's tragic death. Early on, Anthrax was often a touring partner of Burton and co, and it turns out that Scott Ian, Frank Bello, and Charlie Benante are still full of interesting recollections of Metallica's unforgettable bassist.

Hanging with Cliff

Charlie Benante: "Metallica played a place called 'The Rising Sun' in Yonkers, NY, and I remember I was the only person they knew from New York. So I went down there, and I remember going on their Winnebago, and someone took a dump in the bathroom. *No one was supposed to do that.* And they were all blaming Cliff! Cliff was like, 'Fuck you man, I didn't do it!' We were eating breakfast one day, when 'Puppets' was out, and we were talking how sometimes you can't understand what the singer is saying. I'm like "What the hell does James say in that part right before the guitar lead [in the song 'Master of Puppets']?" I think he says 'Fix Me.' So we were all just goofing around, going back in forth, and Cliff goes, "I think he says 'Pancakes!'" Cliff was the coolest guy."

Scott Ian: "Me and him got arrested together in London, in 1984! Metallica was in England 'cause they were supposed to do a tour, and the tour got cancelled. So they were stuck in England 'cause they were in the studio up in Denmark already recording 'Ride the Lighting,' but when they went to England to do this tour, the studio had booked that time so they couldn't just go back. I was there for a few days, and they said 'Hey man, Music for Nations has got us this apartment, you can stay.' One day, Cliff had decided he wanted to go buy a walkman, and we took the subway. We were just waiting in the subway station when some cops came up to us, 'cause we both had really long hair, and the cops asked us if we had any drugs on us. So we were like, 'What are you talking about? We don't have any drugs!' So they arrested us, based on suspicion. They took us into this police station, and threw me in one cell and Cliff into another. It wasn't with bars, it was a little concrete room with a window. They took my clothes—I'm sitting there in my underwear in the freezing cold for like five hours, waiting to find out what's going to happen, and they're not telling us anything. Then at some point I heard voices outside my door. [The cops] said 'We're taking your mate back to the apartment and we're going to search the apartment. If everything turns out fine, then you'll be free to go.' Because when they took us in, Cliff had cold medicine on him, not in a packet. So they took him back, and now I'm really scared 'cause I knew that there was weed at the apartment, I was really getting nervous—all I could think about was 'Midnight Express.' About an hour later they came back, and Cliff had this big smile on his face. We got out of there, and I was like, 'Dude, what the fuck? How did they not find your weed?' He goes, 'Where's the first place you think they'd look? Under the mattress, right? They didn't look! All my weed was under the mattress and they didn't look!' He said that when they got back to the apartment, he came walking in and Kirk is sitting in the living room playing guitar, and [Cliff] walks in with like six cops and Kirk's eyes just got all big. The Metal Gods were smiling upon us that day!"

Cliff's Death

Frank Bello: "We were opening for Metallica on that tour. It was weird, every night before we left the show, the last thing we'd say was 'Hey, I'll see you later,' and Cliff said to me 'Maybe I will.' That's the last thing he said to me. It haunts me."

Scott Ian: "We did the whole U.K. leg of the Metallica/Anthrax tour, which was basically that September of '86. It was on our way from Stockholm to Copenhagen that the accident happened. When I think about it now, it's like a whole other lifetime ago—a weird, terrible dream. We had to get to Copenhagen because there were actually reports that there could be ice on the roads. So we had left before them. I woke up in the morning, walk into the hotel, and see our tour manager standing in the lobby talking to some guy. The tour manager's like, 'There's been an accident. Metallica's bus crashed last night and Cliff Burton was killed.' I totally didn't believe him, it was the last thing in the world I thought he was going to say. And I was like, 'Bullshit!' But he says, 'This is promoter so-and-so here in Copenhagen, he's been on the phone with the police all morning. The bus crashed, it flipped over, Cliff was killed, Lars was taken to the hospital with a broken toe, and James and Kirk are on the way here now.' I was like 'Bullshit, they probably got super fucking drunk last night, [and] can't make the show today.' Then of course, it was real. Still to this day, it's something hard for me to understand and accept. Then there was just this weird limbo because Kirk and James showed up later that day, and obviously they were in a bad state. We spent the night with those guys—keeping [James] from killing anyone around him or himself."

www.anthrax.com

Metal Hammer—Xmas 2003, issue 121

Tony Iommi and Glenn Hughes

Iron Men

*Away from the enormous Black Sabbath Ozzfest gigs of the summer,
Tony Iommi's made a solo album...except in reality, it's a collaboration
with Deep Purple's "voice of rock," Glenn Hughes. Guitarist gets 'Fused'
in New York...*

While quite a few hungry New Yorkers are window shopping and snacking on fresh-baked bread in the downstairs of the Chelsea Market building, Tony Iommi and Glenn Hughes are situated upstairs, in the cushy Sanctuary Records office. And unlike the restless pedestrians you spot scurrying on the city streets outside, Iommi and Hughes are both in "laidback mode"—their English gentlemen manner quickly bubbling to the surface. The subject of discussion? Their third album together overall, 'Fused.'

"When I joined the project, there were five songs musically on tape," explains singer/bassist Hughes. "Five songs that Tony sent me, to say, What do you think of these? And they were fucking brilliant. Very brutal riffs and orchestral things going on. And I said, This could be brilliant." The proof is in the metallic pudding.

Iommi and Hughes have quite a storied history together. Hailing from Birmingham and Cannock respectively, the duo's paths crossed often as members of Black Sabbath and Deep Purple in the early '70s. Come the mid '80s, Iommi was eyeing a solo album, and nabbed Hughes as his singer. Only problem was Warner Bros. demanded the album be released under the Black Sabbath banner. With Iommi the only familiar Sabbath face in the line-up, 1986's 'Seventh Star' fell on deaf ears, while Hughes only lasted for a handful of tour dates (Hughes would later admit to be battling drug addiction during this period).

Almost exactly a decade later, the duo reunited for a recording session, but the fruits of the sessions remained unreleased until last year, when 'The 1996 DEP Sessions' finally landed. Iommi- "I think after we released 'The DEP Sessions,' it just seemed like an obvious thing to go into. And that sat there for nine years, before we released that. I started writing some tracks, and [thought] Glenn's there, why not get together—I'm looking for singers, and he's an actual singer. He has a great voice. So I spoke to Glenn and he was up for that. He came over to England, and started writing."

But instead of following in the more melodically based direction of its predecessor, 'Fused' puts the focus back on Iommi's almighty riffs. "It's a lot more riff-oriented I think," says Iommi. "It's a more powerful album. 'The DEP Sessions' is a more softer album. We wanted to do a few things—we wanted a 'band' as such, who could go in, record the album, and it would come out—not like ten years. And have a band we could tour with."

The band that Iommi mentions will obviously include Hughes, as well as veteran drummer Kenny Aronoff, who has played with everyone from John Mellencamp to Smashing Pumpkins, as well as on Iommi's self-titled 2000 solo outing. "He's been talking about, 'If you ever do an album, call me.' So I did—he's a great player." Hughes seconds the praise of Aronoff. "Kenny Aronoff is the most amazing drummer—you've got to be on your toes when you play with guys like this. Aronoff to me is another nut job—a lovely man."

With the players now securely in place, Iommi, Hughes, and Aronoff met up late last year to whip the songs into shape, under the watchful eye of producer Bob Marlette. "I already wrote some songs," remembers Iommi, "Just the tunes themselves, not the melodies. I had a few done, then Glenn came over, and we started writing new stuff. And then I got to play him a couple of the ones from before, and he liked them." Hughes explains even further. "Tony had written the music with Bob Marlette, my job was to come in and fuse it together. Tony always gives me free reign to bring my ideas in, and we change a couple of things, we always do. I take things home, and sometimes write three, four sets of lyrics and melodies to the songs. Normally, the first melody is the one I keep, because it's the most spontaneous. I wanted this to be a focused album. When working with Tony, it's going to be more metal than what I'd normally do with my projects. You've got to be in this headspace, and the content I think was appropriate for where we were going."

With Marlette having previously worked with Iommi on such past projects as Black Sabbath's 'Reunion' live album and the aforementioned self-titled solo outing, the trio welcomed an extra pair of ears to bounce ideas off of. "I stuck with Bob through a few years, and we actually started off with a couple of the tracks I'd done with Bob. I invited him over to my house, to my studio, and we just put ideas down. I work well with Bob, so we used him on this album. I don't know—if we just had Glenn and myself now, we may have just done it ourselves. But it was good having Bob involved."

Hughes adds that Marlette also gave him vocal suggestions that helped shape the sound of 'Fused.' "He suggested the way I sang on the album [be] more modern, stripped down—rather than the stuff I would sing on my albums, which is more R n' B. He wanted me to sing in the box, and not really go out of it. We wanted to keep it so the kids could understand it more. I love what he did for Tony—very stripped down with a couple of really interesting signature things. Marlette had a vision on the album, and I think it's very good."

While 'Fused' contains plenty of riffs to keep Iommi's legion of fans content, it also sees the guitarist pen songs in a very aggressive manner, such as the album-opener, 'Dopamine,' plus the epic album closer, 'Insane.' These just happen to be among two of Hughes' favorite tracks. "['Dopamine'] is the first intense rock track we wrote—I love the lyric I wrote, I must say. Insane is mega-long and mega-cool. We pulled it off—with nine minutes and fourteen seconds; it was originally twelve and a half. We cut three minutes out, there were six movements, then there were four. I think what we created there was a showcase for [Tony's] guitar, and it's a very showcase-y vocal performance. I also love 'Grace'—'the centerpiece of the album,' I call it." Iommi on the other hand, is non-committal as far as selecting a favorite track. "I haven't got a favorite yet, because it's still relatively new. I think that normally comes down the line."

When asked about if any memories stick out from the sessions, Iommi tells a humorous tale when a certain bandmate indulged a bit too heavily in a dangerous substance...coffee. "One memory I've got was when Glenn and myself first got back together again. The first day of writing—and I hadn't worked with him for ten years—we sat down and I had a cup of coffee and he had a cup of coffee. And he doesn't drink coffee. God, he bombarded me [mimics someone talking a mile-a-minute]—bloody hell! I thought, 'God, is this what it's going to be like?' So the next day, he came in, 'Oh, I'm so sorry about yesterday—I don't drink coffee!' We had some great times, it's all been very much fun, because we've all been into it."

Hughes also offers some memories of the sessions. "[Tony's] nuts, he's a prankster. We recorded a lot of it live initially, and then Tony overdubbed, and I overdubbed some of the bass. I've always spent time watching him do his thing. He only lets certain people be there, and I think he feels comfortable with me. He's the best timekeeper we've got in rock music. I kind of rush—

he's right on the money. When you're standing next to [Tony's amps], even when you have the headphones on, he's so fucking loud."

With Iommi busy until the end of the summer due to Sabbath landing another Ozzfest headlining spot, tour plans for 'Fused' had to be pushed back—to autumn. But Iommi and Hughes are already discussing what songs to include in their setlist, which is sure to please fans old and new. Iommi mentioned that he'd enjoy playing material from 'Seventh Star,' and possibly even Dio-era Sabbath tracks. "It would be refreshing, because the last few years, [Sabbath] played a lot of the same songs. There's a whole variety of songs we could play which is great."

Hughes fully embraces the idea of playing Sabbath tunes—going as far as suggesting they dig out a few uncommon gems. "I suggested to Tony, if we're going to do like ten songs from our project 'Fused,' we should have two or three 'chestnuts,' I like to call them. I would like to do some very early Sabbath classics that Ozzy hasn't done. Something that [Sabbath] hasn't done yet. He's excited about that. And maybe something we can change—change the setlist. Sabbath don't really change their setlist." And what are the chances of a song or two appearing from the three Deep Purple albums that Hughes appeared on? "I wouldn't. I haven't even asked him—let's embrace Tony on this. I wouldn't want him to play Ritchie Blackmore riffs. I think he could, but I wouldn't want him to."

Thus far, the Iommi-Hughes tandem has averaged only an album per decade. Will release number four appear in the foreseeable future? Iommi offers a promising forecast. "I'd imagine we will, yeah, because we work well together. I think for the next album, we'll have Kenny come over and get involved. Because we actually wrote some of these tracks without Kenny, then got Kenny in and started playing them. I think if he was involved from the scratch, we'd do a lot more stuff." Hughes also believes that their best days lay ahead. "I think Tony and I have started something that is pretty much a bankable thing if we commit to doing more."

All hail the new Iron Men.

Bonus Bit #1: Guitar Fusion

'Fused' sees Tony Iommi's signature guitar sound remain intact, but in addition to the expected line-up of axes, this album featured one model he's not been associated with since his brief days in Jethro Tull in the late '60s. "I used a couple of different SG's, a Les Paul. I actually used a Strat on one track, which I haven't used for I can't remember when. I had a Strat for years and always played a Strat, then I went to Gibson on the first album [1970's 'Black Sabbath']. I just thought for one track, 'Deep Inside His Shell,' I could hear a Strat sound. So I said, 'Get me a Strat,' and I started playing that. I used my Laney Iommi model amplifier, and I think for some of the quieter bits I used an AC-30."

Hughes was also particular about what equipment he played on the album. "I used my Manne signature bass—go online and check it out—it's basically a bass that I designed myself, kind of looks like a Rickenbacker a little bit. It's got a vintage p-bass jazz pickup—great bass. I used on this project Ampeg amplification [and] Digitech Effects—that's a company I love to pieces."

Bonus Bit #2: Feeling Paranoid

How do you follow up a metal classic? That was the question Iommi and his Sabbath mates wondered while recording 'Master of Reality'—the follow-up to 'Paranoid.' "There's always pressure when your last album goes to number one. What do you do then? There's only one way down. We were under pressure to come up with an album to equal ['Paranoid']." Spawning the classics "Sweet Leaf" and "Children of the Grave," 'Master' cemented Sabbath's standing as metal giants. The catalyst? "We [would] go in a room and just start playing—I play a riff and then they join in. We worked like we've done with every one." Still, drummer Bill Ward experienced turbulence. "There was one track on that album that became a pain, I can't remember which one. Bill was really struggling—he just couldn't get it right. It was probably all the drugs and drinking!"

www.iommi.com
www.glennhughes.com

Guitarist—July 2005, issue 265

Soundgarden

Black Hole Sons

Think of the Seattle scene and you think of Nirvana. But it was Soundgarden who led the grunge explosion. Classic Rock caught up with Matt Cameron and Ben Shepherd, producers Jack Endino and Steve Fisk, and photographer Ross Halfin, to look back at the band that killed glam metal.

When Soundgarden's world tour wrapped up in 1997, it seemed like just another successful record-tour cycle for the band. Their latest album, 'Down on the Upside,' was a global hit, they'd become the first-ever band to appear twice on Lollapalooza, and had just wrapped up a lengthy headlining tour of their own. But behind the scenes, it was an entirely different story. "The [recording] sessions were certainly strained," remembers Matt Cameron. "So I knew something was up, something was certainly going on. And then once when we started touring for that record, the shows were just increasingly bad. It was just horrible. A lot of drinking, a lot of bad vibes, a lot of temper tantrums, a lot of rock star bullshit. I was actually thinking about bailing at that point. It was really tough—we couldn't get through a show basically, without someone storming off the stage. It was so not about music." On February 9th, Soundgarden played the tour's final show at the Blaisdell Arena in Hawaii. On April 9th, the group would announce their break-up.

But before their aforementioned "downfall," Soundgarden was one mean rockin' machine. Equally influenced by Black Sabbath and the Bad Brains, the group perfected a style touched upon in the early '80s by the likes of the Melvins and Black Flag—slowing punk's fury to a sludgy crawl. And while Nirvana was the band that blew the roof off the '90s Seattle rock movement, Soundgarden was the band that provided the legwork—one of the first groups of the scene to record for Sub Pop, tour nationally, and sign to a major label. Oh yes, and the group was responsible for some of the '90s best rock albums ('Badmotorfinger' and 'Superunknown') and songs ("Rusty Cage," "Outshined," "Black Hole Sun," etc.). And along with Pearl Jam, Alice in Chains, and the aforementioned Nirvana, Soundgarden did us all a favor by exterminating glam metal.

Meet Chris Cornell and Kim Thayil—an ex-cook and a college grad with a degree in philosophy, respectively. Quite an unlikely duo that co-formed one of the biggest rock groups of modern times. Both hailing from around the Seattle, Washington area, Cornell and Thayil crossed paths thanks to a mutual friend, Hiro Yamamoto. Cornell was a roommate of Yamamoto's, and played in a band together, the Shemps, while Thayil and Yamamoto were friends since their early days in Chicago, before relocating to Washington together to attend college.

Come 1984, the trio decided to form their own group—Thayil on guitar, Yamamoto on bass, and Cornell pulling a "Phil Collins" (handling drum and vocal duties). Taking their name from a nearby artsy sculpture, Soundgarden was born. The trio line-up only lasted for a few shows however, before drummer Scott Sundquist signed on, and Cornell focused solely on vocals. Producer Jack Endino happened to catch their debut as a quartet. "They played half the set with Chris on drums, then he came out, and said, 'OK, we want to introduce our new drummer, and I'm just going to sing now.' Scott came out, finished the set, and Chris just stood there and sang. That was the first time I saw them—it would have been one of their very early shows—probably in early '85."

Endino, who was then a member of another up-and-coming Seattle act, Skin Yard, recalls Soundgarden's early sound. "Scott was an older guy, he had kind of a Ginger Baker touch on the drums. A rolling, jazzy sort of feel, that was really dynamic, and very fluid. It wasn't so 'conventional heavy rock' as they became later. It was a slightly psychedelic kind of vibe. And at times, it was really pretty amazing. Even though he wasn't technically anywhere near the drummer that [Matt Cameron would be]."

"After they got Matt in the band, they became more focused—'We're just going to play these big rock riffs,' and zeroed in on the sound they became known for later. Soundgarden was a little inconsistent live—you never knew what was going to happen. There was definitely an element of 'chance' going on, craziness, and fun. There were some amazing Soundgarden shows in the early days. I remember them playing the Ditto Tavern, and I think the only people in the audience were like five people! I was doing sound and a couple of my friends. I have a poster from those days—'Soundgarden/Skin Yard $2' [laughs]. It's from like a Tuesday. Those were the days."

1986 would prove to be an important year in Soundgarden's development. The group would make their first-ever appearance on album, the CZ Records compilation 'Deep Six,' as well as experience their first line-up flutter. With it becoming clear that touring outside the region was going to become a requirement soon, Sundquist (who was a husband/father) opted to leave the group before the going got tough. This made way for Matt Cameron, previously a bandmate of Endino's in Skin Yard.

"I'd seen them play a few times, and they were my favorite band in Seattle," remembers Cameron. "I heard that Scott left, and I called Kim. I said, 'I'd like to try out,' and I did. I knew a few of their songs—there was one called 'Heretic' that I knew, and I knew 'Incessant Mace,' and a few of their other earlier songs. So I showed up semi-prepared. I remember Chris really liked the way I played—he said that I played everything perfectly. They had a gig in a week's time at the Central Tavern, so it was baptism by fire. I just threw myself in there and never looked back."

Making believers out of local rock fans, the group especially left an impression on one admirer, Ben Shepherd. "They were playing a show down in Olympia, one of those 'daylight shows,' there was a bunch of bands. Seattle was totally cool back then—the music scene was totally happening. People were fun, life was cool as fuck, and there they were. So that was the first time in Olympia getting to see Matt play. It was like, 'Wow, they're the real thing now.' Chris was just singing, and Hiro and Kim—that was the true Soundgarden. The very first show I saw they blew some national act away."

With the Cornell-Thayil-Yamamoto-Cameron line-up now in place, Soundgarden set out to go beyond the demo stage and do a pro-recording. Already pals with Endino, the quartet asked the producer to oversee the sessions, as he'd landed a job at the nearby Reciprocal Recording Studio. Endino- "We worked very hard at getting the right performances. We spent a ridiculous amount of time mixing it, just making it exactly so. Just as good as we could possibly get it, with the gear and the budget that we had available— nobody had any money around here. Sub Pop didn't really exist yet. I think it was something that came up partly through the recording—'Oh, these guys we know are talking to us about maybe releasing it'."

Recorded quickly and mostly live (Cameron- "We only had three or four days to get the rhythm tracks done, because we had day jobs"), the six tracks were released in October of 1987, through a label that was co-run by an old pal of Thayil's, Bruce Pavitt (and his business partner, Jonathan Poneman)— Sub Pop. "I remember listening back to the mix of 'Nothing To Say'," recalls Cameron, "and I just couldn't believe that I was playing in a band so good, at such an early stage of development." Shepherd agrees with Cameron's assessment. "'Screaming Life' is still my favorite record of theirs. That's what Soundgarden sounds like to me—dark, black and blue. It sounds like the overcast days of Seattle. They sounded huge, and their riffs weren't stupid or anything—something more to them. Something disturbing and huge."

Wasting little time, a follow-up EP, 'Fopp,' was issued again via Sub Pop in August 1988. The EP's producer, Steve Fisk, recalls a Soundgarden-Faith No More show from around this time that won him over. "Some kids got it together, to spend all of the College of Ellensburg's entertainment budget. I guess if they didn't blow it on this, it was going to go to Stryper or some horrible band. It was interesting—[Soundgarden] closed with 'Iron Man,' and Faith No More opened with 'War Pigs.' I was impressed with that more than anything else. I was impressed with the terrible phase shifter Kim was using. I thought his guitar sound was great, and then he turned on this cheesy phase shifter, and they sounded like a bar band. This is before anybody knew who the fuck they were."

Recorded at Seattle's Moore Theater during an afternoon with a mobile truck, Fisk recalls realizing that Seattle's buzz was growing. "At one point, a jackhammer crew went to work on pavement, and we couldn't hear anything in the truck. This is another thing that tells you what the time was—we got the crew to move and come back later in the day, because they didn't know who Soundgarden was, but they knew Seattle bands were starting to get some attention. So they did to be cool [laughs]."

With major labels starting to sniff around Soundgarden and other local acts, the group opted to stay 'indie' for their full-length debut, 'Ultramega OK,' released in November of '88. Issued via Black Flag's SST label, the album would be nominated for a Grammy Award (Best Metal Performance) a year later. Cameron remembers more rapid-fire recording. "We had a little more money to record with. We went down to this kind of homemade studio that was pretty good. It was in this place called Newberg, Oregon—this gay couple lived out in the woods, and they let us record there. Again, we didn't have a lot of time—I think we had two weeks to do it all. We recorded some up here in Seattle, in an abandoned warehouse. Recorded some drums there, then we finished the rest in Newberg."

With other Seattle groups following Soundgarden up the ladder (Screaming Trees, Mudhoney, Nirvana, Mother Love Bone), the band decided that the time was finally right to go with a major label. Inking with A&M, 'Louder Than Love' was issued in September 1989. Produced by Terry Date, the album wasn't the one that would break Soundgarden commercially. But it certainly helped set the stage, as the videos for both "Hands All Over" and "Loud Love" received late night MTV rotation. It was also supported with a year's worth of live dates.

But it certainly was not a smooth-sailing period, as Yamamoto exited after the album sessions wrapped. With an extensive U.S. tour coming up with Faith No More and Voivod, Soundgarden arranged bassist try-outs, and whittled the competition down to two—ex-Nirvana guitarist Jason Everman and ex-Nirvana roadie Ben Shepherd. "They were crunched for time," remembers Shepherd. "Once we got to the rehearsal room, I didn't say anything; I just walked over to the amp, turned it up, and started playing. We jammed for three hours—we didn't play any of their songs. We didn't even talk; we just played music the whole time. They took Jason because he knew the songs—he was more connected and on-beat with it."

While they completed the ensuing tour with Everman, Soundgarden soon realized they had chosen the wrong bassist. Upon returning home in the spring of 1990, Shepherd was asked to join. "We rehearsed for a couple of weeks, then we went straight to touring Europe. The first place I played was the Roskilde Festival [broadcast live]. So we come on stage and the crowd is chanting, 'Hiro! Hiro!' I'm like, 'Oh, goddamit!' We did this three-week tour, then we came home, then we had another tour all ready to go. So it was like jumping right into the fire, it was awesome. So fucking fun."

After a tour with Danzig wrapped in September, the group focused on their next studio effort, produced once more by Terry Date. But unlike earlier releases, there was something in the air about the Seattle scene, which Shepherd remembered noticing. "You could see everybody was 'on music' at that point. Music was suddenly alive again and doing something. Sometimes it's film and writing that does that culturally, but that time it was music."

Setting up shop at Studio D in Sausalito, California (at the behest of their Faith No More pals), Shepherd remembers the sessions being extremely laid back. "It was so fun, we invented this game—it takes a Frisbee and a Nerf ball to play, two man teams. We'd play that all the time when we weren't tracking. A home away from home. It's way outside the city—a cool old barn turned into a recording studio. Really comfortable. Kim would be outside at night, smoking cigarettes in his van, listening to the Mariners games."

Just as sessions wrapped, a side project featuring Cornell and Cameron, as well as members of the then-unknown Pearl Jam, released 'Temple of the Dog.' It turned out to be a tribute to Andrew Wood, the singer of the pre-Pearl Jam outfit Mother Love Bone, who had recently died from a drug overdose. Cameron- "Chris and Andy had been roommates. I think the original idea was to do a single on Sub Pop in tribute to Andy. We got together, and just started to write more songs. Chris of course had a bunch of really cool songs, so we decided just to track it. A&M really liked it and put it out, so it was once again, organically-produced."

Released in October of 1991, 'Badmotorfinger' was where it first all came together for Soundgarden in the studio, as it was their strongest and most consistent album front-to-back. It also didn't hurt that they issued it right as the 'grunge movement' was erupting, thanks to two albums released around this time, Pearl Jam's 'Ten' and Nirvana's 'Nevermind' (and earlier, Alice in Chains' 'Facelift'). Additionally, Soundgarden happened to land some prime touring spots.

The same week as the release of 'Badmotorfinger,' Soundgarden played alongside Metallica as part of the mammoth Day on the Green Festival in Oakland, California. Two months later, the band opened a string of arena dates for Guns N' Roses, who were still in all of their out-of-control glory, followed by dates with Skid Row. Cameron- "We were in the metal trenches at that point, just fully paying our dues. We were kind of like 'the opening act' for '91/'92."

Despite coming from complete opposite ends of the spectrum, Shepherd remembers the G n' R tour fondly. "We had a blast. The whole crew of theirs and their whole band are really fucking nice. And me, I'm like a punk rocker fuck-up, and I'm all cantankerous—my nickname was Manimal back then, and we were called Frowngarden. We weren't rock stars and shit, we're not like that. I'm all grumpy—'Goddamn it, these guys are nice, I can't even fucking hate 'em! I hate their music, but they're nice.' Same thing with Skid Row—fucking hated their music, they knew it, but they're all so fucking cool. Pissed me off, now I don't even have a reason to be pissed off. What the hell is this? My life is going to shit and it's beautiful at the same time."

It was also around this time that renowned rock photographer Ross Halfin began working with the band. "The thing about them—they were all actually quite quiet. They were very nice, but they were one of those bands that as soon as they started drinking...when people drink, everybody becomes a wanker. Matt Cameron, I never saw him like that. Kim Thayil would always get very morose and started wanting to be your best friend—crying and stuff. Chris would be alright to a point, and then he'd start doing things like kicking doors or tables. And Ben Shepherd would just go crazy. It would be like 'Fuck you and fuck you!' to whoever he could. It got to a point where they ended up getting security in England. Ben was walking across Camden Town, there was a bunch of English guys outside a pub, and he's like, 'Fuck you assholes,' and they came over and whacked him. So security was [needed] because they would just go off when they drank."

With such tracks as "Outshined" and "Rusty Cage" getting major attention on the airwaves, 'Badmotorfinger' served as Soundgarden's commercial breakthrough. And as a "reward," the group nabbed a spot on Lollapalooza II in the summer of 1992, alongside the Red Hot Chili Peppers and their pals Pearl Jam. Cameron- "That was our payback for opening for all these weird heavy metal bands that we had nothing in common with. Once we got to Lollapalooza, we were back with our friends. That was a really fun tour."

But it was also during this time that Shepherd began hitting the bottle heavily. "I would hang out with Jesus and Mary Chain, I was the only guy that would talk to them—share my whiskey with them or whatever. I started drinking too much on that first Guns N' Roses tour. I would just get really depressed and that was the only way out, or so it seemed. A lot of touring is 'hurry up and wait'—you get there and then you wait. You'd see guys that had been out for a couple of years in a row—you hit this wall where it's like, 'Why go back? Why go home? There is no home, there's nothing! Let's just keep going, we'll play another show.' It gets really surreal."

By the time their 1991-92 tour wrapped up, there were three Soundgarden-related albums on the charts—'Badmotorfinger,' 'Singles Motion Picture Soundtrack,' and 'Temple of the Dog.' Having toured non-stop for over a year, Soundgarden took a much-deserved break for most of 1993, during which Cornell "celebrated" by shaving off his long mane of hair, and Cameron/Shepherd launched a garage rock outfit, Hater. In fact, the only shows Soundgarden played the whole year were two weeks worth of dates opening for Neil Young in August.

But the majority of the year was spent pent up at Seattle's Bad Animals studios with producer Michael Beinhorn, preparing the album that they hoped would be the final push over the top. Cameron- "I think creatively we were really peaking at that point. All pistons were firing—we were writing really cool music and we were playing really good together. I think the arch of the band was fully peaking at that point. We really wanted to be prepared and we rehearsed a lot. Worked on the arrangements of the songs and everything."

"I remember those sessions being pretty intense—it took like four or five months to track that record. There was a lot of wheel spinning going on—like we would spend three days on a guitar part. It got really silly. We knew we had a good record in there, but I think we were all just sick of it, we just didn't care anymore. Then Brendan O'Brien mixed it, and he did it in like two weeks—the complete opposite of the way we were working. Just knocked it out. At that point, when I took the mixes home, I realized we had a really good record."

Shortly before the album's arrival, a press release was issued, in which Shepherd explained, "Bands like Aerosmith and Led Zeppelin made records where every song counted, and I think that's what we did." Boy, he wasn't fooling, as 'Superunknown' was not only one of the greatest rock albums of the '90s, but of all time.

Released in March of 1994, 'Superunknown' would debut at the top of the U.S. album charts, and prove to be a worldwide smash, on the strength of such hits as "Spoonman," "Fell on Black Days," and especially, the moody-yet-melodic "Black Hole Sun."

With the album's mass chart success, Soundgarden found themselves in the same league as rock's elite. But a month after the album's release, the world was shocked by the suicide of Kurt Cobain, which spelled the end of Nirvana. Couple that with Pearl Jam losing the plot and touring less (due to a battle with Ticketmaster), and suddenly, Soundgarden was the leaders of the pack. On 1 March 1995, Soundgarden took home two Grammy Awards—Best Hard Rock Performance ("Black Hole Sun") and Best Metal Performance ("Spoonman").

How did the group handle their new status? Halfin remembers that the band "Were fine with that, I just think they didn't care. It's very much that 'down' Seattle-way mentality. One of the things I think they [had] over Pearl Jam—Pearl Jam, with all their anti-everything, still very much liked the trappings of being rock stars. The body guards, the this, the that. Whereas Soundgarden didn't really have that—they were very accessible—where Pearl Jam was 'Keep everyone away'."

Despite the success, Cameron remembers the first chinks in the armor showing around this time. "For the most part, [the tour] was pretty fun, and then towards the end of that tour, the whole fabric of our group was starting to unravel a little bit. We weren't really getting along that good. The pressures of touring so much, just being on the major label machine of record-tour-record-tour just sort of took its toll after a while. After that, I think we took a little break, then we started to try and get some songs going for 'Down on the Upside'."

Produced by Adam Kasper, 'Down on the Upside' was released in May of 1996. While the album peaked at #2 on the U.S. charts and contained its share of highlights ("Pretty Noose," "Blow Up the Outside World"), it didn't exactly measure up to its stellar predecessor. Cameron- "It was my idea to record it at Studio Litho with Adam Kasper, because I felt our last situation was so kind of intense with all these big named producer guys involved. It just wasn't our scene at all—we just went back to the homemade method of making records with our buddy Adam. It was good, but we weren't all on the same page. I was certainly trying to keep everyone motivated and just try to get it off the ground, but if people don't want to do things, it's really hard to get them going. I just think that at that time, we just weren't enjoying the process as much as we had been."

And as Cameron recollected earlier, things only got worse once Soundgarden hit the road in support of 'Upside,' first as part of Lollapalooza once more, and then their own headlining tour. By the time the tour was winding down in Australia and Hawaii, Halfin could see the writing on the wall. "[Shepherd] kept walking off stage halfway through the last few shows—you got an idea they weren't getting on. You'd be in Australia, and they'd just be holed up all day—Chris would just stay in his room all day, you never saw him."

Shepherd recalls what put him in such a foul mood during their last few shows. "That last show we played in Hawaii was the night that I found out it was our last show. Because our bass tech, I'd gotten him out of rehab, which is another harsh thing about our family that was going on—but that's a whole other story. But anyway, I got him over to Hawaii, and he called a band meeting. He's the only guy besides one of us that can call a band meeting—he had seniority. He goes, 'What's this shit I hear [that] this is your last show and you're breaking up?' And I'm like, 'What?!' And everyone didn't rebut that, they just sat there. I was like, 'Oh my God, what the fuck'?"

"And of course, my equipment died that night. It completely died, and the other opening band had already left, so there was no other fucking equipment in the building. So I got all pissed off and smashed my bass. I was totally out of my head—angry and pissed off, drunk. I left the stage because there was no sound. I'm not going to stand up there and monkey around like I'm playing. It was almost right away; I think I got to play six songs, if that. And I was so lividly sad, because that was the end of the tour after my honey had left me. And that was it, the last show of the tour that she should have been with me on. It was the most creative and destructive music that I'd ever heard or been part of. The final magic."

Two months later, Cameron was surprised to find a mystery visitor one morning at his Seattle home. "I took my dog out for a walk, came back, and Chris' truck was in my driveway. I was like, 'Cool, Chris never comes to visit. Awesome man—we'll work on some stuff. What a great opportunity.' So I go into the house, and my girlfriend—who's now my wife—she goes, 'Hey, Chris is in the basement.' I go down there, and he just reeked of alcohol. I think he'd been up all night drinking, and he looked a little odd, so I said, 'Hey, what's up man?' And he was like, 'Well, I'm here because I'm leaving the band'."

Shepherd also recalls getting a similar visit from Cornell that day. "We're all standing in my living room, and my friend goes, 'Today's the day the Beatles broke up.' And Chris goes, 'Here man,' and hands me the bottle [of whiskey]. I take a swig, we go down to my car, and he says, 'I'm quitting, I'm breaking up the band. How do you feel about that?' I looked down at the ground, I spit, and I went, 'Alright.' That's how I joined the band—they asked me, 'Do you want to join the band?' I looked down at the ground, I spit, looked up, and said, 'Fuck yeah!' So it was kind of fitting for me." Just like that, one of Seattle's finest was over.

In Soundgarden's wake, Cornell initially launched a solo career, before uniting with 3/4's of Rage Against the Machine as Audioslave. Cameron has remained busy with another garage rock outfit, Wellwater Conspiracy, as well as keeping the beat in Pearl Jam. Shepherd appeared to disappear for a spell, before returning this year with a belatedly released second album from Hater, and focusing on an all-new outfit, Unkmongoni. Thayil on the other hand has appeared to completely vanish, as his ex-bandmates do not even have contact info for him. Jack Endino offers this update, "Kim is basically hanging out, reading books, watching TV. I'm not sure what he's doing."

Looking back at Soundgarden's split nearly ten years later, it's clear the group did the noble thing, and shut things down at their peak (a la the Police and the Beatles). But perhaps it's Halfin who sums it up best with a comparison. "Whereas a band like Metallica got progressively worse, [Soundgarden] were getting progressively better when it fell apart. Soundgarden albums improve as they go, where the Metallica albums don't. They start well—'Kill 'Em All' is probably their best album, and then it just goes all downhill from there."

Bonus Bit #1: Nevermind

How Ben Shepherd turned down Nirvana.

With Nirvana readying the material that would appear on their landmark album, 'Nevermind,' Shepherd almost found himself as a member of the band. "Yeah, I was supposed to play the other guitar. But I kinda really didn't do anything, except be a friend with them on tour. I was supposed to be another guitar player for them, but I was always like, 'You guys should just stay a three-piece man.' Then it came to us being in Ann Arbor for a couple of days. What happened was I'd rehearsed all the new stuff that they didn't even play on that tour—that was a make up tour, because Jason had quit, or they'd kicked him out. Then they came home for a little while, then I went on the road with them for a little while. And before we left, we rehearsed everything that basically became 'Nevermind,' and never played that shit live. They only played 'Bleach' back then. That's pretty close to how it was. The day before Soundgarden asked me to try out, Nirvana asked me to try out. I said, 'Well, shit, I've got to do Nirvana first you guys,' and they were like, 'Alright, cool.' Because they asked first, or it would have been the other way around—I would have said the same thing. But with Nirvana I would have gotten to play guitar, which was my first love. Hiro made me feel really good when I joined, he's like, 'Man, I'm really glad you're doing it Ben. You're good at it, so go for it.'

I was like, 'Thanks brother.' All the rest of the guys in the band were fucking awesome, and made it really cool and smooth. Made it easy, y'know? It could have been really trippy, but it wasn't."

Bonus Bit #2: Double the Pleasure

If Ben Shepherd had his way, there would have been more 'Garden albums during their commercial peak, 1991-1996.

Soundgarden's last three albums were definitely epic in length, averaging well over an hour. But the grand prize went to the hour and ten minute long 'Superunknown,' whose vinyl version had to be issued as a double LP set. With such an outpouring of songwriting by Shepherd and his bandmates, the bassist wanted to issue even more music. "Every record we made, there were so many extra songs. We didn't even bother to rehearse them, or we'd get them to the point where they could be tracked and then decide not to. We always had an extra album's worth of shit to do. That's what I always wanted to do, like, 'Fuck this, let's record two records now, go on the road for this one record, and then while we're on the road, we can release the second record.' No one ever liked that idea [laughs]. We could have recorded two records in a row every time. Just eliminate the middle process and go for it every time— have one in the vaults, so when you're touring, you can have more time off. Like working to get ahead, instead of just subsistence. I think towards the end, we started just bringing in songs almost finished to each other. There would probably be logistically more, because the time of accumulation of songs and stuff."

Bonus Bit #3: Brothers in Arms

Faith No More and Soundgarden, two of the era's biggest bands, often found themselves sharing the stage. Matt Cameron recalls the blood, sweat, and beers.

During late 1989/early 1990, Soundgarden found themselves participating in a three-band-bill with Faith No More and prog-metallists Voivod, jokingly dubbed "The Munsters of Rock" amongst its participants. "That was probably one of our best tours ever," admits Cameron. "It was just so memorable. We loved the bands we were touring with—everyone got along great. At the time,

Faith No More was just starting to break—Voivod at the time was the biggest draw. During that tour, Faith No More started to just get mega huge, so we had to flip the line-up around a few times—depending on what city we were at. I just couldn't believe how great Voivod was back then. They would just smoke the biggest fatties before they went on stage—the most technical, most involved music you could ever imagine, and it was just spot-on. So they must have learned it that way, y'know? We got along great. I'm still in touch with Mike Bordin. It was just killer. I think Patton and Chris—the two singers were egging each other on each night, who could sing the highest or who could do the craziest acrobatics. I remember once, Patton played before us and he threw the mic cable over the lighting rig, and he said, 'I predict Chris Cornell will do this tonight!' And he started to crawl up the mic cable and dangle from the lights." A few years later, Soundgarden and Faith No More would cross paths again. "We actually toured with Faith No More and Guns N' Roses a little bit later on in Europe, in '92. That's when Faith No More was at their full, mighty power, and they were just incredible. Oh my god. They were just one of the most stunning live bands I've ever seen in my life."

Classic Rock—Summer 2005, issue 83

Ratt

Ratt Trap

With the Mötley Crüe reunion and nostalgia for '80s metal at a peak, Ratt are one band that won't be reforming. Yet, between 1984 and '86, they were the band who battled Nikki Sixx and friends for cover stories, chart positions, and spots on MTV. Classic Rock speaks to those ruled— and destroyed—by "the Three P's."

[Robbin Crosby interview by Mitch Lafon]

The world of Ratt circa 2005 is a turbulent one. For starters, it's unclear who is entitled to the "Ratt" name—singer Stephen Pearcy (who tours as Stephen Pearcy & the Rat Bastards), or guitarist Warren DeMartini and drummer Bobby Blotzer (who tour as Ratt, with replacement members)? Add to it that one of their most identifiable members, Robbin Crosby, recently died, and bassist Juan Croucier is out of the picture, and you have a dicey situation.

But roughly 23 years ago, the band was a tight unit. Hollywood's Sunset Strip was a punk rock haven in the late '70s/early '80s, but come 1982, one-time Strip regulars Van Halen had inspired a legion of bands. "It was crazy, anything went," remembers Pearcy. "People were fucking and pissing and partying and drinking. It was like that Doors movie, but it was in the early '80s."

And there was a wave of groups that in a few years would spearhead the glam/pop metal movement—Mötley Crüe, Quiet Riot, W.A.S.P., Stryper, and Great White. Additionally, you had Mickey Ratt.

San Diego native Pearcy recalls stumbling upon a then-unknown band, which changed his life. "I used to travel up [to L.A.], and got to meet Van Halen before they got signed. I used to sit on the stage at the Whiskey when Van Halen played in front of 18 people. I'd be shitting my pants—'This is crazy, I have to tell my friends'—and nobody believed me that there was a new thing. I said, 'I'm going to L.A.'." Soon after, Mickey Ratt was born.

But few failed to match Pearcy's desire to "rock n' roll all night and party every day," as bandmates came and went, including guitarist Jake E. Lee. "Jake was in the band for nearly a year, he was getting noticed as we were getting noticed. Dio auditioned him, then Ozzy auditioned him."

Knowing that he needed a six-string hero to launch the group, Pearcy tracked down another San Diego musician, Warren DeMartini. Soon after, mutual friend Robbin Crosby was enlisted as second guitarist, and through the local musician grapevine, a rhythm section of bassist Juan Croucier and drummer Bobby Blotzer was solidified. Mickey Ratt was now simply known as Ratt.

Blotzer recalls "Hunger, lack of food, fire in our veins—a lot of fun and good times" and "A lot of camaraderie going on" with other bands. But one group stuck out among all the party hearty acts—Metallica—who Blotzer not-so-fondly remembers sharing a stage with.

"I remember Metallica opening for us in some church in Pasadena. It wasn't an active church anymore; they were using it for shows. Metallica always had an attitude like they were better than everybody else. I didn't get their trip then. We were trying to write catchy 'airplay' songs, that still had a rough edge. Hook-heavy. They were playing the shit that we wouldn't want to play—over-riffing and not catchy. But, who's got the last laugh?"

With their peers getting signed, Ratt felt left out in the cold. Quickly, a plan was devised—record an indie EP in hopes of attracting major labels. But friction reared its head. DeMartini- "When you rehearse all week, you get up on stage, and someone is wasted on Jack Daniels, it's easy to blame 'that guy'." DeMartini exited briefly, before Crosby convinced him to reconsider.

This proved to be a tricky time for Croucier, who was under contract by Q Prime Management to play bass in Dokken, but was smitten with Ratt. "[Q Prime] had me on a small salary—I was a starving musician. It came down to deep soul searching. I'd rather be happy and be in Ratt, than be miserable and have a deal with Dokken. I chose Ratt."

Recorded in two days, Ratt's self-titled EP quickly created a buzz. DeMartini- "KLOS had a show called 'Local Licks'—at the peak of rush hour—and 'You Think You're Tough' was played. That led to Atlantic coming down." With a showcase set for July 27, 1983, at the Beverly Theater, Ratt delivered. Blotzer- "It was like one of those stories that you hear about where backstage are all these labels, and they're all jockeying to get into the dressing room. Doug Morris, the president of Atlantic, made it in. We got the deal that night."

With a label now in place, Ratt got to work on their full-length debut with producer Beau Hill (Pearcy- "All I remember is having a great time— fucking chicks in the lobby"). While the resulting album, 1984's 'Out of the Cellar,' contained several subsequent Ratt staples—"Wanted Man," "Back for

More"—there was one that would break the band. Pearcy- "When Beau heard 'Round and Round,' he said, 'What's this?' We're like, 'I don't know, it's not really tight.' Beau's like, 'We're going to make it tight.' The next thing you know, it's the single."

DeMartini- "We did all the things to assemble [the album]. Then there was this 'calm before the storm'—for six or eight months, nothing. Out of the blue, we got a call that we were going to make a video. It just exploded. We were doing our own club tour, and then we got on a national tour."

It seemed like pop metal was all the rage during the summer of 1984, as Van Halen, Mötley Crüe, Quiet Riot, and Twisted Sister were all over MTV. And Ratt thrived under this rock-friendly climate, as the Don Letts-directed "Round and Round" video and a tour supporting Ozzy Osbourne catapulted 'Cellar' into the U.S. top-ten.

In addition to all the U.S. attention, Ratt was massive in Japan. Blotzer- "That was fully the films you see of the Beatles. The hotels were mobbed with people, police escorts, couldn't go in and out of the hotel at will, hundreds of people outside at all time. It was true rock stardom."

While the others were enjoying the wave of success, Pearcy looked beyond. "We wanted business, we wanted seats, we wanted records, we wanted fun. Big party, big money, big everything." As a result, the singer followed a motto that the great philosophers of the 21st century adhered to. "The Three P's—pussy, party, paycheck. I live [by] that motto to this day."

After the tour wrapped, Ratt regrouped in Maui to pen their second long player. But the good vibes quickly turned sour for Crosby. "Everybody got their own little room, or condo, but that was the beginning of the end. Everybody took their girlfriends, wives, and kids, but in my opinion it was a time to work."

"Everybody was doing their own thing. We were supposed to write together, but Warren had his wife and a new baby that he hadn't seen in months. Juan same thing. Stephen had his own place. I just remember feeling really alone. Nobody ever came over to my place. We all wanted to get some time off, but if we went surfing or fucked around, the manager was saying, 'When are you guys going to get together and write?'"

Released in 1985, 'Invasion of Your Privacy' was another U.S. top-ten hit, on the strength of "Lay It Down" and "You're in Love." But it was easy to detect the group was favoring pop gloss over their early raw/rocking approach.

Regardless, the album established Ratt as a major U.S. concert draw (especially when teamed with a pre-'Slippery When Wet' Bon Jovi). Blotzer- "Sold out, a lot of money, hot chicks. Young and fucking rich was a good way to be. After 'Cellar,' I bought a new car and house. After 'Invasion,' I bought everybody in my family cars and my mom a house."

Like most successful '80s groups, Ratt wasn't immune to the trappings of stardom. Pearcy- "You had big everything. Big drugs, big money, big parties. And it's all free, the more the merrier. Heroin, booze, blow—it was everywhere. Me, I always went towards the pussy and the paycheck." Blotzer recalls that drug use was "Not really a problem—the problem was getting them, like when were in places like Montana [laughs]! We snorted blow and drank, smoked weed. But then, everybody snorted blow—you'd snort blow so you could drink longer." DeMartini admits not learning from others' mistakes. "Everybody ignored what happened to our heroes in the '60s. It was a free-for-all."

While the other Ratt members appeared to handle their vices, Crosby went off the rails. "I met my wife [Playboy model Laurie Carr] at the very end of the 'Invasion' tour. When I got home I was really burned out, so I started smoking heroin. That became a ritual. I was doing a couple of hundred bucks a day. I just liked the way it made me feel better and I didn't get all drunk and hung over. I thought it was great. I went through the whole 'It's not going to happen to me' and 'I can handle it' thing."

With Ratt rapidly becoming 'pop metal elite,' Ratt committed a blunder while preparing 1986's 'Dancing Undercover.' Blotzer- "We weren't even ready. Our manager supposedly put down some deposit on a studio that we'd lose. We were in rehearsal with just a handful of ideas—Pearcy never showed up. It ended up being OK and it sold well, but for me, side two I can't even hear because of Stephen's lyrics."

But it was alleged shady dealings that also hampered the recording. Croucier- "I realized Beau Hill really didn't care about Ratt—he cared about making money. He told us, 'Be at the studio at 9am sharp, and I'm going to leave at 6pm. If you guys aren't here, we aren't going to make the record.' Subsequently, I came to find out that he was recording vocal tracks for Fiona Flanagan, on Ratt's dime, after Ratt had left the studio."

Still, MTV backed 'Undercover'—especially "Dance," "Body Talk," and "Slip of the Lip." And the resulting tour did respectfully, as power pop veterans Cheap Trick and a fast-rising Poison opened, resulting in stronger ticket sales as the dates progressed.

On Ratt's next release, 1988's 'Reach for the Sky,' a union with ex-Queen producer Mike Stone seemed promising. However, Stone was fired before the sessions wrapped, and replaced with Hill. DeMartini- "I think it fell short again. I really liked working with Mike Stone—great with sounds, and great to be around. That record started out one way, and then finished another way." Pearcy agrees that the album marked "A weird time. I think the cover says it all—everybody was into their own 'worlds'."

Crosby recalled even the tour rehearsals being stressful. "For live shows, [Stephen] rarely sang in rehearsals. He'd show up a week before and maybe make it through a set and then that was that." And it didn't get any better for Crosby once the tour began. "I'd never 'use' on tour. I'd just go cold turkey and the first couple of weeks were kind of a drag, but the 'Reach' tour was difficult for me 'cause I got strung out from all that time off."

Despite the album not being up-to-snuff, the Aerosmith-esque "Way Cool Jr." earned quite a few spins, and a career highpoint occurred—a gig at Japan's Tokyo Dome. Pearcy- "We played New Year's Eve with Bon Jovi. It was the craziest show ever—like 80,000 people, indoors. You're looking at 'dots' and the stage is like 50 feet high, trying to figure out how this could even be a purpose!" Blotzer also recalls a sweet paycheck. "We did five dates, and got paid like a million dollars."

For 1990's 'Detonator,' Ratt enlisted the songwriting aid of Desmond Child and Diane Warren. However, changing musical tastes couldn't be ignored. DeMartini- "If we had done ['Detonator'] when 'Undercover' or 'Sky' came out, it would have done better. The genre had changed so much— as good as it was, it was kind of an anachronism."

Croucier had other ideas for the album. "I wanted to go back to the EP. Lose the big production, get right back in-your-face. Someone said to our manager, 'How about if we get someone like…Desmond Child?' Which was the last thing I wanted to do."

Blotzer remains unimpressed with the genre that killed glam. "By and large, I didn't really like grunge. I thought [Nirvana] had a handful of good songs, but to this day, I hear ['Nevermind'], and after four or five songs, I've had enough. I didn't think [grunge] had anywhere near the staying power that our genre—hard rock/metal—had. But it definitely put us all out of business."

As if changing musical tastes wasn't detrimental enough, Crosby's addiction worsened. Blotzer- "I didn't know Robbin was taking heroin. He went to rehab, came out, we toured Japan, then he relapsed. He was really out of it. Going on tour was not going to help his plight. He couldn't be around that atmosphere and stay clean."

It was obvious to Croucier that his friend was quickly becoming a drug casualty. "What was affected the most was his creativity. He started withdrawing from the band and isolating himself. There became an issue between Warren and Robbin about the guitar work—Warren wanted to play more lead, and wanted Robbin to play less lead. Robbin's feelings were really hurt by that. It launched him into a depression and more drug abuse."

With Michael Schenker taking Crosby's spot, the tension increased. Blotzer- "We weren't selling tickets like normal. We'd be at a 12,000 seater with 5,000 people there—it was wearing on everybody's nerves. We were fighting within the band—it was a shitty tour." Shortly after the 1991 collection, 'Ratt & Roll 81-91,' Pearcy exited, spelling Ratt's first break-up.

From a business standpoint, it was the worst time to split. Blotzer- "It put us in a world of shit, because we had already taken an advance from Atlantic on a record that never got recorded. We owed a lot of money from a merchandise advance we took for the 'Detonator' tour. Only a quarter of that was paid back, and we took a million bucks. We all were on the hook for about $150,000 we had to pay back. Typical Pearcy move—doesn't care about anybody but himself." Soon, lawsuits were a-flyin'.

While the others were able to fend for themselves, Crosby was the worst off. Croucier- "He got the old 'one-two rock n' roll punch.' He loses the band, and out the door goes the old wife. 'Love you too, honey!' She files for divorce, and they held his feet over the fire. His bankruptcy had to do with his personal thing following his divorce. I'm sure the Ratt problems didn't help."

Later in the decade, talk of a reunion began. But the others soon realized Crosby was in no shape to tour, as he had contracted AIDS from intravenous drug use, gained weight from a thyroid condition, and was bedridden for extended periods. Crosby- "I have full-blown AIDS. Basically, it's killing me. I've got a terminal disease. Recently, I went in for surgery 'cause my back hurt so bad, and they got all this infectious fluid out. Then they found that my bones were not getting oxygen under the infectious fluid [a condition called osteomyelitis]. I've been in the hospital for eight straight months and in and out for over seven years."

Without Crosby present and Croucier opting out ("Nothing had changed with Stephen—he was still drinking heavily, very stubborn, just a tense situation"), Pearcy-DeMartini-Blotzer re-launched Ratt. The trio compiled an album of unused tunes, 1997's 'Collage,' and hit the road—eventually releasing a 1999 self-titled album (on John Kalodner's Portrait label). Croucier- "Bobby, Stephen, and Warren decided [Robbin] wasn't going to be in the band. But they didn't so much as call him to tell him. So Robbin was really upset about that. His disease became worse—eventually they put him in a hospice."

On June 6, 2002, Crosby died at the age of 41. Croucier- "All of his friends basically abandoned him. The truth is that he was furious with the guys from Ratt, because they hadn't shown any interest until the last maybe six months of his life. That's what he told me. Which is really sad because he loved those guys."

But before Crosby's passing, Pearcy was no longer seeing eye-to-eye with the others. "I was playing guitar, and I'm like, 'This isn't it, this is wrong.' Then comes the end of that record in 2000, and I told them, 'Stop. We have to take a step back and look at things. You're going into [secondary] markets and people aren't showing up. There's no single, no video, no development—this is a brick wall.' They wanted to go to Japan, I said, 'I ain't payin' for my own trip. That should be the label's responsibility. I'm going to take a break.' They said, 'We're going to grab a new singer.' I went, 'Well, don't forget that I have major interests in both entities.' Long story short—went to court, they sued, I tried to get them back, and they got away with making the courts believe [otherwise]."

DeMartini's accounts of what went down differs. "The final leg of the tour was booked. Then we had a falling out, and Stephen decided to leave the band, start a solo band, and go on the road with that. We learned through the testimony in this trial, he was already working on the solo thing when he assembled the tour. We could have just taken a break. I never understood why he insisted that we book a Ratt tour, and then at the same time start working on a solo thing. Anyway, he quit the band and the tour had to be cancelled. He went on the road with a solo band, so we got a new singer and continued."

And continue they did. DeMartini and Blotzer toured this summer with ex-Love/Hate singer Jizzy Pearl, as part of the 'Rock Never Stops' tour. Pearcy also remained busy this summer—touring as part of 'American Metal Blast 2005.' Additionally, Pearcy recently released several albums, including 'Fueler' and 'Rat Attack,' and Croucier is readying 'Demos from the Ratt Years.'

Despite all the lawsuits, there was an attempt to unite Pearcy-DeMartini-Blotzer-Croucier. Blotzer- "[Pearcy] tried to get this thing back together, but his terms were asinine beyond belief. He sent some nutty email stating he wants half the merchandise, he wants to manage, produce, call all the shots. It was a joke. I laughed in a sick way, 'God, this guy, is he ever going to change?' Stephen needs counseling badly in my opinion."

On the other side, Pearcy offers a different take. "I made a proposal to them. 'Alright, let's stop—this is business to me. These are mostly my songs, it's my band down to the logo. I propose an album and a tour.' DeMartini shot it down, and I said, 'OK, I can see you're staying true to your destruction of this band.' It would have given the fans a 20 year anniversary record and a tour, like Mötley, actually before the Mötley thing was exposed. So they dropped the ball on that, and actually put the end to Ratt."

Croucier on the other hand, doesn't agree with either side. "Frankly, I'm embarrassed by Bobby and Warren calling themselves Ratt. I think it's wrong—it's not Ratt. 3/5's of the guys are gone; the guys who did most of the writing are no longer in the band. I can understand they need to make money, but to take the name and abuse it doesn't seem like a respectful and intelligent thing to do. Ironically, I know if Stephen had the chance, he'd be out there doing it too. The damage is done at this point."

Looking back, Crosby offered an honest assessment before his passing. "I ate, slept and drank rock 'n roll since I was ten years old, and my dreams have all come true. And then some have been dashed against the rocks, by some people that I didn't even really respect at times."

Bonus Bit #1: Strip Tease

How the members of two of the biggest L.A. bands of the '80s ruled the Strip.

"In the early days, Nikki used to come and see Mickey Ratt, and we became friends," explains Stephen Pearcy. "They were trolling the Strip—needing food and housing—just like me. I had 'Ratt Mansion West,' it was a one-bedroom apartment in Palms, a few miles from the Strip. We used to hang out and made a gang, 'The Gladiators.' We found girls to take us home, feed us, breed us, and do whatever to survive. Nikki was 'Nikki Leader Sixx,' Robbin was 'King Crosby,' I was 'Ratt Patrol Leader,' Tommy was 'Sergeant in Arms.' We all looked after each other, and made sure everybody partied as hard as they could." Bobby Blotzer also recalls hangin' with the Crüe. "I used to dirt bike with Tommy and Vince. My ex-wife and I, and Tommy and Heather [Locklear] used to go on trips together. We would go out, and just fucking dominate any club or wherever we went." The Crüe-connection also ran deep for Juan Croucier. "Mick Mars and I were going to start a band. We're sitting in my apartment, talking about names, and he goes, 'I got a name for you, Motley Crew.' He said he was watching a documentary on the Beatles, and they were interviewing this little old lady in Hamburg. They asked her what she thought of the Beatles, and she said, 'They're a motley crew, aren't they?' I saw him about two weeks later. He goes, 'I just auditioned with this guy, Nikki Sixx…'" Additionally, Robbin Crosby formed a bad habit with Sixx. "Nikki Sixx and I had gotten into the heroin thing together. He was supposed to be the best man at my wedding and he didn't come, 'cause there was going to be people drinking. That was when he had just gone through his rehab thing."

Bonus Bit #2: The Pop Metal Wars

If you were a U.S. hairspray rocker circa '85, the Ratt/Bon Jovi arena tour was the place to be. But the groups weren't always so chummy…

"We had played some shows with Bon Jovi, when we first went out," remembers Bobby Blotzer. "Our first shows out on the road in '84, we played with them in Portland, Maine and Seattle, Washington. We were going to keep playing with them, then we got the Ozzy tour, so we hightailed it down to San Diego to start the tour with Ozzy. Bon Jovi were shitty to us—moved their gear way up, we had no stage room when there was plenty of room for them to move back. Shitty attitudes, y'know, 'east coast versus west coast.' So when we were headlining an arena tour for '85, and Bon Jovi were offered up, we were like, 'Alright, bring them out—let's get some payback [laughs]!' They came out, and we were going to show them who did what—their album went gold, and we had multi-platinum status. Quickly though, we became friends, so all that shit went down the tubes. That tour was huge man, sold out arenas every night. It was just amazing—crazy." But for Robbin Crosby, the tour showed that both groups were headed in opposite directions. "Every night, [Bon Jovi] had a great time in their dressing room before the show, but go into our dressing room and everybody is bitching at each other. Every fucking night, Stephen would go out, watch about two seconds of their show and would come back in just raging pissed that Jonny was ripping off his shtick. It was like 'Stephen, you don't have a shtick to rip off. You're not David Lee Roth. You don't say anything special. You barely know what fucking city we're in. So, what do you mean he's stealing your shtick?' It became the feud of the century."

www.therattpack.com

Classic Rock—Summer 2005, issue 83

Faith No More

The Real Things

When a rock band signs to a major label, the goal for most is to build a nice and comfortable career—even if it means being a bit predictable at times to please the mainstream. No one ever bothered telling that to Faith No More. Every single Faith No More member from their first album through their last (as well as their longest-tenured producer) charts the progress of the band that made a career out of keeping listeners on their toes.

"They were really like a spider web, pulling equally in five different directions," recalls long-time Faith No More producer Matt Wallace. "There was no de facto leader of the band. If any guy tried to be the leader, the other guys would just say, 'Fuck you.' They would laugh him out of there. It was pretty much the most democratic band I've ever worked with. No guy could lead that thing. Patton was really into Sade, as was Roddy Bottum. And Roddy was really into the techno thing, and Mike Bordin was into Killing Joke and studied African drumming at U.C. Berkeley. And Bill Gould was the glue of the whole thing."

For a period of time, the ever stretching "spider web" had plenty of elasticity, as Faith No More rocketed out of the underground and straight up the charts, with a sound that soaked in countless styles. And for a period of time in the early-mid 1990's, they were one of the top rock bands on the planet. But ultimately, line-up hiccups and bickering would derail one of the most influential and respected rock bands of all-time.

The Faith No More story begins with the aforementioned "glue"—bassist Bill Gould. Hailing from Hollywood, California, Gould began playing in local bands during the late '70s, just as the Sunset Strip was being infiltrated with such punk outfits as the Germs (and soon after, Black Flag). By the time he had reached 18, Gould had enrolled in college in Berkeley. Gould- "The first thing I did after I unpacked all my stuff in the dorm room, I walked down to the record store on Telegraph Avenue, and looked on the bulletin boards to get in a new band. There was a phone number for this guy Mike Morris, who was putting a band together. And that was what became Faith No Man."

Yes dear readers, before Faith No More, there was Faith No Man. Joining Gould and singer/guitarist Morris was keyboardist Wade Worthington, and a drummer by the name of Mike Bordin. But according to Gould, Faith No Man's sound was far from the all-encompassing sound of what Faith No More would one day be. "It was a little more derivative of what was happening in Great Britain—Theatre of Hate and Killing Joke. And there was a post-punk thing that was kind of new. I was kind of getting out of punk rock by then, because the Black Flag crowd started becoming saturated with football players and meatheads. So this post-punk thing was very appealing."

Looking to get their sound down on tape, Bordin recounts that producer Matt Wallace entered the picture the same way Gould did. "[Gould] saw a flyer around Berkeley, saying 'Dangerous Rhythm Studios—cheap demos, I'll do anything.' We did some demos with him, and we loved him. A good, fucking fun-loving guy, he was willing to work as hard as he had to." Recording soon began in Wallace's parents' garage, which led to Faith No Man' debut single, 1982's "Song of Liberty" b/w "All Quiet in Heaven." Gould- "I had pneumonia—a really bad bronchial infection, where I couldn't hear. My ears completely plugged up, so I recorded that record deaf!"

Soon, Faith No Man was playing live (Gould- "Pretty horrible shows"), but it was during rehearsals that it became apparent that the rest of the members didn't see eye-to-eye with Morris. Worthington saw the writing on the wall and exited, replaced by a roommate of Gould's, Roddy Bottum. But with tensions increasing between Morris and the rest of the band, a move had to be made.

Bordin- "We all just kind of quit. We said, 'We're going to start playing [without Morris]. We like each other, we've got a vibe. We've got an itch that we want to scratch.' So that's why there was keyboard, bass, and drums, and that's why we switched guitarists so much, because it was just us three. The 'Man' was gone—the man was 'No More'."

Now christened Faith No More, the trio began playing out with another guitarist, Mark Bowen, but instead of getting a permanent singer, the group played with a variety of singers. One singer that stuck around a while longer than the rest was none other than Courtney Love. "Courtney was one of the revolving singers we had," explains Bottum. "She sang with us for probably six months. She was an awesome performer; she liked to sing in her nightgown, adorned with flowers." But as Gould points out, it just didn't work out. "She was a very chaotic personality—she took a lot of work. It just got too much after a while."

With Faith No More having lined up an L.A. gig, Gould invited an old friend, Chuck Mosley, to man the mic. Gould- "He had a couple of 40-ouncers of beer—I don't think he'd ever sang before—he just got on the mic and yelled. I think we had a show in San Francisco after that, and he came up for that and did it. It just started becoming a band thing."

Mosley recalls his early days as a singer. "The thing I hear most often is, 'Did you ever think of going into stand up?' I learned early on the devastating effect [of] the in-between song silence and the band trying to talk amongst themselves and tune up. The unfamiliarity of relating to the crowd was always an 'energy black hole,' so I always tried to fill it up with whatever's going on at that present time—just saying really stupid stuff."

Around the same time, Bowen exited the band, and an old friend of Bordin's, Metallica's Cliff Burton, suggested who Faith No More should consider as their next guitarist. Bordin- "I was with Billy Gould eating at a Mexican restaurant in the East Bay, and lo and behold, there's Cliff. He goes, 'Y'know, you've got to get Jim in your band, because Jim is working a regular job, it's fucking killing him. You know he can do what you want him to do'."

According to Gould however, Martin's name came with a disclaimer from Bordin, who had previously played with Martin (and Burton) in a band called EZ Street. "Jim and Mike Bordin never really liked each other, apparently. The way it was put to me was through Bordin—'There's this guy Cliff knows. He's an asshole, he's always been an asshole. I was in a band with him and I quit because he was such an asshole. But he can play guitar'."

With Martin's arrival, the final piece was in place for Faith No More musical puzzle, according to Wallace. "I always liked to compare him [to] the guy who comes in with big army boots and stomps—wearing muddy shoes—across your floor. He came from a Black Sabbath and Corrosion of Conformity [background]. He was really into the much heavier stuff. It was an essential ingredient to weigh the band properly."

And in addition to bringing an extra-added music weight, Wallace points out that Martin was an unmistakable original. "At the time we met, he looked like the star of that movie 'Eraserhead.' He almost looked like Kid N' Play, where he had this slightly tallish, curly head of hair that looked really weird, and he had these really thick glasses. He would just say whatever's on his mind—there was no governor between his brain and his mouth. It was kind of refreshing to have that."

Martin remembers these early shows as a time where the group looked towards non-musical areas for inspiration and guidance. "We burned a lot of sage at those early shows and some of the band members liked playing on significant days of the Wicca calendar; such as the summer solstice or the spring equinox. These were the really early shows. Once we started in earnest, we left the Paganism behind."

As a result of the group's then-still interest in all things Wiccan, Wallace was met with apprehension from a few friends when he went to work with the group on their next set of demos in 1985, which would turn out to be half of their debut album, 'We Care A Lot.' "Everybody kind of freaked out, because the band were this...a lot of people thought of it as a Satanic thing, but I think they were, for lack of a better phrase, more into the Wiccan thing. We walked into Prairie Sun to record—they were doing these sage smudges. They had this slightly metaphysical thing about them—people were always like, 'Dude, they're into Satan!' But it never phased me, I knew they were creative guys, and that they were going to do what they were going to do."

With several new songs in the can, Gould handed the tape to a friend that worked at a nearby record store—with specific instructions. "'Just play it when people are shopping for records.' It turns out that Ruth Schwartz, who started Mordam Records, was shopping for records when he played the tape, and came up to the desk to ask what music that was. He told her, 'It's just my roommate's band. She said, 'What label?' and he said, 'They're not signed.' And she called us up like two days after that. It's kind of bizarre, but that's what happened."

The group returned back to the studio to finish off the second half of the album—the entire album being done in two three-day weekends, according to Wallace. But it was during these sessions that a recurring pattern with Mosley sprung up. "I probably 'mental cased' myself into a cold, a sore throat, or [lost] my voice. It just never changed. And I was never fully prepared—I was always working on stuff as we were recording. That's kind of been a trademark of mine—coming to the studio mostly prepared, but not really knowing what I'm going to do on certain parts and having to work them out right there."

With the album released in 1985, college radio latched onto the album's contagious title track, which would become one of the decade's great underground rock anthems. Gould- "I think that we didn't know how damn good it was until we were actually recording it and heard it on two speakers. We were kind of surprised that we had this song that seemed to have a life of its own." Bottum also remembers what inspired him to pen the lyrics. "I wrote the lyrics to that song after listening to a whole lot of Run-DMC."

The supporting tour was a whole other story, however. Gould- "We got in a four-door pick-up truck, with a little trailer hitch, and just hit the road. Great fun, great tour, very hard work—had no fucking money whatsoever." Martin also recalls this early FNM touring era. "We traveled across the country and had about 30 dates in 90 days. It was brutal. We saw very little money, and as a consequence, we ate very little. Chuck was an asshole. The wheels fell off the truck. We met many generous people who let us stay with them. We lived in the Metroplex in Atlanta, Georgia for a couple of weeks. Rats ate hot and sour soup out of my beard!"

Shortly after returning from their inaugural Stateside tour, work began on their sophomore effort (which saw the group jump from Mordam to Slash/ Reprise). Released in 1987, 'Introduce Yourself' featured a more focused sound and approach than their debut; the album also featured a re-recording of 'We Care A Lot.'

The album's ensuing tour saw Faith No More hook up with another up-and-coming band, the Red Hot Chili Peppers. Martin- "We were traveling in a box van with no windows. Drove all the way to the east coast for the first show. Flea asked me if we liked to smoke weed. When I said 'Yes,' he said, 'We're going to get along just fine.' We did something like 52 dates in 56 days."

But it was during the group's first-ever European shows where it was clear that Mosley was going to be the next in-line to exit. The problems became exacerbated when a roadie friend of the singer's was fired after getting into a fistfight with Martin. "By the time that happened, Chuck was already kind of out of it for me. I guess Jim and [the roadie] had been drinking and they got in a fight. It came a point where Jim was our guitar player—he broke his hand fighting the guy. It's the first night of our European tour, and somebody had to go—it obviously wasn't going to be our guitar player. Chuck's reaction… he took it very personally—to stick up for this roadie." On the same tour, tensions ran so high that Gould punched Mosley on stage.

Gould recalls the final straw with Mosley, after the band returned home.

"There was a certain point when I went to rehearsal, and Chuck wanted to do all acoustic guitar songs. It was just so far off the mark—I think I actually attacked him again [laughs]!" Instead of simply firing Mosley, Gould employed a similar tactic that ousted Morris several years earlier. "The upshot of [the confrontation] was that I got up, walked out, and quit the band. Just said, 'I'm done—I can't take this any longer. It's just so ridiculous.' The same day, I talked to Bordin, and he said, 'Well, I still want to play with you,' and Bottum did the same thing. It was another one of these 'firing somebody without firing them'."

After Mosley's exit, rumors began circulating about the singer's alleged party-hearty lifestyle. "I've never been addicted to heroin," explains Mosley. "But I've done everything from PCP to acid. Had a problem with coke, which I don't touch anymore." Looking back on the split today, Mosley offers his take. "I said, 'I don't want to [leave], I want to work this out.' I even made moves before that to make them say, 'Look, I'm on your guys' team. We're all shooting for a common goal here.' I did a couple things to gesture that I was going to work along them, not against them. But by that point, they were already too sick of me. I felt bad about it, but what can you do?"

Despite being singer-less, the remaining members of Faith No More set out to pen "album number three." Bordin- "The music was written in shifts on that record, in that that was the first record we wrote and recorded in L.A. We were staying down in the Oakwood [Apartments]. Jim and I were sharing a place. We were partying hard, and Metallica was in town—people getting fucked up and drinking Jägermeister. That was that whole beginning of the bad period that Hetfield talked about when he got sober—that was 'Alcoholica'."

"Billy and Roddy were working probably 10:00 to 3:00. Jim was drinking all night with his buddies—he wouldn't go to sleep until 7:00 or 8:00 in the morning. We would get up at fucking 4:00 and go into the studio around 7:00, and work 'til probably 10:00 or 11:00. So we were totally doing shifts. We didn't even have each other's phone numbers! We just went into the rehearsal room and thought we'd see each other eventually. And then one day, Billy stayed late or we came early—'Hey, where have you been?' And then Billy started getting on our own schedule too. We just started writing shit—we were all working on stuff. And then ultimately, it all came together. It was very fucking fully realized—this is us, this is what we are."

Eventually, a singer search began, and a name that was being thrown around early on was Soundgarden's Chris Cornell. Gould- "Soundgarden opened up for us a few times in Seattle. We were friends with them. I think one day, Mike and I went to [Cornell's] house to jam, but I don't think that we had a musical connection."

Soon after, it was a then-teenaged singer (who gave Bordin a tape of his band a few years earlier in Eureka, California) that the band began talking about—Mr. Mike Patton. Bottum recalls not being exactly wild about the idea initially. "Mike Bordin really liked his Mr. Bungle tape he gave us. So did Jim Martin. I didn't—not my cup of tea."

Martin recalls a conversation he had with Patton around this time. "We auditioned about five other people, and it was pretty clear that Patton had superior natural ability. We called him and told him to come down; we wanted him to go to work immediately. He was very hesitant like, 'I can't do this right now; it's not a good day. I have a school box social to go to. And tomorrow is show and tell. If I had plenty of advance warning, I might be able to come down for a little while, but today is not good.' I informed him he was at a crossroads in life—one way was to become a singer, the other way was to be a record store clerk in a shitty little town in Northern California. He really was like that. Very clean and shiny, nice kid. Milk and cookies type." Patton wisely lined up a tryout, and soon became Faith No More's new singer.

With the music already written, Wallace recalls that the group was adamant that Patton work with what he was given. "Patton was asked to write the lyrics for that record, and he did that within twelve days—he wrote all the lyrics and melodies. And basically, he said, 'Hey guys, can I make this part longer or this part shorter,' and they said, 'No.' So the interesting part of that story is the music was done, and they were taking no input from Patton about arrangements."

In return, Patton was adamant about his singing style. Wallace- "He was singing really nasally and also, his pitch on record was not as good as I knew it could be. I was just like, 'Why don't you just hit the notes?' And he goes, 'No man, this is my style.' Because he'd sing the song on tape, and he'd do this amazing, really full voice. I'm like, 'That's the voice! Get that on the darn tape!' He was like, 'No man, I don't want to do it'."

"I never asked Patton this directly, but one of two things happened—one, he was trying to keep that kind of snotty, punky, rap persona, and that was important for him to have that snotty attitude on the recording. Or another possibility was that he still had a lot of loyalties with Mr. Bungle, and I think he wanted to separate himself as the singer from Mr. Bungle and Faith No More." But Patton himself looked upon it from a different perspective, "It was my first record, and I was just happy to be there."

Released in 1989, 'The Real Thing' stuck out like a sore thumb amongst what was going on in the world of hard rock around that time. Name a style, and it's probably represented here—rap ("Epic"), pop ("Underwater Love"), prog ("Woodpecker from Mars"), piano jazz ("Edge of the World"), and thrash metal ("Surprise! You're Dead!"). The U.S. was slow to latch onto the band, but the U.K. wasted little time—as a sold-out London show was taped in early 1990, and later issued as the CD/home video, 'Live at the Brixton Academy.'

With FNM's U.S. label deeming 'The Real Thing' "dead" and that it was time to start thinking about the next album, they granted the band one more video—for "Epic." A wise move, as it became a huge hit in the summer of 1990—the single peaked at #9 and the album at #11 Stateside—and finally broke the band commercially.

Patton- "More than anything, I remember us being in Europe, in this van that smelled like vomit, from the day we got it. And our manager [would] check in with us maybe once a week. He called and said, 'Your single is blowing up over here.' We didn't believe him—we thought he was joking. We thought he was kind of buttering us up, so he could keep us on the road, and we all wanted to go home. I remember landing in the airport and going to a hotel, we were going back to the States, and seeing the damn video. Turning on the TV by chance and seeing the video, and going 'Oh shit…the joke's on us'!"

Staying on the road for nearly two years, the group took most of 1991 to pen/record songs for its all-important next album. Patton filled his free time with Mr. Bungle (who issued/toured behind their self-titled debut around this time), while also looking towards outside sources for 'artistic inspiration.' Wallace- "He was into this weird, twisted porn stuff. I remember he was showing me some of these videos he got from Japan. I was like, 'Dude, why are you watching that for?!' Crazy shit."

But when the suits at the label heard the material, they were not pleased to hear no "Epic II." Martin- "After listening to some of the rough tracks, the president of Slash Records said, 'I hope nobody bought any houses.' Of course, some of the band members did, and this comment made those members very agitated and anxious. With all the pressure of fame on top of the financial responsibility of home ownership, I began to think this record was too contrived and wanted to take a more freeform approach in the recording process. This was met with great opposition from the new homeowners."

Wallace also remembers Martin's dissatisfaction with the material. "He kept referring to the music as 'gay disco.' He just hated the material on the record. And I kept saying, 'But we really need you—your guitar playing is what's going to keep it from being 'gay disco.' We need your big army boots in here.' He couldn't get his head around it, and the band was furious."

Even with all the tension, Faith No More defied the odds, and released one of the greatest and most influential rock records of all-time, 1992's 'Angel Dust.' Unlike 'The Real Thing,' 'Angel Dust' touched upon fewer styles, but it more than made up for it in focus, performance, and uncompromising brilliance. No other band sounded like 'Angel Dust' upon its initial release (with Patton earning the "Most Valuable Player" award here, as he matured into one of rock's great singers and lyricists). Fast forward ten years, and every metal band has knowingly or unknowingly borrowed a thing or two from 'Angel Dust.' Despite this, it sold below expectations Stateside (debuting at #10, but soon falling), yet performed strong in Europe, after a hit cover of the Commodores' "Easy" was added on.

Upon its release however, it appeared as though the band had it made, when Guns N' Roses offered the quintet a long stretch of opening stadium dates in the U.K. and the U.S. (the latter tour also joined by Metallica). But FNM and G n' R were coming from two completely different worlds. Gould- "There was a rumor that Axl brought his psychic on tour with him, and it would be bad luck in any city that started with the letter 'M.' So he cancelled Manchester, Madrid, and Munich. He did Montreal, and that's when the riot happened."

"It got very bizarre. We saw Axl once or twice the whole time. We did a lot of interviews talking about how it was, and I think the band didn't appreciate that very much. We got busted one day, and we had to go apologize. It was like getting in the principal's office. We went and met Axl in his room, and to tell you the truth, he was super-cool and super-gracious. Then some guy comes in, and says, 'Now that everything's good, come over here.' We went into some trailer where there's some 'lesbian love act' going on. It just blew the whole thing. It was so fucking gross that we were just like, 'Oh God.' We thought that we came to some kind of meeting of the minds, and obviously, we hadn't."

During this time, Bottum also decided to "come out" as a gay man. Bottum- "I don't know, it happens at different times in all gay people's lives. To the rest of the band I think it might have come out of the blue and was awkward—but only initially. We were all free thinkers, independently motivated and proud of who we are and it's never been an issue with any of the band members. Including Jim Martin, the guy who you'd typically think would have issues regarding such."

However, other issues had separated Martin from the rest of the band. Bordin- "Jim wasn't stoked on a lot of 'Angel Dust.' I think in some ways, maybe he just wasn't ready to accept something different, like, 'Here's this formula we hit on that works, let's work on that for a while.' But that's not how we work. That was never the idea. I mean, think back on 'Angel Dust' and 'Real Thing,' and then compare it to what I said at the very beginning. Faith No More was a band that started out that was writing a particular set of music for a show. And you can even look at those albums as particular sets of music. They weren't going to be the same—they were never going to be the same. Even the album itself was always incredibly varied within the album—making it a satisfying fucking listening experience."

"But Jim's contributions, I got to say, between 'Real Thing' and 'Angel Dust,' dropped off. I mean, I can think of 'Jizzlobber' on 'Angel Dust,' but I can tell you half of fucking 'Zombie Eaters,' a good portion of that whole middle section of 'Woodpecker from Mars,' the whole of 'Surprise! You're Dead!' He was all over that album, y'know? Those were all parts that he brought, and all of a sudden, those parts weren't there. It was like, 'What the fuck is this? What the fuck is that'?"

Martin however casts the blame for tension within the band on two different things around this time. "Patton. He had some weird mind control over Bill and Puffy. There were many embarrassing displays of megalomania expressed in the music press. Our presentation became very undignified, and as a result, I began to lose interest. Axl Rose and management confronted Bill and Patton for their awkward remarks in the press concerning Axl. Puffy denied association, Bill said it was something else, Patton was excused because he was an idiot. I began to avoid interviews and photo shoots, you know, all the things you need to do when you're in this business. It was exhausting. The band became more hostile because they didn't think I was pulling my weight, and they accused me of being one of 'them.' There was also a dishonest attempt to realign our business agreement. My disinterest deepened. We became estranged."

The strained relationship between singer and guitarist managed to spill over into the press during this time—on more than one occasion. It was never more evident than in a Melody Maker feature dated 8 August 1992, in which writer Mat Smith (who spent time with the band during the aforementioned Guns N' Roses/Metallica/FNM U.S. tour) chronicled the rapidly growing animosity. "The trouble with modern music," [Martin] continues, "Is that there ain't enough guitar solos anymore." "I hate guitar solos," Patton hisses. "Every time our guitarist tries to do one, we stand in front of him." The bit ends with Smith observing that "[Patton] fixes Jim with a beaming smile. The guitarist ignores him."

And according to Steffan Chirazi (in his 1994 book, 'Faith No More: The Real Story'), the author recounts one of the final performances of the 'Angel Dust' tour, at a festival in Werchter, Belgium. "Then, with his back to the stage, Patton instinctively hurls a bottle of water over his shoulder towards Martin...it misses by two feet. Had it been a strike, that surely would have been the catalyst necessary to bring this thing boiling over."

The "Martin era" officially came to an end in the fall of 1993, when the guitarist was fired...via fax. Martin- "I actually felt relieved; a great pressure had been suddenly removed and the pain began to leave my body."

Martin's replacement turned out to be Patton's bandmate in Mr. Bungle, Trey Spruance. But Spruance recalls the singer not being so hot about the idea. "It definitely was not Mike's idea—he was not really into it. And really, he was right. He made sure that I knew he felt like that—I didn't really understand what he meant at the time, but in retrospect, I definitely knew what he meant. They needed a fucking guitar player, and they were having a lot of trouble finding somebody suitable. They hated the thing of doing a repetitive riff that Jim Martin would do, but that was a mistake. I mean, their chemistry—it seems to me that the chemistry of that band depended on every band member."

The resulting album, 1995's 'King for a Day...Fool for a Lifetime' was

FNM's first-ever recording to not be produced by Matt Wallace, who was replaced by Andy Wallace (no relation). Spruance- "It was at Bearsville, it was a fucking amazing studio. I thought Andy was in a weird position—he's being told to make this band that usually sounds like they're made of diamonds and has a billion dollar production, to make it sound like a garage band. And here we were in Bearsville, the one place where Puffy's drum sound sounds like his drums—that huge fucking sound of his. But, 'Nah, get rid of the room mics, we're tightening this thing up to make it sound like a chunky Black Flag record.' I'm like, 'What the fuck'?"

Additionally, the death of Kurt Cobain was a contributing factor in Bottum entering rehab around this time, to address a heroin addiction. "I was friends with Kurt mostly through Courtney. We became close fast. His death was really a serious blow to me—but reinforcing, because I'd stopped doing dope myself and it was a reminder of where I could have gone with it."

Similar to the absence of Martin's presence on the 'Angel Dust' material, FNM had a similar situation with 'King for a Day.' Gould- "Roddy wasn't really into the music, so that was difficult. Roddy was just coming out of rehab, and I guess this is common with people with substance abuse and quit—they reevaluate all of their relationships, to see what put them there in the first place. And I think we were one of the biggest things that were occupying his life, and I think he saw us in a very negative light. He definitely wasn't carrying his weight. We wanted him to—he just wasn't there."

Although another strong album, it appeared as though the record buying public in the U.S. had completely forgotten about the band, as 'King' peaked at #31 (despite landing in the top ten in the U.K.). Yet just a few weeks before the supporting tour was supposed to launch, Spruance abruptly exited. Taking his spot for the dates was the group's keyboard roadie, Dean Menta. Menta recalls band relations during the supporting tour as such—"They talked shit behind each other's backs constantly and avoided each other...pretty much as they always did."

Faith No More's shows however remained wild and wooly affairs, as Patton's unpredictable on-stage antics kept Menta on his toes. "The peeing, the pooing, the drinking the pee, the peeing in the shoe and drinking. The peeing in a cup and handing it to a young girl in the front row who I think assumed it was water and guzzled it. Things of that nature."

Cutting the tour short to focus on their next album, it was agreed amongst the band that songwriting-wise, Menta wasn't a good fit, which saw a friend of Gould's, Jon Hudson, become the latest FNM guitarist. Looking back at the recording sessions for the group's 1997 release, 'Album of the Year' (which the group co-produced with ex-Swans drummer Roli Mosimann), Hudson describes the sessions as "Fragmented. I don't know what the other studio experiences were like for Faith No More, I just know that this one was sort of piecemeal. There were a few different stages of making the record. I think the band was having a more difficult time putting this record together. I don't think it was a lack of creativity, I just think people's interests were starting to go elsewhere."

The group held it together long enough to launch a supporting tour in support of 'Album' (which peaked at only #41 in the U.S.), which was prefaced by Bordin doing double duty in Ozzy Osbourne's band. But by the summer of '98, it was clearly over. Patton- "I think it was the right time to turn off the lights before we became a pathetic band. Creatively, we hit the wall as a band and it was important to some of us that we end it with integrity."

Despite all the ups and downs, Faith No More's hard work certainly paid off, as they're constantly name-checked by new bands. Gould- "It is very cool to see even though it didn't seem to work at the time. If you look at it in the long term, our gut instincts were correct. It's super cool to see—to make an influence like that."

As a result, the question has come up time and time again over the years…could there ever be a Faith No More reunion? Let's hand the mic to Patton. "If I personally stood to make three million dollars after taxes I would consider it. Really! Why bother unless it is for stupid money. At this point it would not have anything to do with the music. Most of these reunions are sad cash ins, but to each his own." Gould has other ideas. "I think the only thing that would make me interested in it is maybe to do it in a club in Bakersfield without telling anybody—for 50 bucks! Then I would do it. If it was a human thing between human beings, I would do it. If we couldn't do that, I don't think there would be any reason to do that. I think it would be fake."

And as for how FNM is perceived by others, Bordin adds this parting shot. "We loved this band. This band was our fucking lives. So for people to say, 'It's a bad story' or 'They didn't care' is bullshit. Don't believe the fucking hype."

Bonus Bit: Where Are They Now?

Catching up with FNM's cast of characters.

Bill Gould: Runs his own record label, Kool Arrow, produces bands (the latest group he worked with was the German heavy rock/noise trio, Harmful), and continues to write music.

Mike Bordin: Continued on as Ozzy Osbourne's drummer—currently working on a new Ozzy solo album. Also played on Jerry Cantrell's 2002 solo release, 'Degradation Trip.'

Roddy Bottum: Plays guitar in the band Imperial Teen and does film score work. Reunited with Courtney Love on a song for the 2005 indie film, 'Adam & Steve.'

Chuck Mosley: Currently recording a debut album with a new outfit, Vandals Against Illiteracy (V.U.A.), which will include a new version of "We Care A Lot"—featuring a guest appearance by Bottum. Briefly a member of the Bad Brains in the early '90s.

Jim Martin: Owns a real estate holding and development company, and is also a "world-class giant pumpkin grower." Has also released a solo album, 1997's 'Milk and Blood,' appeared on Primus' 1999 release, 'Antipop,' and collaborated with singer Anand Bhatt on 2000's 'Conflict.'

Mike Patton: Runs his own record label, Ipecac, and fronts a variety of bands—chiefly Tomahawk and Fantômas. Currently touring behind his latest project, Peeping Tom. Also made his acting debut in the 2004 film, 'Firecracker.'

Trey Spruance: Runs his own record label, Mimicry. After Mr. Bungle's split in the early 21st century, Spruance focused primarily on his own band, Secret **Chiefs 3.** Their latest release was 2004's 'Book of Horizons.'

Dean Menta: Has been the guitarist for Sparks for the past five years. Also writes music for video games, works as a music editor for TV and film, and has collaborated with Bottum recently on film scores and TV commercials.

Jon Hudson: Is now in the property management field—manages "common interest developments."

Matt Wallace: Is still a much sought-after producer. Has since worked with a variety of acts—including Blues Traveler, H20, and Mushroomhead—and also produced the 2002 U.S. top ten hit for Maroon 5, 'Songs About Jane.'

Classic Rock—October 2006, issue 98

Metallica/Cliff Burton

Cliff's Deaf Jam

Greg Prato uncovers a bunch of obscure tapes

After Faith No More hit it big in the early '90s, it became widely known among fans that FNM guitarist Jim Martin was an old pal of Cliff Burton (you could even spot Martin wearing a "Cliff tribute" shirt in FNM's "Epic" video). Soon after, it came to light that tapes existed of jam sessions the pair held with drummer pal Dave DiDonato back in the early-mid '80s. Instead of cashing in, these much-fabled tapes were kept away from the public, until now. Martin—"This is Dave's dream, this is Dave's nightmare. He's put all the energy behind this thing. He felt that he wanted to make this music available to people. He talked to me about it, and talked to Cliff's father, Ray Burton. Everybody said, 'Fine man, go ahead'."

Available for sale via DiDonato's website, www.rotgrub.com, the drummer explains the need to release these recordings as such, "We decided that we needed to at least preserve the tapes, and then we didn't know what they would come up in the future [as]. There's a lot of stories that go behind the tapes and Maxwell—some of the stories I'll be posting to the website. But there's just a whole lifetime of good times and events that took place, and this music was the focal point of it. I'm just trying to put it back out there because people have contacted us." The "Maxwell" that DiDonato refers to is the name of the CD's that are being released, as well as the town where the jams were held. Martin—"We had this property that my folks bought, I think it was in 1969. It's up in the Coastal Mountain Range, in California. And it's well off the beaten path. So you can go up there, and you won't see anybody for the duration of your stay. Guys run some cattle up that way and stuff, but generally, you never see anybody. So pretty much, anything goes. That's where we did most of our exploratory music projects. And we recorded them on the spot as they happened. It's tapes and stuff of just whatever was coming right off the top. So, we did quite a few of them, and it was a good experience. A lot of material came out of it that you might be familiar with—[Faith No More's] 'Woodpecker From Mars' has a section in there. A Metallica song would be 'For Whom the Bell Tolls'."

As far as the instruments' set-up, DiDonato recalls, "Cliff and Jimmy brought all their gear. At night, we'd go out and start jamming. We had a little generator there, that we put up at the back of the cabin, and ran some power cords down to the front. In some of the tapes, when we stop playing, you'll hear the generator humming away. But they would have like six or eight effects boxes on the ground—basically on the dirt or on plywood, in front of the cabin. This is where they did a lot of experimenting on their tones, and what plugged into the sequences, and a lot of the settings. A lot of it was just trial and error, and they would hook up into these pretty huge riffs, tones, chords, whatever, and we would just jam for hours. The tape would catch 30 minutes, [before] someone would go over there and flip the tape back over." But be forewarned, these jams are very loose and unconventional—empty oil drums are used for percussion, while DiDonato admits, "At times, Jim did not care what Cliff was doing and vice versa."

www.rotgrub.com

Classic Rock—January 2005, issue 75

Guns N' Roses [Producer Mike Clink]

If You Want It, You're Gonna Bleed

Get in the Clink

"It holds up great. 'Appetite for Destruction' is a timeless record," recalls the album's producer, Mike Clink.

By the mid '80s, producer Mike Clink's background was primarily mainstream rock (Survivor, Heart, Triumph). But it was a little live record that he'd worked on in 1979, UFO's classic 'Strangers in the Night,' that perked up G n' R's interest when Clink's name came up as a potential producer for their debut album. On paper, it should never have worked. Instead, the world received one of rock's all-time classic recordings.

How did you come to work with G n' R?

I came in contact with them when my manager, Terry Lippman, called me, and said that I had a meeting at Geffen Records. I went to Tom Zutaut's office and met with Alan Niven, Axl, and Terry was there and myself. They had been in the studio a couple of times with some other people, so they played me what they didn't like about those sessions, and asked me if I could do what I do.

What were your initial impressions of the band?

I had met the rest of the band at S.I.R. Rehearsal on Santa Monica Boulevard. And I had never met a band like that before—these were rock n' rollers and they lived the life. They were the real deal. But they were all great guys. They were very wary of me—it was a matter of gaining their trust. They didn't trust anyone—they had already had some bad experiences, and they weren't willing to open up immediately to anyone.

How were they getting along?

I think they got along great. It was a volatile band, but they really did get along with each other. They would come to the studio in the morning, work hard through the evening, and then when it came time to leave, they would party hard. And they always partied together. I always say they were a gang.

They did everything together.

Memories of the sessions?

We worked hard on all the vocals. Axl and I would be in the studio, and we would work and make sure that every single line projected the feeling of what the lyrics were saying. I was putting in 14-16 hour days every day to get that record done.

Is it true that G n' R had "Don't Cry" written/demoed before the first album?

Some of the ones that we had for the very first record, we spun over towards ['Use Your Illusion']. That and "November Rain"—there were a bunch of them. They were demoed—demoed meaning we played them in rehearsal. But "Don't Cry," there is a demo somewhere that exists of that song. That was done maybe a year before I was introduced to the band—that's probably one of their oldest songs.

It's impressive how sonically undated 'Appetite' sounds today.

I think that we set out to make a classic record—more "old school," a la early Aerosmith. We had the two guitar players playing off each other, we didn't go into samples—sampling was just becoming en vogue, and people were triggering the snare drum, and using this bombastic snare verb.

How does the album hold up today?

It holds up great. It's a great, timeless record. Someone comes up to me every week and says how much that record influenced them and touched their lives. I respect that and am very thankful for that. It's always nice when people pay me compliments about how important that record was in their lives.

www.gunsnroses.com
www.mikeclinkproductions.com

Classic Rock—July 2007, issue 107

The Stories Behind the Songs

"Sabbath Bloody Sabbath" Black Sabbath

Devastated by writer's block and pestered by ghosts: the inside story of the song that saved Sabbath's career...

Early in their career, Black Sabbath released albums and launched tours at a breakneck pace. For a while, the relentless record-tour-record cycle helped fuel their creativity—from 1970 though 1973, Sabbath issued four classic albums, which spawned numerous anthems—"Paranoid," "Iron Man," "N.I.B.," "Sweet Leaf," etc. But when the group tried to settle down and pen their fifth album in the summer of 1973, guitarist/songwriter Tony Iommi experienced something that he never had previously with Sabbath—a wicked case of writer's block.

"Well, what happened was we had done 'Volume 4' in Los Angeles, and we had a house in Los Angeles," recalls Iommi. "We all lived there and everything was great on that album. We came to England and toured and all the rest of the stuff, and then we were due to make another album. We went back to the [Los Angeles] house again, to do 'Sabbath Bloody Sabbath.' We got in there, and I got writer's block. It just went dead. We had the studio booked, same everything booked. And it was just one of those times. I really panicked—'Oh my God, I can't seem to think of anything that we like!' I could play stuff, but it just wasn't sinking in. I didn't like it. So what we had done is that we canceled the whole thing, came back to England."

Instead of jumping right back into the songwriting process, the band took a little time off to recharge their batteries, before getting back to work. But rather than rent an ordinary house to write and record, the members had something else in mind. Iommi: "We rented an old castle here in Wales [Clearwell Castle]. This old big castle, and it was just us there. What we did is we set up the equipment in the dungeons of the castle, to try and get some vibe going. And then that was it—came up with 'Sabbath Bloody Sabbath,' and the rest came fairly shortly afterwards. The block had gone."

In the Brian Ives-penned essay, 'A Hard Road 1973-1978,' from Sabbath's 2004 'Black Box' multi-disc set, bassist Geezer Butler recalled how he and the band felt when Iommi presented the "Sabbath Bloody Sabbath" riff to them.

"When Tony came up with the riff to 'Sabbath Bloody Sabbath,' it was almost like seeing your first child being born. It was the end of our musical drought, the beginning of our new direction, an affirmation of life. It meant the band had a present—and a future—again."

As with the majority of Sabbath's early material, Butler was the song's wordsmith, describing the song's meaning in the same 'Black Box' essay. "The lyrics to 'Sabbath Bloody Sabbath' were about he Sabbath experience, the ups and downs, the good times and the bad times, the rip-offs, the business side of it all. 'Bog blast all of you' was directed at the critics, the record 'business' in general, the lawyers, the accountants, management, and everyone who was trying to cash in on us. It was a backs-to-the-wall rant at everyone."

Musically, 'Sabbath Bloody Sabbath' is comparable to past Sabbath classics—featuring a mammoth Iommi riff, and also including a musical trademark long associated with the band—merging a heavy section ("You seen right through distorted lies, You know you have to learn," etc.) with a lighter one ("Nobody will ever let you know, When you ask the reason why," etc.)—to create "light and shade," if you will. And harkening back to such past compositions as "Black Sabbath" and "Children of the Grave," the song concludes with a long-and-winding instrumental jam section. Vocally, the song is one of the few Sabbath songs to feature Ozzy utilizing (gasp!) high pitched, almost falsetto vocals ("Where can you run to, What more can you do," etc.).

While the band would begin to fracture soon after (due to drug abuse and burnout), Iommi recalls that Sabbath was getting along quite well on both a musical and personal level around the time of the song's recording. "I think pretty good. We'd done what we always do—we go to a studio, lock ourselves in, and record the album. Everything seemed to go all right on that album I think. We didn't have all the problems we had with some of the others."

But there were a few unordinary occurrences outside the band's circle that happened during the recording. Iommi: "I recall walking from the dungeons one day, with I think it was Geezer, Bill, or somebody. We were walking along the hallway, and saw this figure coming towards us. It's a long corridor. This figure turned left into this room, which was the armory room, where they had all the weapons. We followed, and went in there. There was nobody in there, and there was no way out or anything—no other door. Very odd. Anyway, a few days later, the people who own the castle came to see if we were OK, and we said, 'We've seen a few strange things happening here,' and we told them. They said, 'Oh God, that's whatever his name was, Harry, the castle ghost, don't worry about him'!"

Issued as the album's lead off single, "Sabbath Bloody Sabbath" also has the honor of being the first Sabbath song to ever have a promo film accompany it. Unlike earlier Sabbath TV appearances that have popped up over the years on various music video channels (namely the group's Beat Club appearances from 1970), the group does not mime the lyrics or fake playing their instruments in the clip. In fact, they don't even bother to pick up their instruments at all, as they waltz through what appears to be a forest. Iommi: "Yes, that was at Geezer's house. We'd done that in Geezer's garden that was, we were walking around in. That's what I remember about that, just turned up, and that was it really—we're doing a video!"

Bonus Bit: Sabbath Covered

Since they left such an identifiable stamp on the heavy metal world, it's only natural that countless metal bands have covered Sabbath tunes over the years. Among the best known include Soundgarden's "Into the Void," Faith No More's "War Pigs," Guns N' Roses' "It's Alright," and Metallica's "Sabbra Cadabra." But there's been a gaggle of non-metal bands who've also voiced their admiration of Sabbath—"Sweet Leaf" has been covered by both Mogwai and Galactic, "Iron Man" by the Cardigans, "Snowblind" by John Frusciante, "Planet Caravan" by Mercury Rev, "Paranoid" by Big Country, and another reading of "War Pigs," this time by Ween.

www.blacksabbath.com
www.iommi.com

Classic Rock—April 2005, issue 78

"From Out of Nowhere" Faith No More

In 1989, the keyboard-driven "From Out of Nowhere" helped catapult alt-metallists Faith No More to major stardom.

Just before the '80s ended in an explosion of Aqua Net and spandex, alt-metallists Faith No More found themselves at a crossroads. While the San Francisco-based act had already issued a pair of albums, 1985's 'We Care A Lot' and 1987's 'Introduce Yourself,' relations had soured between singer Chuck Mosley and the rest of the band—Roddy Bottum (keyboards), Jim Martin (guitar), Bill Gould (bass), and Mike Bordin (drums)—resulting in Mosley's ousting. "We were in a weird place at the time," recalls Bottum, "Having just lost a singer. I think I felt it more than the others—I was pretty close to Chuck. We were taking stock and starting over, but the mood amongst the four of us was pretty optimistic." And the group soon had good reason to feel optimistic—the arrival of singer Mike Patton. Shortly after the dawn of the '90s, Faith No More would be one of the world's top rock bands, as their first album with Patton, 'The Real Thing,' would scale the charts, along with their hit single, the rap-metal groundbreaker, "Epic." But it was another track, the album opening "From Out of Nowhere," which helped the band get back on track initially.

Bottum recalls that the song's music was penned before Patton's arrival. "Billy, Mike Bordin, and I wrote that song together at our rehearsal space in Hunter's Point. It was amongst the first batch of songs that we wrote after Chuck left the band. Typically, the three of us would get the skeleton of a song going on, and then get Jim Martin to put his guitar part on. Sometimes Billy would write [Martin's] guitar part for him but I think in the case of 'From Out of Nowhere,' he wrote his own part." But Bottum does admit that Patton lent a major hand in how the song came out—"[Patton] came in and did the melody and the lyrics. All of the music of the songs on 'The Real Thing' was written prior to Mike joining the band. He sat with the songs for a couple weeks and wrote all his vocal parts. Really fast." Gould also recalls that the track was demoed beforehand—"We tracked a cassette demo in the rehearsal room. [Patton] took it home and worked on the melody and lyrics, then he would come to my house and we'd put the parts down on four-track to hone them down. The majority of the lyrics and singing melody was from him."

Lyrically, there has been some debate over the years concerning exactly what the song is about. This is evident by the fact that Bottum and Patton's thoughts differ wildly. Bottum reckons that the song "Seems to be about a chance meeting and how chance plays a role in interaction," while Patton explains it as "Jello shots, Hermetic Philosophy, Ptolemaic Cosmology...you know, your average commie/junkie jibber jabber." Perhaps the reason that the lyrics came out the way they did was because of Patton's "state" at the time. "I think I was on some sort of macho endurance trip—doing sleep deprivation experiments."

In the '80s, keyboards in heavy metal were delegated almost exclusively to power ballads, but Faith No More was one of the first metal bands to use keyboards for texture—which is quite evident in "From Out of Nowhere." Beginning with Martin bashing out a C chord repeatedly, the keyboards soon come floating in, before we are introduced to FNM's then-new guy, Patton (who sings in quite a nasally voice—a technique he would drop on future recordings). The song also proved to be one of the shortest on the album, and was completely guitar solo-less.

When it came to actually record the song, the quintet was well prepared. Looking back however, Patton's memories are a bit fuzzy—"I have no recollections of recording the song whatsoever. But I'm sure it was nothing short of a full-scale hootenanny." Bottum on the other hand, recalls the sessions that transpired at Sausalito's Studio D as being "A weird 'getting to know each other' time with Mike Patton. We all got along and worked together pretty easily. Everyone was pretty proactive in the studio. Jim Martin was becoming very particular about his guitar sound, I remember that."

Indeed, Martin had become quite particular about his guitar sound. He recalls at the time consulting two renowned names in the rock world for advice—producer Rick Rubin and Metallica's James Hetfield. "What happened was I drove down to Los Angeles one day, to see Rick. He was recording Wolfsbane. So I went down there, and I sat in while he was working on that—they were working on getting guitar sounds that day. He let me see what process he was going through to do it. I talked to other people about it as well. I talked to Big Mick Hughes, Metallica's live soundman—he told me some things also. James Hetfield told me some things that they did in the studio to get the guitar sound. So pretty much, I was checking around to find out how to get what I was looking for—getting more ideas."

Due to its fast pace and intensity, the song also served as the opening number for the mammoth tour in support of 'The Real Thing,' which lasted from 1989 through 1991. Gould—"That song was good because most of our stuff was so mid-tempo that the set was always in danger of dragging. With this one, we could at least start things on a high note and hopefully this spark would keep the rest of the set alive. There is nothing worse than being on stage for 80 or so minutes when things are not working correctly. Generally this seemed to work out well, and we stuck with it as an opener until we hated it so much we scrapped it from the set altogether." Bottum also recalls how the song put the crowd over the top at one gig. "I remember playing in London for like the millionth time on that tour. We were pretty popular in England, but hadn't really taken off at all in the U.S., and all our American label people came to London to our show to see what all the hubbub was. We opened with that song and the crowd went bananas and broke through the barrier between the stage and the audience. We had to stop the song midway through because people were getting hurt. We left the stage and came back after the barrier was rebuilt. The American label people were aghast."

Bonus Bit: Bjork's Flipping Fish

Who could forget Faith No More's video for "Epic," the song that finally broke the group commercially? One of the most memorable parts of the clip was its ending, when a little fishy is flip-flopping around—out of water—to Roddy Bottum's solo piano accompaniment. Years later, fans were surprised to find out that the pet once belonged to Bjork. Given as a present to the Icelandic singer at a poetry reading in San Francisco, Bjork attended a party at Bottum's house later that evening, and left the fish (who she named "Linear Soul Child") behind. Soon, MTV would make the little bugger a star.

Classic Rock—May 2005, issue 79

"Am I Evil?" Diamond Head

It took a year and a half to write, but this metal epic launched one band,
and later on, inspired one of the biggest rock outfits on the planet.

The New Wave of British Heavy Metal certainly spawned its fair share of anthems during the early '80s—Iron Maiden's "Running Free," Saxon's "Wheels of Steel," etc. But one gem that tends to get overlooked is Diamond Head's mighty epic, "Am I Evil?" In fact, some believe it's a Metallica song, since Hetfield and co. gave it a go on their 'Creeping Death EP,' and have often covered it live ever since. According to Diamond Head co-founder/guitarist Brian Tatler, a lot of work and planning went into the construction of this metal classic.

"I can remember wanting to write a song *heavier* than 'Symptom of the Universe,' the Black Sabbath classic. So when I came up with that riff, I think we all said, 'Oh, that's good—we should work on that.' The song evolved over a period of 18 months. We seemed to keep adding to it. We added the fast section, and then I must have come up with the intro, that was kind of based on 'Mars' from 'The Planet' suite [an orchestral composition by Gustav Holst]. And that got sewn onto the beginning. I can remember coming up with the ending, and the very last thing to be written was the guitar solo section, where it changes key and the tapping. That was finished in the studio as we were recording it—right in the nick of time. I think we started it around 1978, and probably finished around 1980, when we went in to record the album."

To match Tatler's heavy riffing, singer Sean Harris came up with suitably dark lyrics, resulting in perhaps the most extreme opening of any metal song up to then—"My mother was a witch, She was burned alive, Thankless little bitch, For the tears I cried." Tatler however, is unsure exactly of the song's lyrical meaning. "I don't know exactly—it's Sean's lyric. But I can remember him being interviewed about this song; he was saying he just wanted to come up with a suitably evil lyric to my heavy riff. So, 'My mother was a witch' was a great opening line. His mum probably took offense, but probably forgave him now! I'm not sure what the whole thing's about—it just kind of works as a rock song. I suppose you could say it's about evil in man—good and bad. The yin and yang."

Shortly after the song's completion, the group tried the song out on a live audience. Tatler recalls it immediately passing the test. "As far as I remember, it always went down well. We soon learned that slow songs didn't work live. The faster ones would stay in the set. With 'Am I Evil?', it must have gone down well, because we probably would have chucked it out, otherwise."

Tatler also points out that the song appeared on two different Diamond Head studio albums. "We recorded it for 'The White Album' (aka 'Lightning to the Nations'). We had to re-record it for the 'Borrowed Time' album, which felt a bit strange doing it again. But on 'The White Album,' I do definitely remember listening back to it, and once I'd got the guitar solo right and all the keys that change underneath the guitar solo, it just blew me away. We put a little bit of keyboards on the intro—I think there might be a little under the solo as well."

Additionally, the guitarist recalls an unorthodox approach to obtaining his uniue guitar sound on "Am I Evil?" "There is a slightly strange sound on the guitar, which is a wah-wah—this Morley Power Wah Boost. It was 'on' for that song, but set at a cutting, nasal position. It gave it a little more of an 'evil' sound, I suppose."

While the song instantly became a favorite among Diamond Head fans, Tatler recalls the day he was introduced to Metallica's version. "We were in the studio, and Sean had gotten a copy of 'Creeping Death,' the twelve inch single, with 'Am I Evil?' on the b-side. We put it on and listened to it, and we thought, 'It's heavier and tighter,' but we didn't think it was any better than our version. Because of course, we're proud of our own recording."

Did Tatler have any idea Metallica was the next big thing? "We had *no idea* that Metallica was going to become the biggest band in the world. At this stage, in 1984, they were on Music for Nations, and it didn't look like they had the potential to conquer the world—to us. We knew Lars, and we knew how ambitious he was, but I don't think any of us had a clue that they were going to take that style of metal and bring it to the masses in the way they did. I'm thankful that they did, because I don't know what I'd do without the songwriter's royalties of those four songs that they've covered [in addition to "Am I Evil?", Metallica has covered "Helpless," "The Prince," and "It's Electric"]. Imitation is the sincerest form of flattery, so we're of course flattered that they covered us. They could have covered Witchfinder General, couldn't they [laughs]?"

Having split up in the mid '80s, Diamond Head reunited sporadically throughout the '90s, before Tatler soldiered on sans Harris. To this day, "Am

I Evil?" remains in the set list. "Every time we play it live, that riff seems to stir up something in the audience, and it's always a winner. You just can't fail if you fire into that riff. The crowd duly responds—it's just got something about it. It's fairly easy to play as well. I've taught people how to play it, and it almost seems like, if you like rock, it's one of the first riffs you learn. And I quite like that—it's not some clever, complicated thing. It's like a 'Smoke on the Water'—a nice, simple, heavy riff that you can hum and remember."

Perhaps unsurprisingly, Tatler agrees that the song is among Diamond Head's best. "I would say it's one of the best, yes. But it had all the ingredients—a good riff, a good chorus, it went fast, there's a big guitar solo in it, it had good dynamics. Songs like that are hard to write. I don't know how we did some of those songs, looking back. They don't obey rules of songwriting—we did whatever we felt, rather than followed any rules like 'verse-bridge-chorus.' There was a naiveté in the early songs. Like I said, it always works. You never play it and think, 'That's a bag of shit'—it always seems to sound good. *Some* songs sound a bag of shit, y'know [laughs]."

Bonus Bit: Did Lars Jam with the 'Head?

Lars Ulrich took in many a Diamond Head gig during the early '80s—going as far as crashing in the homes of both Tatler and Harris for a period. Ulrich was also present at several Diamond Head rehearsals at the time, which leads one to wonder, did the future Metallica drummer ever jam with the band, or even mention a desire to give it a go himself?

"He didn't say, 'I'm a drummer' or 'I'm going to form a band.' He didn't say anything like that. Maybe he was too shy—I mean, it's hard to imagine Lars being shy, but it's either that or I suppose, if I picture myself hanging with a band that I like, I probably wouldn't have the nerve to say, 'Let's have a go on your guitar.' He probably was slightly in awe and thought, 'I ain't got the nerve to sit on the same drum stool as Duncan [Scott] and take over'."

www.diamond-head.net

Classic Rock—April 2007, issue 104

"No One Knows" Queens of the Stone Age

One of the few all-time classic songs of recent years, this unlikely single was lyrically opaque, five minutes long, had a "jam part"—and ended up giving QOTSA a huge hit.

If there ever were a modern day rock classic, it would be Queens of the Stone Age's "No One Knows." While rock radio nowadays has become quite a predictable beast—with most of the same-sounding bands droning into one another—"No One Knows" was an exception during 2002-2003. But while there's no denying the song's catchy riff and vocal melody, if you pay close attention to the song's structure, it makes an unlikely single. Even to former QOTSA bassist Nick Oliveri. "When they were talking about doing it as a single, I was like, 'This is a five minute song, dude.' There's a jam part in here, a bass part, a drum thing. What do you mean, single—y'know? They're going to cut this song up. The last thing I want to do is have anybody edit up [our] song. But we kind of felt we could get behind any of the songs, and whatever single they wanted to choose—the one *they* wanted to get behind, we just said, 'Go ahead'."

And Oliveri is right—2002's 'Songs for the Deaf' contained a multitude of potential singles—"Go with the Flow," "Gonna Leave You," "First It Giveth," etc. Following in the footsteps of 2000's 'Rated R,' QOTSA's third release overall was yet another incredibly consistent recording front to back. But 'Deaf' also featured the group's unquestionably strongest line-up ever—Oliveri, singer/guitarist Josh Homme, and drummer Dave Grohl (yes, *the* Dave Grohl) were the main players. Additionally, such guests as Mark Lanegan guested on a few tracks—"A Song for the Dead," "Hangin' Tree," and "A Song for the Deaf."

When Oliveri first heard an early version of the song, he was reminded of one of the standouts on 'Rated R.' "I remember thinking the staccato thing is like 'Lost Art [of Keeping a Secret]' or something. I was like, 'Is this the brother song or the sister song?' I liked that." And when asked about if he had any memories of the writing and recording sessions that birthed "No One Knows," he replied, "When we were recording it I was thinking, 'This is badass, we're playing with Dave Grohl!' No, I'm kidding [laughs]. That was pretty much a Homme tune—from start to finish. I think Lanegan lent a hand in that one as well."

While there was no denying that the song was quite a catchy little ditty, the hard-to-decipher lyrics made fans wonder just exactly what the song was about. Drugs ("We get these pills to swallow")? An expedition via desert ("I journey through the desert)…or ocean ("I drift along the ocean")? Or a love song ("I realize you're mine")? When interviewed by MTV shortly after the release of 'Songs for the Deaf,' Homme admitted that he was in the dark as much as the listener. "It's a mystery what that song's about. No one knows. It's kind of almost Beatle-esque with a driving beat, and it's kind of jumpy."

In addition to the song's catchiness, its whacked out video received numerous airings worldwide on MTV. A trio of bandmembers (Homme, Oliveri, and Lanegan) play the part of hunters, traveling by jeep, who accidentally hit a deer in the road. But the deer has the last laugh on the Queens, when he snaps back to life, smacks each member upside their head, takes their vehicle, and terrorizes a pack of boy scouts singing fireside—before mounting the Queens' members heads on a wall (!). Sounds like some sort of drug-fueled hallucination, but it somehow worked well, resulting in an incredibly original and popular video.

Speaking to the SBI: Generation site, Homme explained that the group had little to do with the video's plot, as he wanted to leave it in the hands of the director, Dean Karr. "Our thing is that we like to party, and you can't have every video be like two guys bouncing off each other, it's gotta have some kind of sexuality and alcohol abuse and some kind of looseness to it. We are that vague." Additionally, Karr explained the video to Homme supposedly at 5:30 in the morning, during a birthday party for the director. "Basically it's the drunken ramblings of Dean Karr's. This guy is basically certifiable, he's the only guy I know who has broken his leg partying. Twice, two different legs." Despite all the partying, Karr has become one of rock's most in-demand video directors, having also worked with Marilyn Manson (the infamous "Sweet Dreams" clip), Ozzy Osbourne, and Slayer, among others.

Queens of the Stone Age was so eager to play their 'Songs for the Deaf' tunes that they hit the concert trail a few months before its August 2002 release—remaining on the road from May 2002 through January 2004. "I remember playing it every night and people adding new life to it," recalls Oliveri. "If you're playing something every night for a year on end, sometimes you can go, 'God, I wish I could throw a different song in there right now.'

But it's a bad jam, I enjoyed playing it, and it was one of those things where you can get new life from somebody singing it."

With such an intense touring schedule (perhaps *too intense*, as Oliveri was dismissed from the band after it wrapped up), it shouldn't come as a surprise that it was while on the road that an incident made the bassist realize 'No One Knows' was breaking the band to the next level. "When we started getting hotel rooms! Nah, I'm kidding [laughs]."

Bonus Bit: Talking Points

Throughout the 'Songs for the Deaf' album, several "DJ's" can be heard jive talkin' between the tracks. Since none reveal their identities during their respective spiels, it's hard to discern who the mystery DJ's are. Turns out that a few are quite renown in the hard rock community. The Dwarves' Blag Dahlia ("Millionaire"), Amen's Casey Chaos ("Six Shooter"), Eleven's Alain Johannes ("First It Giveth") and Natasha Shneider ("Song for the Deaf"), Mondo Generator's Dave Catching (the unlisted "Feel Good Hit of the Summer" reprise), and ex-Marilyn Manson member Twiggy Ramirez ("God is in the Radio") are all heard talking prior to each aforementioned song.

www.qotsa.com
www.myspace.com/nickoliveri

Classic Rock—October 2007, issue 111

Every Home Should Have One

Kyuss 'Blues For The Red Sun'

An undervalued or forgotten gem you may have overlooked.

The desert. Heat, sand, vastness, and swirling winds providing the only soundtrack. In other words...the last place you'd expect Kyuss to hail from. Judging from their molasses-slow tempos and detuned riffs, it's understandable to assume that Kyuss was influenced by the usual suspects (Sabbath, etc.), but in reality, Kyuss was a bunch of Palm Desert, California-based punkers. With Black Flag and G.B.H. records dispersed throughout their collections, singer/screamer John Garcia, guitarist Josh Homme, bassist Nick Oliveri, and drummer Brant Bjork originally congregated during the late '80s (rehearsing in air conditioned bedrooms—the heat rendered garages useless).

Local punkers Across the River had created a new forum for Palm Desert bands—generator parties. Held outdoors at night, large groups would congregate to a central location—where bands would play power generated-sets, for beer-drinking/dope-smoking friends. When Across the River split (later mutating into Fatso Jetson), Kyuss inherited the generator party throne—issuing their debut, 'Wretch,' in 1991. Soon after, Kyuss found a kindred spirit in producer Chris Goss, who brought a raw/retro-ish approach to their sophomore outing.

"We were just kids," remembers Nick Oliveri. "We didn't know what we were doing—we were just out playing, having fun. 'Wretch' was just kinda like songs in sessions that were already done. And I think it's a cool record, it's fun, but 'Blues' was a really good time. Chris was awesome man, he's all about 'vibe' and his ideas are great."

Sounding like a volcano erupting from your speakers, 1992's 'Blues for the Red Sun' paved the way for what is now known as "stoner rock." Heavy yet trippy, the album recalled such bands as Alice in Chains, but Kyuss took riff-rock to a whole new level. Oliveri—"It was at Sound City in the big room—Studio A. I remember little moments that were like *'Wow man!'* Just hearing things coming back from the tape was new and exciting, 'cause I was so young—you don't hear it that way when you're playing. Especially when you're 19 or 20. I remember singing through a walkie talkie mic going to a big muff pedal and this effects rack thing for 'Mondo Generator.'"

Ah yes, "Mondo Generator." Originally a song on 'Blues,' the phrase would eventually be used as the name of an Oliveri-led band. So how did it originate? "Brant named my bass amp 'The Mondo Generator.' It's actually spray-painted down the side of that Sunn cabinet that's on the inside [of the CD booklet]."

Starting with the slow-building "Thumb," such vicious rockers as "Green Machine," "50 Million Year Trip," and "Allen's Wrench" followed, as well as the near eight-minute epic, "Freedom Run." Additionally, Kyuss made great use of instrumentals ("Molten Universe," "Apothecaries' Weight," etc.), which tied the album into a long-and-winding journey. However, several tracks stand out for Oliveri—"My favorite is probably 'Green Machine,' that song is really badass. '50 Million Years' is really good, 'Allen's Wrench' was always a favorite of mine."

But just as it seemed that another heavyweight metal contender had arrived, Kyuss began to splinter. Oliveri—"There was a lot of stuff going on, and I was moving in a different direction. I wanted to go join the Dwarves, basically! [laughs] I was getting a little messed up in my life at the time— my dad jumped off a cliff before we made the record, and I may have been drinking too much. So Josh, I'll say, 'let me go.'"

Oliveri split shortly after the album's completion (reuniting later in the decade with Homme in Queens of the Stone Age, before being ousted earlier this year), while Bjork stuck around for another release, 1994's 'Welcome to Sky Valley,' before exiting himself (later launching a solo career, and joining Oliveri in Mondo Generator). Garcia and Homme meanwhile soldiered on for another album, 1995's '…And the Circus Leaves Town,' before packing it in.

Despite issuing only a handful of commercially-ignored albums, Kyuss' contribution remains significant—especially judging from the amount of bands that appeared in their wake, and just happened to share the same sound/ approach as the boys from the desert.

www.myspace.com/kyussmyspace
www.myspace.com/nickoliveri

Classic Rock—September 2004, issue 70

Kiss 'Alive'

By Charlie Benante

Anthrax's Charlie Benante on the glam metal classic that changed his life, and made him realize that you can never have too many drums.

"The first time I heard that album, I was at a party at a friend's house. The only thing I heard prior to that as far as Kiss was 'Dressed To Kill.' I was a fan, but when 'Alive' came out, it was a totally different thing. The thing that I remember most about it was just staring at the package—it opened out to a gatefold, and there was a huge booklet in it. I just remember staring at it, and being like, 'What the hell?!' Because you would listen to the record and you would visualize in your own mind how it was.

You had all these different things. And I remember early on, when I first heard Kiss, I used to think that Paul Stanley's voice was Gene Simmons' voice. It was very weird when I saw them on a TV show called 'The Midnight Special,' and I was like, 'Wait a minute—he's not supposed to be singing that!'

I don't think there were any of [the songs] were my least favorite. I loved every single one on that record. I remember playing it continuously, over and over again. I loved the way side one would kick in, it was like the introduction is the beginning of the show. Then you get to the middle portions—sides two and three—and side four was the big ending. I'll never forget listening to 'Black Diamond' and being like, 'What the hell is going on?' The explosions and everything. [The tracklist] is a bit out of sequence—actually, it's not even a live show, they totally re-recorded it—but who cares. It fooled me back then.

I loved [Peter Criss'] drumming on 'Alive.' I think he was one of the big influences as far as having a huge drum kit. It was like, 'Look at all these drums, what is he doing with all these?' Because at the time, you had like the 'five-piece-kit-drummers' out there, like John Bonham and Joey Kramer. After Peter, Neil Peart had the big kit also.

The end of '76 was when I saw them for the first time—['Alive'] prepared me. 'Dude, this is fucking crazy!' I just couldn't believe it. Everything was going on, I couldn't focus on just one thing. It was just an assault on my senses. Because most of the bands at the time really didn't put on that type of a show the way they were doing. It was more or less getting up on stage and playing. It wasn't, y'know, Kiss.

Kiss made me realize that this is what I'm going to do. And that mindset just stayed with me—it never left. Before that, I wasn't really taking it as serious as, 'I'm going to make a living doing this.'

I absolutely still listen to ['Alive']. I listen to it sometimes before we play, it pumps me up. It puts me in a different state of mind."

www.kissonline.com
www.anthrax.com

Classic Rock—Summer 2005, issue 83

The Beatles 'Sgt. Pepper's Lonely Hearts Club Band'

By Ronnie James Dio

Ronnie James Dio on the Beatles' most experimental—
and arguably most groundbreaking—album of their career.

"I think that the greatest album that has ever been made is 'Sgt. Pepper's Lonely Hearts Club Band.' I can't think of a losing track on that album. It was at a time when the Beatles were let alone being great musicians and incredible songwriters—it was at a time when experimentation was really being done by them. Especially in the studio. And that's what you can hear throughout this album I think—you can hear the tape loops that were done, the way George Martin manipulated things, the way that Paul McCartney and John Lennon had those kind of ideas, George Harrison's contribution with the Indian influence, the look of the album because it was so different. Just everything about it."

"[It includes] my favorite song probably on earth—'A Day in the Life'—which I think is just an absolutely brilliant song. I think that it has the greatest ending that there ever was, and it's just one piano note going on for eleven minutes or something. I just think that it's an album that if anyone hasn't heard it, I'm sure even to this day, will listen and say, 'Wow, what was that?' The melodic content of it all, just the way the Beatles always were. I find no flaws in that album."

"The first time I heard 'A Day in the Life' I was in a car, and I had to pull over to the side of the road. I was just absolutely stunned by it."

"I like everything [on the album]. For some strange reason, I like 'Being for the Benefit of Mr. Kite!' I like that song a lot. I couldn't point to one. I even like 'When I'm Sixty-Four,' I guess that's because I'm thinking about that now. Just everything on it—brilliant."

'It was far reaching. It was beyond belief—I don't think that anyone could fathom what they had done. I mean, this was the Beatles, the Beatles didn't do that. It wasn't that immediate of a jump, because 'Revolver' was starting to that get that way as well. It was because of the experimentation that it was absolutely phenomenal.'

"It always holds up for me. Even if I'd never head it remastered, it doesn't matter to me—a good song is a good song. Remastering is great for the audiophile. For me, it really doesn't matter—I just hear the song and I can envision all the other things that are in it. Of course, a bad recording is a bad recording. But it holds up for me because of its content, not so terribly much because of its recording. Although I think, once again, it's experimentation is phenomenal."

www.thebeatles.com
www.ronniejamesdio.com

Classic Rock—September 2006, issue 97

Kiss 'Destroyer'

By Mr. Lordi

Lordi's Mr. Lordi on one of the most experimental albums Kiss released during their long and winding career.

"It was the first Kiss album I owned. It wasn't the first Kiss album that I heard—the first one was 'Creatures of the Night.' I was a little kid back then. I went to a record store, and I thought I'd buy just *the* Kiss album—I didn't know that there were *plenty* of Kiss albums. I was like, '*Whoa,* there are so many to choose from!' I had no idea where to start. I made the decision from the picture on the cover—I thought 'Destroyer' was the coolest cover of the albums, and I chose that one.

It has so much nostalgia for me. It has 'God of Thunder'—my all time favorite song from Kiss...not from Kiss, but one of my favorite songs, *period*. I remember the first time I was listening to the album with all the theatrical parts on the album—the few seconds of 'radio theater,' if you will, at the beginning [of 'Detroit Rock City'], I was scared shitless. It was terrifying, but I loved it!

I often wonder, if I was to have chosen another album, if I chose 'Rock and Roll Over,' would that be my favorite album? Is it just my personality that I'm so locked on the nostalgia of the album—my first rock album? I have no idea...I guess I'll never know.

Because Kiss has so many different albums and so many different musical styles—more than some people change their underwear—it's like a deck of cards. 'Destroyer' is different—I think it's the first 'big sounding' album they did. The first three albums, they're more like 'rock n' roll albums.' 'Destroyer,' it's a *huge* album—it doesn't matter how low the volume you're listening to, it sounds big.

Of course, there are so many production tricks there, with the piano powering up the chords, and the orchestrations and stuff. If you took 'Dressed to Kill,' 'Rock and Roll Over,' or 'Love Gun,' I still think 'Destroyer' really has something unique in its feel. As a whole, it has something really fresh—to this day. I think a lot of 'thank yous' go to Bob Ezrin, because the next album that really sticks out from the catalog is 'The Elder,' and then from the non-make up era, you see the 'Revenge' album, which is Bob Ezrin once again.

I'm a huge Gene Simmons fan—that was my favorite member of Kiss. It's always been Gene. And it's kind of funny that 'God of Thunder' is a Paul Stanley song—the ultimate Gene Simmons song is written by Paul Stanley. That's kind of weird—it's like an exception to the rule. I think it's perfect, there's nothing that I would change on that song.

'Sweet Pain' is one of my favorite songs, also. Once again, surprise, surprise—a Gene song. A simple melody and in the end it has a really cool off-time rhythm. The riff at the end is really cool, because it's something that you don't expect to happen in the song.

'Detroit Rock City' as an opening track...I have a friend who said that 'Detroit Rock City' is the best song in the world, ever. And he was surprised when he realized that not all the Kiss fans think that 'Detroit Rock City' is the best song in the world [laughs]. The bass line in the verses is excellent, that bass lick is something you would have never expected from Gene, if you listened to the first three albums. It's so technical and non-Kiss at the time. And the guitar solo in 'Detroit Rock City,' that's larger than life also. Actually, it was written by Bob Ezrin [laughs].

I still listen to it quite a lot actually. I'm the kind of person that my knowledge of music and interest in new music kind of stops somewhere before the mid '90s. I just didn't find any more new bands and new albums that I would really get into—I don't get that rush. Kiss' 'Destroyer' stands the test of time. I don't know what it is about it. It's still my favorite. Every show, before our intro tape starts to roll, we play 'God of Thunder'."

www.kissonline.com
www.lordi.fi

Classic Rock—June 2007, issue 106

Tour Bus Survival

Rob Halford/Judas Priest

Music: My iPod is with me wherever I go. My iPod is all over the place—it's got Beethoven, Bach, Mozart, Tchaikovsky, Vivaldi, Wagner, and then it goes into Slayer, Emperor, everything by Sabbath, everything by Queen, Tool, Pantera. I could just go and on. I'm just a chameleon when it comes to music—all kinds of music touch my senses.

DVDs: 'Lord of the Rings' is *de rigueur* for me, because it's so metal. Anything with some action and anything that's got some reality-based drama. I'm all over the place with movies. I'm a huge Martin Scorsese fan, Jack Nicholson, Al Pacino, Meryl Streep. To me, it's a combination of dimensions, so I've always got 'The Godfather' with me, I've always got 'Scarface' with me. I like movies like the music that I like—I can keep looking at and experiencing them over and over again, without it getting tedious.

Books: The trilogy by Mervyn Peake that was written in the '30s, called 'Gormenghast'—I've always got that with me. Or I can go to Carl Hiaason with his 'Skinny Dip' and 'Lucky You.' I've read all the Dan Brown books back-to-back—I just consumed every one of those in about two weeks. Anything that takes you on a journey. All of the Metal Maniacs, Metal Hammer, Kerrang, Billboard—I just try to keep up to speed in everything as much as I possibly can.

Essential Tour Bus Rule: Give each other space, and don't raid one person's part of the refrigerator. You all have a certain part of the refrigerator, and if someone takes your particular brand of beer or fast food…keep your hands off my McDonald's, that kind of thing. Your bus is your home away from home, really—to escape the "madness," so to speak. So it's a combination of listening to music, watching movies, reading, and anything to get 300 miles under your feet. Sleep is also an option [laughs].

www.robhalford.com

Classic Rock—September 2006, issue 97

Q and A's

Steve Vai

The master of the seven-string releases his first new album for six years, and hopes to play UK dates in the autumn.

It's been six years since the arrival of 1999's 'Ultra Zone,' but Steve Vai has a hugely ambitious concept work all cooked up and ready to be served, 'Real Illusions: Reflections'—with a projected two additional albums on the horizon. And it also turns out to be one of his most musically diverse albums, featuring everything from hard rock ("Building the Church") and funk ("Firewall") to sprawling epics ("Under It All"). Touring plans include both U.S. and Japanese dates in the spring, with European dates to hopefully follow in the fall. Mr. Vai recently explained his 'Reflections' of his latest outing.

So how did 'Real Illusions: Reflections' come about?

It started out with all these characters in mind, but I kind of abandoned that idea because it was too difficult to get the kind of artists that I wanted to play some of these characters on the record. The record took quite a long time. There was a lot of material that I recorded for it that didn't make it to the record—that's not uncommon. A lot of times artists will make records, have 25 songs, and just pick their favorite twelve or whatever. I did something very similar; I just pulled out all the things that didn't have a particular message in them, or feeling. When an artist or anybody creates something, they are putting their personality, their likes, their dislikes, their defenses, their confidence, all of these things go into the making of a piece of art or work. With any artist, you listen for those things within your music, and they help you grow, because you identify things about yourself when you're doing it like that. With 'Real Illusions,' I just abandoned anything that didn't give me wood, y'know? That just didn't turn me on in that way that I didn't feel like I was being very sincere about or very honest.

What exactly is the storyline?

It takes place in this town where people are perceived as being very normal, but there's an underlying drama. And we see the story through the eyes of this one character, Captain Drake Mason, who is basically insane as a result of some of the things that he had to go through in his life, and some of the things that he had done. To put it into a nutshell, it's how he discovers himself, in a sense. There's a lot of different elements to it, I mean, there's some funny things, there's some drama. And as it unfolds, it becomes very metaphysical, because we're seeing it through his eyes, and he's sort of a madman. So we see what a madman sees.

Let's talk about your backing band, the Breed.

Well I mean, it's wonderful to have these tremendous musicians. Billy [Sheehan, bass] and I go way back to the David Lee Roth days. He's had a lot of success in the past, [so] we never could get it together. But I had a G3 tour several years ago, and Billy joined me for that. It's just nice, we really get along. And Tony [MacAlpine, guitar/keyboards] is so underrated—people do not know the depths of this guy's musicianship. I mean, yeah he can play guitar and that kind of thing, but he's a totally accomplished pianist, he has perfect pitch. The most important thing about these guys in the band for me, is that they're really wonderful people. When we're together, it's a very special feeling, because it's our family, y'know? It's more rewarding when you're in a band with guys that you love, and the respect is there, everybody is thrilled to be there, and excited about the music. When you go out on tour, there's no secrets—if somebody is a miserable son of a bitch, they only become really miserable when you tour. If they're happy, cool people and just want to have fun, then they become really happy and very cool and we have a lot of fun. I mean Dave Weiner, besides being a very good guitarist with unbelievable retention and dedication, he's just a great guy to hang around with. And Jeremy Colson is just for me, the find of the century on drums. I really love touring with this band.

Any interesting releases coming up on your label, Favored Nations?

Oh, I got some great stuff. I don't know if you remember Al Kooper, he just made this really cool record that we have coming out ['I Am Where I Wanna Be']. I have an Eric Johnson CD that is just unbelievable—his first studio CD in quite some time and it's very nice [projected title—'Bloom']. May be working with Vernon Reid again, I really enjoy his work. Some unbelievable acoustic guitar players—Tommy Emmanuel and Adrian Legg. If you check the website [www.favorednations.com], our release schedule for the year is pretty tapped out.

Are there any other singers or bands that you'd like to play with?

No, I'm not pining for the days of yore. I mean, I'm creating a body of work that I'm trying to keep as undiluted as possible.

www.vai.com

Classic Rock—May 2005, issue 79

Phil Collen

With his new extra-curricular project Man-Raze, the Def Leppard guitarist has definitely changed his spots.

Since Def Leppard has long-been associated with arena rock anthems, it's understandable to assume that a side-project by one of their members would follow the same approach. But longtime Leppard guitarist Phil Collen is looking to cut to the heart of the matter with a new project, Man-Raze. Describing the band's sound as a 'rock version of the Police,' Collen also doubles as lead vocalist, and is joined by his former band mate in Girl, bassist Simon Laffy, as well as Sex Pistols drummer Paul Cook (!). A full-length debut should be arriving later this year (which may be prefaced by an EP), as well as live dates. Collen recently gave Classic Rock the scoop.

How did Man-Raze come together?

We're all from London, that's the thing—me, Simon, and Paul. I was back in London last summer, because my dad passed away, and I was over there looking after him for a while. I just wanted to do some other stuff, and I remembered that Simon...we'd always kept in touch after the Girl thing. We saw the Sex Pistols on tour, and I was like, "Fuck man, we referenced the sound," like the way he hits the snare, which is really aggressive. I'd just bumped into him in the street; me and Simon had already been speaking about doing a three-piece thing. There's no restrictions. Just use every three-piece influence you can thing of—Nirvana, the Police, Hendrix—and it's really just a cross of all those things really. It doesn't sound like Def Leppard or anything like that. It's just three of us, and there's a lot more freedom live. When we've been rehearsing, it was like "Wow, this is cool!" We got in touch with Paul, and said, "We're doing this thing, we'd really like you to play," and he said, "Fine." He heard some of the stuff, we started writing. We just finished the twelve tracks. Really excited.

What does the band's name mean?

Originally, we were just throwing some ideas around, and actually, I was going to call it Fay Wray—y'know, the chick in the 'King Kong' movie. Simon didn't like it, so he said, "How about Man-Raze?" Like the New York artist. So we kicked it around, actually sounded good, and we just went with it—it felt right.

How does the songwriting differ from Leppard?

Again, it's stuff that I could never do with Def Leppard, just different stuff. Me and Simon just started writing. Even when we were in Girl, we never really clicked like that; it was a totally different thing. It's just been really exciting. It's like one person will suggest something, and it'll just go off on a tangent. It's great when songwriting works like that, and it could be anything—Simon playing something on an acoustic guitar, a bass riff, a drum loop. I always liked writing like that, not starting from any specific point, but just going with whatever influences you at the time. So that's really what it's been about. And again, lyrically, you can be a little bit darker, and a little bit more edgy about the stuff. It doesn't have to be a certain way, we can actually write songs about whatever we want, really. There's no real restrictions. I like the idea of that.

Were the songs written together, or by swapping mp3's?

A bit of both really. I live in the States, so I've been coming back and forth. And this is very much a "London band," that's another cool thing about it—we're all from London. It's influenced by what's going on down there. If you actually stroll around and hear something in the street—it's different than what you'd hear in the States. We're into the fact that it's actually a London band.

How did the recording go?

Great. We did it on a bit of a budget—a bit of both really. We'd do some stuff around Simon's house; he's an absolute wiz on computer-based software. With Def Leppard, I always use Pro Tools, and I have stuff at home—I can actually do certain things at home and whiz it over to him in England. We went to Mayfair Studios in London—they got a great drum room. Blur's "Song 2" was all done at that studio; it's got a great sound and a great vibe. Mutt Lange actually [had] done the Bryan Adams album there [1991's 'Waking Up the Neighbors']. We were really thrilled to get this big, huge drum sound—live drum sound. The rest of the stuff we've really been doing at home—bits and pieces, go to the odd studio, it was actually a little demo studio in London. It hasn't been done at one particular time, it's been over an eight-month period, we've been coming back, revisiting stuff—doing it that way. And I think it's great doing it like that, it can get a bit overbearing if you're stuck in one place doing a whole record. It's kind of nice to have a space to breath.

So the EP would be through the website?

Yeah, it's all going to be through there.

Will a tour follow?

I hope so. Again, [Def Leppard] has got a really busy schedule this summer, but I really want to start doing some Man-Raze stuff. Whenever we can fit that in, that would be great.

Has the band played live yet?

Just rehearsing, we haven't actually done any gigs yet, so that's kind of exciting as well.

www.manraze.com

Classic Rock—July 2005, issue 81

King's X

New album in the pipeline; King's X bassist/vocalist Doug Pinnick has extra-curricular albums shaping up for release.

It remains a mystery why King's X didn't become one of the biggest rock bands on the planet back in the late '80s, especially when considering what was going on with rock at the time (unbearable pretty boys posing in spandex). But their Sly-meets-Sabbath-meets-Beatles sound did build them a diehard cult following, which remains standing by their side to this day. Bassist/singer Doug Pinnick tells us about the group's upcoming album (produced by metal vet Michael Wagener), as well as other projects.

How did King's X hook up with Michael Wagener?

We were playing in Nashville, Tennessee. Michael came to a show to see us play and afterwards, wanted to meet us. I mean, me and Ty and Jerry love Michael Wagener—way back with Accept, 'Balls to the Wall.' That was such a great record; it was the best sounding record I heard at the time. We just really admired him, and I didn't know really that he'd done all the stuff with Dokken, Ozzy, and Skid Row. Anyway, he showed up—I don't know who brought it up first, but "We need to record together!" And us not being rich rock stars, we decided to figure out a way to do it that wouldn't cost us a whole lot. So we set up a clinic, for people to subscribe and come in—spending four days with [Wagener], recording King's X. Basically, these people paid to come, and that's what paid our trip there and took care of us. And it worked out so well that we said, "Let's just make a whole record."

I heard you describe the album as a cross between 'Dogman' and 'Gretchen Goes to Nebraska.'

It seemed that those two places kind of guided us to this record, and Michael felt the same way. That was the first thing he said, was those are the two records that our fans like. We didn't want to recreate it, because you can't do that, so we just decided to do it the way we did those two records—blindly go in there and pour out our hearts. Usually, I have problems with everything that I'm involved in, because I'm real picky about what I like and what I do. I always find the flaws. This record, it was such an honest record that I can't find anything wrong because everything was done from our hearts.

What about your collaboration with Pearl Jam's Jeff Ament and Mike McCready?

We did this at Jeff's house—Jeff, I, and a guy named Richard Stuverud— I've known him forever. [Stuverud] is an all-around musician, he can play keyboards and sing, he's been doing all the background harmonies, and I've been doing the lead vocals. I didn't even bring a bass, I just brought my Strat. I was thinking, "Wow, I'm a bass player and I'm bringing my guitar. What am I doing?" But it was so much fun. We wrote eight songs, the three of us together, and we were really happy with them. Flew home, and about four or five months later, got back together, and Mike McCready came. We did eight more songs with Mike—some really good rocking tunes. It's almost southern rock sounding, with a little Stones mixed in, and blues. I've been calling it "Montana," just because that's where we do it at, and that's what I have written all over my CD's.

You're also releasing a solo album.

It's my third solo record, I'm calling this one "Doug Pinnick"—the first two were called Poundhound. I just did it because I liked the Foo Fighters thing— Dave Grohl put his first record out and he called it "Foo Fighters," and it was all him. I thought, "That's cool," it kind of takes the ego away. But on this one, so many people told me that they didn't know I had any records out because they didn't know about Poundhound. I think I'm going to call it 'Emotional Animal,' but I may change the name if something magic pops in my life. I would say ¾ of the record is just straight up, slammin' rock.

And what's the status of project with Reb Beach, the Mob?

I just got all of the mixes of the songs today actually. There's 15 of them I think, I got to sing on them. Basically, Reb wrote all the songs, Kip Winger produced it and played on it too. They're all straight up '80s kind of songs with me singing them, it's so much fun. Reb makes up the melodies—he just mouths words—and he sends the melodies to me. The words just come because it's so easy to make shit up around what he's saying. It's your Bon Jovi, Whitesnake kinda vibe—Dokken kinda stuff.

I remember hearing about a possible collaboration with Chris Cornell—any updates?

Nah. Me and Chris have always talked about doing something together. I don't think he has the time, I know I wish I had the time. Well actually, I would drop *everything* to do a record with Chris...except King's X. We haven't talked about that in a long time.

You once recorded with Dimebag Darrell, right?

Me and Dime were going to do something together. It just bums me out that we never got that chance. We were going to do a blues record—we did this one song, "Born Under A Bad Sign," at his Christmas Eve party, about eight or nine years ago. It was a lot of fun, it's a little bootleg going around [with] Dime playing guitar—that's the only thing I have of 'em, y'know?

www.kingsxrocks.com
www.dugpinnick.com

Classic Rock—July 2005, issue 81

Jason Newsted

With various projects on the go—including working with Voivod—the one-time Metallica bassist is a very busy man.

Since his exit from Metallica in early 2001, Jason Newsted has toured and recorded with Voivod, in addition to working on a plethora of projects, released through his Chophouse site and label. Newsted has recently launched yet another project, the bluesy/psychedelic Heard of Elements, who have opted to forgo record companies entirely, and are putting their music up on the Chophouse site (www.chophouserecords.com). Additionally, a new Voivod album is written, with a release date looking like early 2006. Newsted recently discussed his new projects, as well as his former band.

How did Heard of Elements come together?

I'm constantly seeking out people from different musical worlds, to throw together in the Chophouse. I don't pretend to know jazz; they don't pretend to know metal. On this project was Roy Rogers on slide guitar and a drummer named Carl Coletti, who the most recording he's done is with Ottmar Liebert, the flamenco guitarist. He's got this kind of Latin vibe, but he can hit real hard punk music too. The drummer has that kind of flavor, Roy has his flavor, and I've got my metal thing. So we threw all the ideas together and made our "musical soup." Carl and I have done many projects together—with Andreas [Kisser] from Sepultura, with Devin Townsend. Probably about ten or twelve years we've been recording together. A lot of projects are kind of punky, but this one is considered pretty more complex.

How would you describe the group's material?

I didn't really know what to predict. It's best described I think as "California summer time music." That's what it ended up sounding like to me, once the mixing was happening, production was happening, people were putting on their parts.

When will the new Voivod album come out?

Voivod has just signed a new contract. We can get it going in Montreal in the next couple of months, and we'll probably turn it around at the beginning of the year. I can't promise anything, but that's a rough guess.

How will it sound?

Just another step forward. You can tell it's Voivod within three seconds. Some of it's full-on metal—Venom/Motörhead drumming—then there's some very psychedelic stuff. It's what you would expect from Voivod. It's like, if you go to buy an AC/DC record, you know you're going to get. That's what Voivod is—there's no denying it or no letting anybody down about what they've come to know and love about that band.

What did you think of 'Some Kind of Monster'?

Well, I'll answer you as a "fan of Metallica," because if I look at it from the inside, there's too much personal shit that nobody really gives a crap about.

It's not something that we expected from them. When you have a band like that, the biggest metal band that there's been this last couple of generations or whatever, and people have a certain picture painted of them, and then you go and show the soft white underbelly, and you expose things that maybe people don't really need to see. You know, there's some stuff that's meant to be seen and some stuff that's meant to be sacred, in the inner circle. And they exposed the inner circle. I don't agree with that as a fan. There have been incredible documentary movies made about bands—Dylan, Beatles stuff. There are a lot of really cool band documentaries that out-do that one. I thought they could have done a lot more if they would have shown the things that people wanted to see, at least a little bit. Not just the whole thing about psychiatry sessions, but at least show us three songs of you guys playing live. Give us what we want, *please.* Show us that you're still the powerful monster that we have come to appreciate. I would have liked to see that—the big teeth gnashing—instead of at the very end of the movie, they show it for 30 seconds or something. I would have liked to see some of the real "weight."

Are you still in contact with Metallica?
Only through business.

www.chophouserecords.com

Classic Rock—November 2005, issue 86

My Life Story

Scott Ian

The infamous baldy/goatee ensemble that is the driving force behind Anthrax's catalogue of thrash, Scott Ian talks to Greg Prato about his life in riffology.

Where and when were you born?

"Jamaica, Queens, USA, December 31, 1963."

How was school?

"School was fine, I never really minded school. I did really well in school. I didn't fall into any 'group,' I was kinda in between. In high school, there was a small group of us that were really into music—specifically metal in the late '70s/early '80s. There was only half a dozen of us, so we were really too small to be considered or own clique or anything like that. So I kinda floated in between all different types of groups in school—whether it was the jocks, the nerds, or whoever."

First girlfriend?

"My first girlfriend would be when I was 12 or 13. She was a girl I used to know from where I used to go visit my grandparents in Florida. I didn't really date anybody in my neighborhood growing up—if you weren't 14 and already rich, there was no way to really date the girls in my neighborhood!"

When was the first time you played in front of people?

"I played in a high school talent show. That was in tenth grade—the name of the group was 'Four-X,' and we did 'Rock and Roll All Nite' by Kiss and 'Surrender' by Cheap Trick."

When did you admiration of the New York Yankees begin?

"I've been a Yankees fan since around '71 or '72. My parents weren't really into sports—I don't know how I gravitated to being into the Yankees. I just started watching them on television and started asking my dad to take me to games. The best I went to see would still be the World Series in '77—all the home games. I was at game six when Reggie Jackson hit three home runs, which I would have to say, is the highlight of my baseball experience. Nothing's ever topped that."

What were some of your first concerts?

"I think the first concert I ever went to was Paul Simon. My father took me, and it was soon after that we also went to see Elton John. Then my uncle took me to see Kiss in '76, that was the first concert that I went to that I was like, 'I want to go to this show, can I get tickets, and can somebody please take me?' I saw Kiss quite a bit in the beginning, 'cause they were my favorite band from '75 to '78. Whenever they played New York—I was at all the Garden shows in '77—but then at that time I just really started getting into music, as did all my friends. I remember going to see Ted Nugent back then, Cheap Trick a bunch of times— we pretty much went to anything. Any show that came through, we would go to—from '78 on. At the Palladium especially—I saw Ozzy and Motörhead on the first 'Blizzard of Oz' tour, Priest with Maiden opening for three nights when [Maiden] were still on the 'Killers' tour. Thin Lizzy is the one band I kick myself over. They were a band I just really didn't know about then, then years later I got really into and would think back, and go 'God, I could have seen them so many times at the Palladium!' But outside of Thin Lizzy, pretty much saw everybody—AC/DC, the Ramones at Queens College."

Since you're a big horror movie buff, what are your favorites?

"Definitely 'Halloween,' 'Texas Chainsaw Massacre,' 'The Thing,' the first 'Nightmare on Elm Street,' 'Night of the Living Dead,' 'Dawn of the Dead,' the first three 'Friday the 13th's, 'Phantasm,' 'Zombie.'"

What made you move from the east coast out to the west coast?

"A number of things—the biggest one being 'cause I could! I loved coming out here since I was a kid. In the summer of '77, I had saved up all my bar mitzvah money, and I bought tickets for my brother and I to spend the whole summer in Laguna Beach, where a friend of my mom's lived. Ever since then, I pretty much loved California. So when I had the opportunity to move out here, I grabbed it. At the end of '89, when the band was coming out to record 'Persistence of Time,' we had a truck coming out here with all our crap on it, so it just enabled me to make my move a lot easier. 'Cause I was able to put a bunch of stuff on the truck and just have it driven out here."

Give us your side of the story on the S.O.D. reunion in 1999.
Charlie didn't seem too pleased.

"I don't have a side—I did an S.O.D. reunion. He feels the way he feels about it. We decided to make a record, and everybody agreed to that, nobody was forced to do anything, as far as I know. I just think there was probably a little too much touring. We went around and we did one tour which I thought was killer, and then I think we spread ourselves a little too thin and tried to come around a second time. The shows in the States just weren't as good and the places were half full. The reason why it never was a full time band was because I never wanted it to be something that just became a job, or had baggage, or any of that stuff that a normal band has. So as far as I was concerned, it was cool to go around once, give everyone an opportunity to check it out, but that's when we should have ended it. For whatever reasons, maybe we got greedy or whatever it was, trying to go around a second time kinda killed the fun of what S.O.D. was about."

What's a day in the life of V.J. like? [Scott formerly hosted 'Rock Show'
on VH-1 in the U.S.]

"V.J.'s do nothing! A V.J. is the easiest job in the whole world. It's what I should have been doing from the beginning. You do nothing—especially for me. I'm doing a show where I already know everything about all these bands, so I would get a script, look it over, show up on the set the next day, it would take about 40 minutes to tape the hour show, and I'd be done. All you are is a talking head, who's trying to make a subject seem interesting, whether it is or not."

What's your most cherished item?

"My book collection. That's really the only thing I 'collect.' I have a pretty huge book collection—first editions and limited edition stuff from Stephen King, James Ellroy, Anne Rice, J.K. Rowling, and Charles Bukowski. I couldn't tell you how many I have, but I've got quite a bit. Too many to fit in my house, let's put it that way. I hate having stuff in storage. I have two storage places, and I'm getting it down to one."

www.anthrax.com

Metal Hammer—March 2004, issue 124

Classic Show Review

Metallica/Queensrÿche

Nassau Coliseum, New York, March 8, 1989

It was one hell of a three-year period for Metallica. Between 1986 and '89, just about everything that could go right did so (building a massive fan base by opening for rock's big guns; issuing the classic 'Master of Puppets'), as well as go wrong (Cliff Burton's tragic death).

But James Hetfield, Kirk Hammett, Jason Newsted, and Lars Ulrich had weathered the storm by early '89, and had officially hit the big time—embarking on their first Stateside headlining arena tour, in support of their top ten album, '... And Justice for All.' Never mind that the group would reject the album's musical direction soon after, they were still content and had assembled quite a concert bill.

Opening were Queensrÿche, fresh from supporting Def Leppard and plugging their prog-metal epic, 'Operation: Mindcrime.' So when the tour hit New York's Nassau Coliseum on a frigid March night, it was no surprise that all 18,000 seats were occupied.

If you were looking for an evening of tricky time changes and an overabundance of riffs per square song, you were at the right place, as the high-water mark of '80s-era "thinking man's metal" remain 'Mindcrime' and 'Justice.' The sign that an opening band will soon make the jump to headliner is usually when they can escape unscathed in front of another band's audience, and that's precisely what Queensrÿche accomplished. Focusing primarily on 'Mindcrime,' it didn't take a genius to realize that they would soon make that career leap (two years later, they returned back to this same venue...as a headliner).

But Metallica was what the crowd wanted. And they got a whole lot of them. While you practically needed a compass to follow the newer epics—including show opener "Blackened," plus the subsequently rarely-played-live "Eye of the Beholder" and the never-ending title track of 'Justice' (during which a lighting truss and a replica of the album cover's statue came a-tumblin')—all stood their own among the classics. And plenty of classics there were, including such finely tuned steamrollers as "The Four Horsemen," "Master of Puppets," "Fade to Black," and "Creeping Death," the latter having the crowd chant "DIE!" during the breakdown. While Hetfield was fast becoming an arena-worthy frontman, his introduction of "new member" Jason Newsted raised a few eyebrows, since by now he'd been in the line-up over two years.

And speaking of Newsted, not even his god-awful, toilet break-inducing bass solo could derail the show, as a few cover-song snippets peppered the set, including bits of Jimi Hendrix's "Little Wing," and Zeppelin's "How Many More Times" segueing into Deep Purple's "Black Night."

But the big Metallica story at this time was that they had finally taken the "MTV plunge" by issuing a video for "One," the mood-shifter on 'Justice.' Unsurprisingly, live it was a pyro-heavy rendition of the song that received one of the evening's strongest responses. And what better way to sign off than with a wink to long-time fans, which a tremendous one-two punch of "Am I Evil?" and "Whiplash."

On this night in New York's suburbs, Metallica still mattered—mightily.

Bonus Bit: Also Happening in 1989

— Germany's Berlin Wall comes crashing down after standing for 28 years.
— The Exxon Valdez oil tanker sprouts one hell of a leak, as 11 million gallons of crude oil flows into Alaska's Prince William Sound.
— Artist Salvador Dali dies from heart failure and respiratory complications.
— Michael Keaton and Jack Nicholson wow audiences in the year's top grossing movie, 'Batman.'
— The Nobel Peace Prize is awarded to the Dalai Lama.
— Faith No More release 'The Real Thing.' Accidentally, rap metal is created.

www.metallica.com
www.queensryche.com

Classic Rock—June 2004, issue 67

Show Review

Ozzfest

Jones Beach Theater, Wantagh, New York—July 14, 2004

The Punks Meet the Godfathers

Metal Gods old and new embark in epic battle against Mother Nature.
Yea verily, the flame of heavy metal doth burn brightly.

Wind nor rain could extinguish this heavy metal flame. And what a flame it was at this year's Ozzfest—showcasing such legends as Black Sabbath, Judas Priest, and Slayer (all featuring their classic line-ups), as well as potential throne inheritors (Slipknot, Lamb of God, etc.). One of the tour's first stops was New York's Jones Beach Theater, an outdoor venue right on the bay. But when you're near the water, the weather gets tricky—a breeze turns into a wind chill, and drizzle turns into a typhoon. So when thunderstorms were forecasted, New York metalheads kept their fingers crossed.

As with most festivals, two stages were utilized—a main stage in the theater section (for heavy hitters), with a second stage in the parking lot (for up-and-comer's). Unlike earlier Ozzfests, both stages were not going simultaneously—the second stage ran from morning 'til afternoon, before the main stage opened its gates.

Most second stage bands tended to blend into one another, but booths offered an alternative (mostly adverts), as well as an autograph tent, where several Ozzfest participants parked their bums to sign tchotchkes. With the sky overcast early, the sun appeared by noon, and turned the second stage into a scorcher—making those "sunblock-less" pay dearly (especially your humble narrator). It quickly became apparent that the second stage audience was comprised largely of youngins, the type of metal youth that will slam/surf to anything.

One of the first bands to leave an impression is Lamb of God. It's easy to figure out the band merely by look—a bunch of longhairs represent the "metal," while singer Randy Blythe's shorter locks (and anti-George Bush t-shirt) hint he's the "hardcore." But the main attraction of the second stage is Slipknot, who agreed to tour only if they could play on the second stage. Their peculiar wish was granted, and you can tell their set is nearing by the amount of children accompanied by daddies (which leads you to wonder—is Slipknot this generation's Kiss?). Wearing masks in the boiling heat doesn't slow down the nine-man band, as they leap, headbang, and give the middle finger salute. The group's two percussionists repeatedly bash their drums with baseball bats, while each test their kit's sturdiness, by jumping on them throughout.

Soon after, the throng takes refuge in the shaded main stage, as three-time Ozzfest vets Black Label Society greet them. Guitarist Zakk Wylde alternates between his trusty Les Pauls and a Randy Rhoads Flying V, and soon turns out to be the only person serving beer (Jones Beach doesn't allow alcohol)—handing the front row a cool one. We then go from pro-beer to pro-marijuana, as Superjoint Ritual's backdrop logo contains a "sweet leaf." Fresh off Pantera's split, singer Phil Anselmo (sporting a 'Cowboys From Hell'-era long haired Mohawk) rallies his new troops, and does an admirable job initially. But the crowd soon turns ugly, as Anselmo rambles between songs, and unwisely, disses Pantera. Winning over the crowd is soon out of reach.

Sweating bullets in makeup and studded knee guards, black metallists Dimmu Borgir are up next. While the crowd digs 'em, Dimmu's stage show is best suited for the dark, *not* outdoors during daylight. Slayer fares much better (random "SLAYER!" shouts were heard throughout the day)—with Dave Lombardo back, this is the first look at the classic Slayer for many new fans. A setlist comprised of classics transpires, including raging versions of 'Mandatory Suicide' and 'Raining Blood,' the latter of which was accompanied by a perfectly timed thunderstorm. Roadies scramble to cover amps, while audience members in only tees and shorts are punished.

With it still pouring, the drenched crowd awaits the return of Judas Halford. And the leather boys don't disappoint, as they blow away the competition with a near hour and a half set that balances lesser-known ("The Sentinel," "Beyond the Realms of Death") with classics ("Green Manalishi," "Breaking the Law," "Metal Gods"—the latter of which sees the leather-trenchcoated Halford marching like a *Probot*). With nil stage props (although Halford's motorbike makes an appearance), the mighty Priest prove they're back in business.

Due to the weather, pockets of the crowd are on their way home by the time the pre-recorded strains of "Supertzar" announce Black Sabbath. The day's ongoing anti-Bush stance continues during set-opener "War Pigs," as images comparing Bush to Hitler are flashed on a projection screen. And the screen gets quite a workout, as Tony Montana's doomed 'Scarface' character appears during "Snowblind," and a clock ticking towards 4:20 appears prior to "Sweet Leaf." With the storm easing, Ozzy takes mercy on still-soggy fans by not throwing his trademark water buckets (instead, dunking one over his head)—and later, singing a sample of "Singing in the Rain." While the audience adores Sabbath, if you've seen them on one of their many recent reunion tours, the setlist is predictable, as the long day finally ends after Ozzy implores the crowd not to drive drunk after "Paranoid."

It didn't matter if you were a headbanger old or new—all things metal were well represented at Ozzfest 2004.

www.ozzfest.com

Classic Rock—October 2004, issue 71

Punk/Alt Rock

Features

Meat Puppets

No Strings Attached

Drugs, record, tour, drugs, record, tour…that's how the Meat Puppets lived it. Ex-members Curt Kirkwood and Derrick Bostrom and manager Tami Blevins take a look back over a career that saw them play with Nirvana, and ended in a blizzard of coke, heroin, and personal tragedy.

"We damn near killed ourselves getting back to Phoenix in order to catch a flight to New York," remembers Derrick Bostrom, about a certain wintry night circa late 1993. "We were in Colorado, and it was blizzarding—we said, 'We have to high tail it back to Phoenix immediately.' They wanted us to go to Telluride in the middle of a snowstorm. We had huge fights with our manager, with the promoter, and we were like, *'We're not going, sorry!'* Just got caught in the blizzard, and it could've gone either way." Ever the road warriors, it was rare that the Meat Puppets would cancel a show, but this was an exception. Oh, and by the way...the main reason the show was cancelled wasn't because of the storm, but because Kurt Cobain had personally invited the Puppets' Kirkwood brothers to appear on a taping of 'MTV Unplugged,' in NYC.

As a result of Cobain ending his life in the spring of '94, MTV incessantly aired the unplugged episode, and the world would see the Kirkwood brothers' mugs non-stop. Add to it an official album release of Nirvana's 'Unplugged In New York' and the release of one of the Puppets' best albums, the gold-certified 'Too High To Die,' and suddenly, the Puppets were *the* overnight success story of 1994. But just when it seemed like years of hard work were about to pay off big time, the group was caput by 1996, due to record company snafus and their bassist's drug addiction.

Although things may have gotten ugly towards the end, things weren't always like that for the band. The Kirkwood brothers, singer/guitarist Curt and bassist Cris, both hailed from Texas originally, before their folks split, and they moved with their mum to Phoenix as youngsters in 1965. The brothers were suspicious of popular music early on, before the elder Curt was turned onto an eclectic mix via a high school chum—Led Zeppelin, the Grateful

Dead, Can, Henry Cow, George Jones, etc. As a result, Curt picked up the guitar himself, and during 1977, met drummer Derrick Bostrom.

"I met him at a party in Paradise Valley," remembers Curt. "It was all his friends from the church that he went to—they were all eccentric people. We didn't start to think about starting a band until years afterwards—it was more just people who partied together." Bostrom's first impression of the Kirkwoods remains clear all these years later. "They were both smart—when [Curt] was younger, he was very full of himself, very funny. I remember he was telling me how he had developed this technique for making everything go black, while he had his eyes open! I remember him describing the process of lying back on his bed, and staring intently at a spot out in space, until the vision just kind of blurred away, and it was all black, and then he could just see hallucinations. He said, 'I've only been able to do this once without acid!' He was just a wild character."

But not too wild to jam with. Bostrom: "[Curt] was playing in his back bedroom with Cris, who was playing the bass. And they were just doing noise jams on their crummy equipment. I happened to stop by their house one time after I had been record shopping, and brought a couple of records over. Curt said, 'Let me see those,' and rather than dismissing them out off hand for being punk—which was the standard thing to do—he expressed some interest. So I filed that away, and then shortly thereafter, he had stopped by the house. He was working as a bus driver for school kids, and got off early. I wasn't working at the time, so he'd come over with pot, and we'd get high. So we jammed, and decided to get Cris over there to make it a trio. We just started jamming on songs from my punk rock record collection." Shortly after the dawn of the '80s, the Meat Puppets were born.

The Puppets quickly fell in with the then still-largely underground punk scene; resulting in the release of a debut EP funded by a band they were friends with, 1981's 'In A Car.' While their hippie appearance and wide ranging musical tastes made them stand out from most of the punk pack, Black Flag became huge fans, and eventually signed them to their SST label.

Bostrom: "[SST] at the time were kind of keying into this aggressive male energy in the audience. Being on SST and rubbing shoulders with Black Flag, word-of-mouth being what it is—and that's all there was back then—[audiences] didn't necessarily know that we were going to come on stage wearing long hair and overalls, doing 15 minute jams on Grateful Dead covers.

Which we did, especially on one tour when we opened for Black Flag."

Kirkwood remembers many a hostile reaction from crowds early on—"I think the crowds *and* the bands were violent. A lot of those times, people would be out of their minds, and there would be fights. Seeing people who became famous do horrible things. It was chaos. If you got 500 people in there for a Black Flag show, there were definitely *a lot* of assholes. I mean, we always played a lot of different music, but we never tried to service to punk rock. We definitely started rubbing their faces in all the different kinds of crap we liked."

In addition to punk rock, the Kirkwoods and Bostrom discovered another similar interest—drugs. In fact, LSD played a large part in the outcome of their 1982 full length, self-titled debut. Kirkwood: "We did the first SST record when we were out of our minds—it was down at Unicorn Studios on Santa Monica Blvd. For three days, we 'dropped' every day in the morning, just to see if we could make a psychedelic record. It was us on Santa Monica Boulevard, hanging out with prostitutes. Being from Phoenix, we weren't used to that kind of cultural decay, mixed with glam. It was just so otherworldly, because we were tripping the whole time. I don't know how we did it—it was experimentation, trying to pioneer something. We thought that was how it happened. Whether it was George Jones being drunk, the Beatles smoking pot, or Elvis on speed or whatever, we always just figured this is what our heroes did. But we found out probably otherwise."

Unsurprisingly, it was nearly impossible to decipher anything amongst all the white noise. But the trio's second album, 1984's 'Meat Puppets II,' was a different story altogether. There have been few instances in rock history that a band has sounded so *differently* after a single album. Gone (for the most part) was the noise and howling vocals, replaced by songs that somehow incorporated country, folk, and punk—resulting in one of rock's all-time classics. But one thing remained the same with the band—drugs. Kirkwood: "We continued that habit on through—[when] we did 'Meat Puppets II,' we had an ounce of ecstasy, and we just fucking snorted X the whole time. It was "MDA" back then. We were really into putting things into these double locked capsules full of MDA. Just getting high as shit—nobody knew what X was yet."

The Puppets supported the release by opening for Black Flag during their 'My War' tour in 1984, and while they didn't always win over the crowd (Kirkwood: "We'd got 'lugeed' on constantly—hundreds of lugees a night, it was just hideous how people were"), they did leave an impression on a teenaged fan that caught a Seattle performance—Kurt Cobain. Kirkwood recalls what the eventual Nirvana leader later admitted—"It was a pretty early, formative show for him, in terms of punk rock."

For the Puppets' next release, 1985's 'Up on the Sun,' the band somehow caught lightning in a bottle twice. Despite being less country and more psychedelic than its predecessor, 'Sun' has gone on to become another certified '80s indie rock classic. But it was around this time that friction began between band and label. Bostrom: "SST were a little weary about putting out this country rock crap on their punk rock label, and it started to throw a wedge in it. For 'Up on the Sun,' we closed ranks considerably, and we began to develop this 'fuck outsider' thing. Very protective, parental attitude towards what we were doing."

While most punk bands were still keeping things simple, Kirkwood had other ideas for 'Sun.' "I was really into the Who—'Meaty Beaty Big and Bouncy,' 'Sell Out.' And earlier Who, when they were doing three-part harmonies, and stuff that was a little orchestral—that would later become Queen. I was trying to make my own 'Secret Life of Plants' or 'Innervisions.' Rather than 'Sgt. Pepper' or my 'Good Vibrations' record, I was always trying to do a headphone sort of record, like I thought Stevie Wonder would."

The Puppets spent the rest of the decade crisscrossing the states, and issuing further SST releases. Looking back, some catch the band a bit too mesmerized with synths and machinery (1987's 'Mirage,' 1989's 'Monsters'), while others reflected the classic Puppets sound (1986's 'Out My Way,' 1987's 'Huevos'). Bostrom remembers this era as when majors were signing indie bands left and right (Hüsker Dü, the Replacements)...except for the Puppets. And even when the band entertained offers, they left feeling flat. Bostrom: "We saw label guys, and they put us off big time. We'd come into their offices, and they would be wearing robes or whatever, not showing us respect, going, 'Y'know, you guys need to be more like Gene Loves Jezebel, *now there's a band!*' And we were just like, 'Ehhh'."

By the dawn of the '90s, the Puppets had had enough—leaving SST, and aggressively seeking a major label deal. These were lean times for the band, resulting in Bostrom eventually quitting drugs. "It was apparent that the band was mortgaging themselves to their drug habit. Too much money was going into it, money I didn't have. And I was just going, 'God, this is no way to plan for your future.' At the time, and continues to be, the best thing I ever did." By 1991, the waiting game was over, as the Puppets were signed to London Records, and recording their major label debut, 'Forbidden Places.'

While the album was indeed a "return to form" of sorts for the band, the label convinced the band to revisit their country roots—pairing them with Dwight Yoakam's producer, Pete Anderson. Bostrom: "It was a good record, but right around the time, 'Nevermind' came out. So the idea of marketing a band as a country band was a great way to get them ignored." Although Nirvana helped bring alt-rock to the masses in the U.S., Kirkwood remained suspicious. "'Forbidden Places' was not that hard rock, and [we didn't] realize that there was another group of disgruntled teens coming out. And I kind of started seeing that scene like that too, playing to the disenfranchised youth again. That's alright, and they can cloud it with their Mardi Gras beads and stuff—I was pretty cynical about it."

The Meat Puppets convinced their label to let Butthole Surfer Paul Leary produce their next album, 'Too High To Die.' Several months before the album in question was released during early 1994, the Puppets got word of an enticing offer—Nirvana wanted the Puppets to open a few shows on what would ultimately be their final U.S. tour. Bostrom: "Every week [Cobain] was changing the opening bands on that tour. We were lucky to be on the week directly before the 'Unplugged' thing, and we had heard that he wanted to perform 'Oh Me' on the show."

The original plan was for the Puppets to teach Nirvana how to play the song, but when time became a factor, it became apparent that the Kirkwood brothers would fly in for the show, with Cobain singing and drummer Dave Grohl replacing Bostrom. Eventually, the one song turned into three 'Meat Puppets II' selections, as "Plateau" and "Lake of Fire" were added. Kirkwood: "We were a 'surprise special guest,' and Nirvana hadn't told anybody until we got there. Literally, the night we were there, [MTV] was still thinking it was going to be Eddie Vedder or somebody. You could tell they were a little like, 'What's this?'"

Easily one of the best MTV 'Unplugged' specials, the episode became one of its most aired a few months later, when the network ran it non-stop in the wake of Cobain's suicide in April 1994. Two months before Cobain's death, 'Too High' found its way into the shops, the most rocking and musically varied release the group had issued since 'II.' As a result of the band's sudden heightened profile, the leadoff single, "Backwater," became a hit. But behind-the-scenes, the Puppets decided it was time to cut ties with their manager, and brought in Tami Blevins ("I thought they were one of the most strangely beautiful bands I'd ever heard").

By the summer of 1994, the Puppets were on top of the world, as they were offered to open the entire summer for Stone Temple Pilots, who had recently topped the U.S. charts with 'Purple.' While drugs were always part of the Puppets, it was during this tour that things spun out of control for Cris, as he became addicted to heroin and cocaine. Blevins: "I think I, like some other people, was in denial about it. I ignored it—just tried to tell myself that it wasn't a huge problem. I hadn't had a lot of experience with people who did heroin. In retrospect, all the signals were there. I think during the STP [tour] is when it was just like 'You've got to be kidding me, this is getting kind of crazy.' Especially during that last week, I was like, 'Oh no, *the ship's going to sink'.*"

Having spent much of '94 on the road, the Puppets decided to go directly back into the studio to follow up their breakthrough hit—releasing 'No Joke' in 1995. But something was a-miss. Bostrom: "It was the same group, but it wasn't the same. I wasn't 100% satisfied with the way it came down—it's difficult to put your finger on it. The record was a little bit over-produced, the material was a little bit down beat." To add insult in injury, the Puppets found themselves entangled in a record company snafu. Blevins: "We were setting up for the release, that's when rumors started—PolyGram being sold. It seemed within a six-month period, the Meat Puppets' entire team either quit or got fired. The single, 'Scum,' came out to radio, and I think it was literally on every rock station in the country. Then their promotions team left, and within two weeks, it went from over 200 stations to 14."

The Puppets tried to breath life into the record by touring with Primus. But this was precisely the same time that Curt recognized his brother's addiction ("He was just zonked out all the time"), and by early 1996, further touring invitations were declined—ultimately ending the group. With the band no longer in his life, Cris spiraled further out of control, as he and his wife, Michelle Tardif, sunk into a drug-fueled abyss. Blevins: "I was talking to [Tardif], she told me, 'Tami, I'm so fucked up.' And I hadn't seen her in quite a while, and I said, 'What do you mean? It'll be OK.' I was trying to get her into rehab, and she goes, 'No, you don't understand, I'm *really* fucked up.' At that point I actually got scared—'What condition are these two really in?' It was a week later that I got the frantic phone call from Cris, that she was dead."

Instead of cleaning up his act, Cris only indulged heavier with drugs. Not even an intervention and a stint at a high-priced rehab could curb his appetite, as he left the facility after only a week. Later, a childhood friend of the Kirkwood's died the same way Tardiff had, and in the same locale—Cris' house. Despite little contact with his brother, Curt continued making music and touring, first as part of a new version of the Meat Puppets (issuing 'Golden Lies' in 2000), and with the all-star Eyes Adrift (2002's underrated 'Eyes Adrift'), while Bostrom retired from music altogether, adapting to the 9-5 life.

Just when you thought it couldn't get any worse for Cris, it did. In December 2003, the ex-Puppet was involved in an altercation over a parking spot, which resulted in a security guard trying to defuse the situation. The confrontation soon turned ugly, as Cris hit the guard with his own baton, before the guard shot Cris in the back with his gun. Although not paralyzed, Cris was seriously wounded, and afterwards, sentenced to 21 months in prison. Curt feels that prison is best for his sibling at this point. "Probably a better thing than running amok and being shot. By habit, over the years [I've] just kind of stayed out of it all, because it's just really alien and unappealing. It goes way beyond feeling like you're trying to take care of a member of the family. It's such a wild story that you have to step back from it. Nothing really surprises me there. It's been a drag for years."

Currently, Kirkwood is hard at work with a new outfit, Volcano, as well as possibly pursuing an acoustic solo album. But fans still inquire about a reunion upon Cris' exit from jail. While it's something that Curt doesn't rule out, it doesn't appear too likely. "It seems so easy in a certain sense to say 'Yeah,' because if Cris got straight it would be pretty easy. It would probably go over as good as it ever did—just because of the history. But Derrick hasn't done any music or toured or anything since the Meat Puppets broke up. It would be a huge shock on his system. Stuff like that I never think is outside the realm of possibilities, just because you have to have an open mind."

www.meatpuppets.com
www.themeatpuppets.com

Classic Rock—March 2005, issue 77

The Dead Boys

Die Young

They had a high-energy, confrontational live show on par with only Iggy Pop, and a debut album only matched by the Ramones. But the Dead Boys lived it like they played it—burning out after only two albums. Band mates Cheetah Chrome, Jeff Magnum, and Johnny Blitz tell their crash n' burn tale.

Guitarist Cheetah Chrome still remembers his initial impressions of New York City. "Dog shit, garbage, smog [laughs]. This is before the pooper scooper law, so you'd get in, and 'Eww, smell that air!'" But this initial "fragrant" impression wouldn't last for long on him, or his band, Cleveland transplants the Dead Boys. "We realized that there was a lot of people like us out there. Why it didn't occur to us earlier, to just jump in the damn van and get a gig out of town…we weren't rocket scientists, we were the Dead Boys [laughs]." But within the span of just a few short months, the Dead Boys would be the toast of the New York punk scene—playing countless shows at CBGB's, signing a major label deal, touring alongside their heroes, and hanging with some of the late '70s biggest celebrities. And seemingly just as fast, the group would go—to borrow one of their song titles—"Down in Flames."

While the New York Bowery possessed quite a fertile music scene circa the mid '70s, the complete opposite could be said about Cleveland—a musical wasteland where cover bands reigned supreme. Chrome- "All cover bands, and I mean Lynyrd Skynyrd, Molly Hatchet. As far as trying to get anywhere in Cleveland, there weren't any places to play. And if you did, it was once every three months." Eventual Dead Boys bassist Jeff Magnum seconds the sentiment. "God, it was the worst. Satin flared trousers on lead singers that desperately tried to look like that insanely popular/grotesque Farrah Fawcett poster."

But there was one exception to this glut of local cover acts, an all-original band called Rocket from the Tombs, whose main influences included Alice Cooper, the Stooges, and the MC5. And the group's guitarist just happened to be Chrome. Also included in the band were future Pere Ubu leader Dave Thomas, and a teenaged drummer, Johnny Blitz. When the Rockets split in 1975, Chrome decided to form a new band with Blitz, along with a then-glammed out singer, Stiv Bators.

Chrome- "Around that time, Stiv showed up on the scene. And he was kind of a fringe character at first—he came from Youngstown, so nobody in Cleveland really knew who he was. And he had moved up there to meet some people and get a band together. So we kinda had the groundwork laid when Rockets broke up, that me and Stiv were going to do something. And that's when we got together with Blitz, and he knew Jimmy [Zero, guitarist]. It really gelled quickly." Ladies and gents, meet Frankenstein.

But conflicting personalities, and lack of gigs, drew a quick close to Frankenstein. However, Bators had a plan up his sleeve to make it work. Chrome- "The guy had more brains than Ralph Kramden. We hadn't talked in months; a couple of us weren't getting along. [Stiv] called everyone up and said he needed a ride—'Can you pick me up at the airport?' We all walked in not knowing that anybody else was going to be there. After Blitz showed up, Jeff showed up, and Jimmy showed up, that's when it started getting interesting. We started talking and Stiv came in. We decided to get back together then." Ladies and gents, meet the Dead Boys.

After hitting it off with the Ramones after the leather-jacketed New Yawkers played Cleveland, Bators realized that the group stood a better chance in NYC. With Joey Ramone landing the Dead Boys a tryout at CBGB's, the band automatically carved their niche—often playing the same club that launched the Ramones, Blondie, and the Talking Heads, while the venue's owner, Hilly Krystal, signed on as manager. Although often hard to create a stir in the city that never sleeps, Bators commanded the utmost attention of New York punkers—flailing around on stage until he was a bloody mess, "hanging" himself over a pipe with his mic chord, and when the mood suited him, introducing the audience to his "willy."

But the Dead Boys weren't all about shocking, as Cheetah had brought along several sure-fire punk anthems with him from his Rocket from the Tombs days—"Sonic Reducer," "Down in Flames," and "What Love Is." It wasn't long before the Dead Boys found themselves signed to the Ramones' label, Sire, and recording their debut album with producer Genya Ravan. Blitz- "I couldn't believe we were letting a female produce our album. That comes with immaturity and age—I was pretty young at the time—but it wound up a great album. It still holds up today, I'll hold it up against anything."

Blitz is indeed correct, 'Young, Loud and Snotty' does hold up incredibly well—nearly 30 years after its 1977 release—as Ravan wisely kept things rough and raw, sounding exactly like the group did on stage. Recorded at Jimi Hendrix's famed Electric Lady Studios, Blitz and his band mates didn't even know they were recording their major label debut. "It was made as a demo tape to shop around to record companies, and Sire said, 'It's good enough, let's just put it out like this.'" Chrome sums up the sessions succinctly—"Hell's Angels, speed, and being unable to go to sleep in the morning!"

Expectedly, the ensuing supporting tour was a no-holds-barred affair, as the Dead Boys played the U.S. alongside Iggy Pop, the Ramones, the Dictators, and Cheap Trick. Blitz- "That was just one big booze and drug-a-thon. To tell you the truth, I don't remember much. I could probably only do it once or twice in a lifetime—I would have burnt myself out so bad."

The tour even included U.K. dates, opening for the Damned. Chrome- "Our record came out three days after we were in England—the day after we played London, of course. So nobody really knew who the hell we were. They were pretty responsive, but it wasn't the best job on Sire's part. I think I did an interview with some guy from Melody Maker. Boy, he hated us. He sat there with his head in his hand the whole time!" Magnum recalls giving the headliner some competition—"I remember the Damned sucked by then, and we smoked those guys night after night."

With the Dead Boys now operating from NYC, the group made friends with two of the era's most recognizable names in music and movies—Sid Vicious and John Belushi. Blitz remembers a chilling conversation he had with Vicious—"He was staying at the Chelsea [Hotel] the same time we were. I was into collecting knives. So Sid started hanging out, and a couple of days before he off'd Nancy, he came down and we were talking. He asked me point blank, 'What would happen to me if I decided to kill somebody in this country?' I said, 'They're going to throw you in jail, if not give you the chair!' Then a few days later, he off'd his old lady."

And while Chrome remembers the ex-Pistol as "A really sweet guy without a lot to say—real funny," Magnum's view differs. "He was a brainless wasted dumb ass who managed to find his female equal in Nancy Spungen. They were both tailor made to drop dead, and just couldn't wait any longer."

With a skyrocketing career in TV ('Saturday Night Live') and film ('Animal House'), John Belushi became a major Dead Boys fan around this time. Chrome- "He started coming to gigs. When they were going 'Saturday Night Live,' a lot of times they'd go out to clubs afterwards, and he discovered us. We stayed friends right up until his death. I saw him a couple of weeks before he died—we used to go out to dinner. John was a really sweet guy. The funny thing was me and him never really got into doing drugs together. I mean, you do a bump now and then, but it wasn't like these stories that I hear about crawling on the floor with these 'lines,' y'know? Wasn't anything like that ever."

Despite all the hoopla, 'Young, Loud and Snotty' failed to connect with a large audience like albums by the Talking Heads and Blondie had. As a result, the group felt pressure to deliver on their sophomore album, 'We Have Come For Your Children.' And in a classic "What the fuck?!" moment, the group head-scratchingly chose ex-Mountain bassist Felix Pappalardi to produce. Blitz recalls realizing things weren't kosher straight away. "[Pappalardi] walks in the room, he has this green suit on—with gold embroidered marijuana leaves! I was like, 'Holy shit, what have we gotten ourselves into?' We went down to Miami to record, and the first night; he invited us to his house. His wife Gail, who was a total whack job, starts talking to their dog, Otis, this old English bulldog. So she's sitting there, talking to this dog like he's a human being, and right then I knew she was out of her mind. And lo and behold, she ends up [allegedly killing] Felix."

Things only deteriorated from there. Chrome- "They set the board flat, walked away, and snorted coke! Nice guy, but I've never been floored by [Pappalardi's] production talent ever. I don't like Cream's production. So why the hell would I want him to do my band? It's like, 'Where does this hippie come off producing the Dead Boys?'" Still, the album spawned one of the group's top classics, "Ain't It Fun."

Soon after sessions wrapped up, Blitz found himself staring death straight in the face one night with roadie/pal Michael Sticca, post-gig. Blitz- "Me and one of my roadies decided to go out to a restaurant. We had two girls with us. So he decided to split early, in the middle of dinner. The next thing I know, his girlfriend is coming in to the restaurant, saying, 'Michael's in trouble!' Michael was flagging down a cab, and something happened with other people in a car. So I walk out, and there's knives and baseball bats out. And the next thing I know, I'm walking into a baseball bat. I get hit right across the forehead. So out comes my knife, I mean fuck, if I'm going down, I'm taking somebody with me. So I proceeded to 'join in,' and the next think I know, I wake up in the hospital, with a guy next to me on the other operating table.

After I got hit with the bat, I was pretty much out of it. I guess I was just going on instinct from there. I was stabbed five times."

To offset hospital bills, the band organized a multi-night "Blitz Benefit" at CBGB's, which included performances by the Ramones and Blondie, as well as appearances by Belushi and the John Waters regular, Divine. Chrome- "Putting that whole thing together was just great. I remember having to sweep up the alley behind CBGB's, which hadn't been touched in years, so we could get the Ramones' equipment truck back there. Anybody who was in town pretty much played. It was great, a real outpouring of friendship."

When Blitz recuperated, the group hit the road once more, but after only a month, the band was called back. With sales not improving, the Dead Boys were dropped by Sire, and just like that, the band was over. Bators would later front goth-punkers Lords of the New Church, while the other ex-Dead Boys slogged it out in lesser-known outfits. But throughout the '80s, the Dead Boys reunited for brief tours, something that is not a good memory for Chrome, who was battling drug addiction. "We had a hard time. The reason that we broke up in the first place was because of reasons. So as soon as we were together for any length of time, they reared their ugly head. There was no management—we were it. And there were no band meetings, except for van rides. Who wants to argue for four hours in a van? It was very unpleasant and stressful." Any chance of further reunions was snuffed out on June 4, 1990, when Bators died from injuries sustained from being hit by a car in Paris.

But throughout the '90s and early 21st century, the Dead Boys finally got their due, as three of the era's biggest bands tackled Dead Boys tunes—Guns N' Roses ("Ain't It Fun"), Pearl Jam ("Sonic Reducer"), and the Beastie Boys (who sampled "Sonic Reducer" in "An Open Letter to NYC"). Also, an over- the-top archival DVD, 2004's 'Live at CBGB 1977,' confirmed the group was one of punk's all-time great live acts. And it appears as though 2005 will see 4/5ths of the Dead Boys reunite for live gigs (with Zero and Chrome switching off on vocals).

But Bators' shadow continues to loom large on the band. Blitz- "He was a great guy, an amazing guy. You'd probably live a lifetime and never meet anybody like that. Very unique, very loving, caring. Wonderful guy—I miss him like you wouldn't believe."

Classic Rock—September 2005, issue 84

Bad Brains

Brainsurgery

So why didn't the Bad Brains become the hugest rock band on the planet? Band members Dr. Know, Darryl Jenifer, and Earl Hudson, as well as longtime manager Anthony Countey and two-time Bad Brains producer Ric Ocasek tell the story of the baddest band of them all.

We all know the famous quote about the Velvet Underground, which goes something like "Few people bought their records, but every one of them formed a band." And the same could be said about the Bad Brains. The list of artists that patterned their sound and approach after this great punk/hardcore/reggae band is staggering—it appears as though each year, there's a new chart-topper raving about the wonders of the Bad Brains. Even though commercial success eluded them, the power of their music prevails. "It's something bigger," explains bassist Darryl Jenifer. "Y'know, I've always said my platinum records and my platinum success is when someone can say that I influenced them in a positive way, through my music. I'll take that more than the money."

Guitarist Dr. Know also adds, "We kind of really...not us but the Father, used us to culturally/musically open up, and just break down the barriers. Here's a bunch of black dudes playing crazy rock n' roll, that you rock n' roll white people can't even play [laughs]. Playing some funk and this and that, and then playing reggae too—it's all relative. Bob Marley has a song called 'Punky Reggae Party,' that's what he was talking about."

And throughout the band's history, they've proven that it's all about the music—not the almighty dollar—time and time again. Admittedly however, usually at the behest of their singer, H.R. (an abbreviation for "Human Rights," and whose real name is Paul Hudson). Jenifer- "In the early days, we had offers from Elektra and Island. [With] Elektra, H.R. introduced the label president to me as 'Satan' [laughs]—at the Plaza Hotel in New York when they were going to offer us a million dollars. And then the Island deal, we had the contracts out to sign, and he said he wanted to use the bathroom, and ran down the street."

While it's hard to pinpoint the exact year hardcore was born, it's safe to say it hails from Washington, D.C. After all, this is where Henry Rollins and Ian MacKaye come from, and of course, the Bad Brains. Jenifer- "We were originally from South East Washington, D.C. The Brains came together about 1978. We were just some teenagers in music." Interestingly, one of punk/hardcore's eventual greats was initially influenced by jazz-fusion—Return to Forever and Mahavishnu Orchestra—as they were originally known as "Mind Power." But that all changed the day a friend of Darryl's paid a visit. "A friend of mine, Sid McCray, came over my house. He had safety pins and stuff all over him, and he had records—Ramones, Dead Boys, Generation X—I found it to be kind of interesting. The cats couldn't really play, but they had something to say." Soon after, fusion was replaced with punk, and Mind Power became the Bad Brains.

Unlike London, New York, and Los Angeles, the punk scene in D.C. was non-existent. Dr. Know- "There was no punk scene. There was a small group of all of us, who were aware. Here's the promoters—it's like, 'Oh, here's some band, we'll put [them] in this restaurant.' It was a restaurant downstairs and they had a space upstairs. Everybody's po-going, and the chandeliers in the ceiling [are] pumping. The club owners are like 'Oh, you've got to stop!' Word gets around—'Don't be booking them dudes man, they make everybody go crazy'." Realizing that they couldn't rely on a record company to back them, the Bad Brains issued their first single D.I.Y.-style, the explosive classic "Pay To Cum." Dr. Know- "We pressed it, licked 'em, sticked 'em. There were no labels signing this, it wasn't like that."

It was also around this time that other soon-to-be integral elements of the Bad Brains were discovered—Rastafarianism, reggae, and "positive mental attitude." Jenifer- "Reggae was discovered at a Bob Marley concert at the Capitol Center. I was taken in by the power of the music. And at the time, we were feeling that to be a real musician, you had to have sort of a 'concept,' like Scientology. But our concept was based around 'positive mental attitude'— we were reading a book, called 'Think and Grow Rich,' by Napoleon Hill. Within that book was a lot of little stuff like adversity, dealing with it, how to get where you want to go. So that tended to fuel our music with P.M.A. If you listen to our early recordings, we'd always be talking about, 'We got that P.M.A.!' But as we kind of progressed, we found that P.M.A. was really through Rastafari for us."

One problem—D.C. was a dead end for the band. By 1980, the Bad Brains had relocated to New York City, setting up shop at CBGB's. Dr. Know- "We played CB's every friggin night. This whole 'Sunday matinee' thing is from us. When we first played, nobody was there. It's like, 'Who are these niggers?' And we're in their face, killing it. We got a weekend day, and by then a little buzz started happening." But still, these were lean times for the band. Jenifer- "We were bumming on benches, selling weed to make food and stuff—we were hustlin'."

But an undeniable buzz was building, which only intensified with the release of their full-length debut, 1982's classic 'Bad Brains.' The album was a complete adrenaline rush, as evidenced by such ragers as "Sailin' On" and a re-recording of "Pay To Cum," while reggae detours momentarily cooled the fury, including the gorgeous "I Luv I Jah." Drummer Earl Hudson remembers that the band followed a golden rule during the recording—"We put 110% into what we did back then. It was totally from the heart, so I guess you could say the intentions were there to do our best."

But still, it was an uphill battle. Jenifer- "[The recording] was a pain in the ass—none of this stuff is like, 'Let's go do this and be that,' it's just like H.R. pushing things this-a-way and that-a-way. It was kind of labor intensive to be in Bad Brains at times—emotionally and physically." Additionally, the album wasn't exactly recorded "state-of-the-art," either. Dr. Know- "I lived at the studio in the control booth—a little loft at 171 Avenue B. [Producer Jerry Williams] had a whole building, but we only had one floor because it was all dilapidated. He built a little stage, and had a four-track."

Up until this point, a few managers had come and gone. But soon, the quartet found their man in the form of a then-NYU film student/punk fan, Anthony Countey. At the behest of friends, Countey made it down to the Roseland Ballroom to see the group open for the Gang of Four, and met/ chatted with the group before the gig. Countey- "I went into the audience kind of halfway back on the dance floor. They came out, and I think they started with 'Big Takeover.' Everybody went totally bonkers—flying through the air. I've never had an experience like that seeing a band, ever. I've seen great shows—the Pretenders, the Stones in their day, Led Zeppelin [during] their first American tour. That was a great show, but this show was even higher energy than that. I went backstage, I said, 'You fuckin' guys were just unbelievable.' And I went home; I didn't think I'd hear more about it."

The following day, Countey was unexpectedly welcomed into the Bad Brains world. "My buzzer rang and I was like, 'Hello?' 'This is the Bad Brains.' 'Huh?' Buzzed them in, they all marched into my living room, sat down, and said, 'We need a manager, we'd like you to do it.' I was like, 'Wait a minute; I'm a film student here. You need a manager who's going to go on tour with you. Somebody's going to have to put in all their time, and I don't think you're going to get me to do that.' And they were like, 'No, you've got to do it' [laughs]."

Despite no previous managerial experience, Countey accepted the position, and hit the road. But perhaps as a precursor of things to come, Countey's managerial intro was rocky, as he found himself defending the band against angry "fans" before a Philadelphia show, which had egged their van and passed out flyers saying the group was homophobic. Countey explains the misconception that followed the group throughout their career. "We played a lot of CBGB's shows, and I saw what was going on. The punk rock scene was full of twelve/thirteen year olds, and also these older homosexual guys. And a few of them who would invite these kids, like, 'Do you need a place to stay? You can come and stay at our place.' But they also molested these kids. This freaked H.R. out, 'cause he thought these people were taking advantage of these young kids. So essentially what H.R. was coming out against wasn't homosexuality per se."

At any rate, these early national tours were a constant battle. Hudson- "A lot of work man—a struggle. It wasn't easy. A lot of days you don't eat, and staying by folks' places. But y'know, it was an experience man, it was fun. You're young, and y'know, for a while it was cool."

On the other side of the rock stratosphere, new wave hit makers the Cars were ruling the U.S. charts. Always interested in discovering new sounds, leader Ric Ocasek became a major Bad Brains fan—playing the group's debut album before shows. When the Bad Brains rolled into the Cars' hometown, Boston, Ocasek met the band, and offered to record/produce them at the Cars' state-of-the-art recording studio. The group accepted, tracking new tunes and re-recording earlier compositions.

"When H.R. does vocals, he always faced the back of the room," recalls Ocasek, "He never watched the control room, as if you were watching him from the back. I guess it took him out of 'studio mode' and put him into 'live.' He's really philosophically into a non-violent thing, even though he's a little violent. You can't say things like, 'Let's punch that part in.' He'll say, 'Don't say punch.' It's down to a little thing like that. So that's a little hard." Soon after, the "Ocasek recordings" caught the attention of the Cars' label, Elektra.

The band especially impressed Elektra's Tom Zutaut, whose keen sense for scoping talent landed the label Mötley Crüe and later, Metallica. After witnessing an extraordinary Bad Brains show at an L.A. club in early 1983, Zutaut set up a meeting to sign the band. "We had this meeting at the Tropicana. Zutaut starts talking—he wants to sign the band. We go through his rap, and then H.R. stops him. He looks at him and says, 'Do you know what happens to people who mess with Rasta?' After the meeting, everyone goes off, and Zutaut says, 'Jesus, this is the first time in my life that anybody's threatened my life over doing something for them in the industry.' And that was it, that definitely cooled Tom." The failed meeting would lead to the group releasing the album (titled 'Rock For Light') independently, and eventually, their first hiatus—as H.R. launched a reggae solo career (with brother Earl), while Dr. Know and Jenifer attempted to launch a new band, Me and I.

After the 'Rock for Light' meltdown, a trend began that the Bad Brains would follow throughout their career—these "breaks" wouldn't last long, and would help re-charge the group's batteries. By the time the quartet got back to work in 1985 with producer Ron St. Germain, they were equipped with a set of tunes more hard rock-based than their early hardcore direction, but compared to what the mainstream considered "rock" at this point, there was simply no comparison. 'I Against I' was infinitely more intense and fierce than most of the competition, and still managed to maintain the group's message-filled lyrics. Even a stint in jail for H.R. (marijuana possession) couldn't stop the band, as he literally "phoned in" the vocals to one of the album's best tracks, "Sacred Love," from the prison to a recording studio.

With such hardcore-like styles as thrash metal infiltrating the mainstream around this time, it appeared as though the time was right once more for the Bad Brains to go the major label route. Everything seemed to fall perfectly into place when Island Records—the label that helped introduce Bob Marley to the masses—expressed interest. But once more, H.R. was opposed to it. Countey—"H.R. decided that there was something wrong with [label head] Chris Blackwell, that Chris had hurt Marley, or had taken advantage of reggae music or something, I don't know. And H.R. wouldn't deal with it; he wouldn't even sit down and talk about it. So it didn't happen."

As a result, the group went their separate ways soon after—H.R. returning to his solo career, while Dr. Know and Jenifer attempted to carry on the group with a different singer. But when producer St. Germain heard the results, he convinced the duo that without H.R., it just didn't hold up. Jenifer- "[We] called H.R., he came up to Woodstock, put him in a motel, gave him a tape of the songs. [In] two days, he wrote all those lyrics. Sent him back, got him in the studio, and he sang over the tracks." Just like that, the classic Bad Brains line-up was back in business, releasing 'Quickness' in 1989. Following in the same metal-esque direction as its predecessor, the album was also one of the group's most progressive—riffs galore and tricky bits abound—while still retaining the group's trademark fury ("Soul Craft") and tranquility ("The Prophet's Eye").

But the rock far-outweighed the reggae, which contributed to the group's next sabbatical. Countey- "H.R. had gotten on stage a couple of times and only played reggae sets. So he was just taking more control, and this was creating tension in the band. There was finally a confrontation about the whole thing, a blow-up. And at that point, it was decided, 'OK, it ends here'."

It was during this time that Bad Brains-disciples Living Colour was tearing up the charts, and possessed quite a bit of clout with their label, Epic. As a result, Living Colour helped hook the Bad Brains up with their first-ever major label contract, resulting in 1993's 'Rise.' Only problem was that neither H.R. nor Earl was included in the proceedings (newcomer Israel Joseph and ex-Cro-Mags drummer Mackie Jayson assumed their spots), and the album fell on deaf ears. The Bad Brains soon were dropped from Epic, but a promising break was around the corner.

It turned out that Madonna must be one heck of a fan, because one of the first signings to her then newly-launched label, Maverick, was a reunited Bad Brains. And with longtime supporters, the Beastie Boys, offering the group an opening spot on their 1995 arena tour, and a new album in the shops, 'God of Love' (with Ocasek producing again), it appeared as though the quartet was possibly finally poised for widespread success. But once more, this prospect did not sit well with H.R. Ocasek- "H.R. was doing some crazy stuff. He was visiting the label on a daily basis and bringing them dead fish, and all kinds of weird shit was going on." Things hadn't improved when the Beasties tour rolled into Montreal.

Countey- "H.R. had a way of isolating himself. He would take over the back lounge on the bus, and not come out for days. We had a road manager—I was just there to see the first show. The road manager came in and said, 'I've been knocking on the door, saying, 'H.R., we got to go on stage, are you ready?' And he doesn't answer.' I knock on the door, he goes, 'Yes, I'll just be a few minutes.' And he came out of the back lounge like a cannonball out of a canon—I don't know why. We rolled around for a while, the bus driver got into it, got me out of there. I walked away from it a bit damaged. I said, 'You got to get him onstage still,' but he didn't."

An attempt to get the tour back on track was derailed a few weeks later, when H.R. had it out with a vicious skinhead at a Kansas club-headlining gig. Countey- "There was this one skinhead who was pushing his girlfriend around. H.R. started talking to this guy, saying, 'Chill out.' They started the next song, and the guy starts beating up his girlfriend again. I saw H.R. pick up the mic stand, and he clipped this skinhead with the heavy end. Knocked him out, cracked his skull." H.R. was arrested after the show, and with the band not having enough money to bail him out; the tour was finished—ending their brief association with Maverick.

Some believed that this would be it for the Bad Brains. But just before the '90s drew to a close, the quartet reunited as the "Soul Brains," playing shows and recording a yet-to-be-released album, with Beastie Boy Adam Yauch producing. Nowadays, most of the group's members are involved in other projects—Dr. Know in Mos Def's band, H.R. with his solo reggae band, while Dr. Know, Jenifer, and Hudson have recorded a new version of their classic, "Re-Ignition," with Lil Jon.

Despite all their musical accomplishments, Jenifer voices displeasure with how the group is viewed by some. "Everything that we went through and rumors that you might have heard about us, every group of our level, has this 'thing' sort of going on. It's just that I really honestly believe because we're black—not to wave any type of racial flag—but I always went on to say, that if Led Zeppelin throw a TV out a window, that's 'rock.' If the Bad Brains smoke up a room with weed and throw bottles all over, we're like 'niggers.' We always had a double standard."

And while some may point to H.R.'s erratic behavior as a detriment to the group, Countey is quick to defend. "As hard as it's been, I know it's harder for H.R. H.R. is a spiritual entity—a prophet—and he's tormented. [But] there's an upside—we remain absolutely human. The corruption potential never was achieved, and the band's name was never commercialized. Something that belongs to the fans that needed that material, needed to hear that kind of commitment, needed to hear a positive message. So whatever H.R.'s done, he's maintained the purity of it."

Bonus Bit #1: Who is Sid McCray?
Meet the Bad Brains' Mystery Member.

H.R.-Doc-Darryl-Earl is the definitive Bad Brains line-up, but early on, they were a quintet—a chap named Sid McCray shared vocal duties with H.R., with H.R. often playing rhythm guitar. Although he never appeared on any albums, McCray is credited with turning the band onto punk. "The partying and all that didn't really make sense with what was going on in the world," recalls McCray. "So I was watching TV one day, and I saw this documentary—I think Don Letts did it. He was showing the England punk scene, it was my first glimpse of it, and it fascinated me." Soon after, McCray was frequenting the famous 9:30 Club (then called the Atlantis), and constantly playing an X-Ray Spex tape, 'Live at the Roxy.' "I went over to Darryl's house, and took albums with me. The next thing I know, I see these other guys coming up—Doc, H.R., and Earl—and we had a little listening party. A couple of them liked it, a couple of them, 'What is this stuff?' That's how it all started." McCray soon joined the group, playing shows and lending a hand in co-penning songs (including the early classic, "The Regulator"). But when the Bad Brains were relocating from D.C. to N.Y.C., McCray opted out. "We were in the car going to the city—I jumped out [of] the car, and they went to New York [laughs]. It was that drastic. I just decided not to go. I had a girl, I had an apartment. I knew they were going to go somewhere, but I had responsibilities. When I think about it now, all those responsibilities kind of faded. I wish I went. That's one of my biggest regrets—not going to New York with them. But we've always kept in contact." Since leaving, McCray has roadied for the band, and is currently putting together a Bad Brains documentary.

Bonus Bit #2 : Never A Dull Moment
Ric Ocasek on H.R.

Looking back at his experiences with the Bad Brains, Ric Ocasek recalls there never being a dull moment while hanging out with H.R. "There are many,

many things that happened. Especially when I'd be hanging out with them, things that would shock your ass off. I don't know if it would be right to tell you about them—crazy stuff. Once we were driving in L.A., and he told me he wanted to get some transmission fluid for his car. He walked into a gas station, just took the can, walked out, and got in the car. I said, 'H.R., you've got to pay for that stuff.' And he was going, 'It's between me and them.' And the guy was running out, banging on the window. I said, 'I'll pay for it, it's only five dollars,' and he's going, 'No, they owe me that.' It almost started into a big fight—I had to get out and give the guy five bucks and drive away. But he didn't even have a car. So it's that kind of insanity that you kind of have to just go with." But Ocasek points out that H.R. also possesses "A nice side. He lives out of his suitcase. Sometimes when they play live, he has a suitcase next to him on stage. And that's all he owns—that's his life right there. That suitcase is his whole life. He won't leave it out of his sight."

www.badbrains.com

Classic Rock—October 2005, issue 85

The Cars

On the Road Again

After motoring up the charts with a trailerful of hits in the '70s and '80s, then having their engine fall out, the Cars are cruising the highway again—this time with Todd Rundgren at the wheel.

Led by singer/guitarist/songwriter Ric Ocasek, the Cars were the prototypical new wave band. Scoring a string of U.S. top 40 hits during the late '70s/early '80s, selling out arena-headlining tours, and becoming darlings of MTV, it appeared the band could do no wrong.

But by 1988, the once tight-knit group had completely come undone, a state that Ocasek explained hadn't improved circa the late '90s. "We don't keep in contact at all. I see Greg quite frequently, I haven't seen Elliot in a few years, I haven't seen Ben in about eight years, and I haven't seen David in about three years. We don't talk on the phone—we're pretty much a dysfunctional family."

It wasn't always dysfunctional, however. Baltimore transplant Ocasek and Cleveland transplant Orr joined forces in the early '70s upon relocating to Boston, when they launched a folk outfit, Milkwood. But shortly after issuing an obscure debut album, 1972's 'How's the Weather,' the group disbanded. Ocasek and Orr then returned to their true love—rock n' roll—and launched Richard and the Rabbits, followed by Cap'n Swing.

It was during this time that Ocasek and Orr welcomed onboard keyboardist Greg Hawkes (who had appeared on Milkwood's album), guitarist Elliot Easton (a Berklee School of Music student), and drummer David Robinson (a member of proto-punkers the Modern Lovers). Easton recounts his first impressions of Ocasek and Orr.

"They were playing at a Warner Bros. party for Foghat at a roller skating rink. I remember being very struck because it was the first local band I'd ever heard in Boston that was doing their own music—really strong. I distinctly remember having the thought, 'I want to play in this band'."

Soon after an introduction. a tryout was arranged for Easton. "I went to Ben's house in Summerville. I went along with my guitar, and the first thing Benjamin said to me was, 'Play something amazing.' So I immediately froze up [laughs]." By 1977, the quintet had settled on a new name, the Cars.

The songs and sound were in place—a merger of new wave (Hawkes' synths, Ocasek's muted power chords) and arena rock (stadium-ready choruses, Easton's guitar heroics)—with Ocasek and Orr splitting the lead vocals. The band had a hard time landing a deal though, despite interest from Kiss' manager, Bill Aucoin.

But the Cars' break was just around the corner, explains Ocasek. "Our demo tape got played on the radio—'Just What I Needed' became a hit before it was even on a record. WBCN in Boston was playing it, and it became the most requested song. Record companies started coming around asking 'What label are they on?' So then we had 20 labels chasing us around Boston."

A record deal with Queen's then-U.S. label, Elektra, was soon secured, with the group flying to England to work with another Queen-connection, producer Roy Thomas Baker. Hawkes- "That was way exciting—we got to go to London, recording at AIR Studios, George Martin's studio. Which was a thrill—got to meet him there. The studio was great, getting to work with Roy Baker was great. We did it in like twelve or fourteen recording days, and then mixing was approximately a day per song. We had the whole thing recorded and mixed during February 1978."

From the get-go, it was clear that the Cars had one single songwriter in the band—Ocasek. "Our band never jammed—I wrote all the songs. I put them down on tape, with the parts on, and people learned the songs. I've never done a song by jamming with somebody else; I don't like the idea of it. I don't like to write with others, it's probably my least favorite thing to do. I started the Cars to play music that I wrote, just like I've started any band that I've ever had in my life—to do music I wrote. I form bands to play my songs."

The Cars' self-titled debut was issued in June of the same year, and began a slow-but-steady climb up the U.S. charts, ultimately hitting the top 20, thanks to the success of such hits as "Good Times Roll," "My Best Friend's Girl," and the aforementioned "Just What I Needed." As with all up-and-coming acts, the Cars "spread the word" by opening for a variety of established bands that year, including Bob Seger, Thin Lizzy, and Cheap Trick. There was one band though that Ocasek was none too pleased playing with.

"We opened for about anybody in the beginning—we opened for bands that we really hated, like Styx. I remember opening for Styx for about a week, and we kept winning over the show, and they got mad. And that would keep happening for bands that we'd open for. And then halfway through the tour we started headlining. But in the beginning we took whatever we could get. Most of those bands would go watch us on the side of the stage to see what the fuck was going on. And it seemed that the people were relating to us and not relating to them. So they all got a little pissed."

It was around this time that renowned rock photographer Ebet Roberts started working closely with the band. It didn't take long for Roberts to realize that each Car had his own distinct personality. "Greg seemed more serious, Ben was very playful, Elliot was just the nicest guy. Ric...warm and unique. David was the visually creative one—he designed the Cars' logo."

One of Roberts' first assignments with the Cars was to shoot the group on the streets of New York City, which yielded one of the group's best-known images. "The photograph I took with the girl running by—we went out to the street, and started photographing in the street, with cars driving by. The energy was wonderful, and then that girl ran by, and the band all reacted to it. It was such timing that I wasn't sure if she was in the middle of the frame, blocking them, or that you could see them. I couldn't believe it worked. After that, Ric called, and wanted to know if I wanted to go to Europe with them."

The tour that Roberts mentions took place in the spring of 1979—the Cars' one-and-only Euro tour—which Hawkes remembers fondly. "The German record company guys took us to some 'beer festival,' and got us all really drunk the night before we had to do 'Musikladen.' We were in no shape to do a TV show the next day, but we had to do it anyway."

"English audiences were generally very positive. I think it was more the English critics that were less positive. It was the heyday of punk rock, so I think we were thought of as an 'American corporate entity,' although I would disagree with that. I guess in comparison to the Sex Pistols and the Clash, we were a little too 'pop'."

With 'The Cars' still riding high in the U.S. charts, the quintet issued their sophomore effort, 'Candy-O,' in 1979. The album stormed the U.S. charts, peaking at #4 (with its leadoff single, "Let's Go," narrowly missing the top ten), which as a result, saw the group playing vast venues. But Hawkes voices the downside of playing hockey arenas. "It starts getting more remote, and it's harder to connect with the audience." Roberts also agrees with this assessment— "I liked clubs over arenas—seeing them in small clubs was just amazing."

Critics were quick to point out the group's often "cold" vibe onstage (they rarely chatted with the audience, while Ocasek hid behind sun glasses), yet Roberts feels that the Cars were one of the top live new wave acts. "Sometimes their live shows got put down—I thought their live shows were great. I just related to their music more."

While the group focused on radio-ready pop ditties for their first two albums, on 1980's 'Panorama,' the mood grew darker and artier, but Easton claims it wasn't intentional. "At the time, people said it was a great departure and it was more experimental. I don't think we were really thinking of it that way—it was just that year and that batch of songs. It's only with hindsight that you say, 'Maybe there were some stylistic departures and maybe we expanded our palette a little bit. I still love 'Touch and Go' off that record."

Barely taking any time off, the group built their own Boston-based studio, Synchro Sound, and dove headlong into their fourth release in as many years, 1981's 'Shake It Up.' With fans wondering if the Cars were going to continue in their newfound arty direction, the group returned back to their earlier, snappy new wave pop style, and enjoyed their fourth consecutive top ten album (and nearly topping the singles chart with the party hearty title track).

Easton recalls the group getting along better than ever. "It was fun. I was a single guy and pretty crazy. The thing that people I don't think totally understand is that it was a very funny band. We had this sort of cool, detached image, but those guys were really funny people. Experiencing all these things for the first time—it was still fresh. We were tight."

Looking to recharge their batteries, the Cars took their first-ever break once the 'Shake It Up' tour wrapped up. Ocasek filled his free time producing others (Suicide, Romeo Void, the Bad Brains), and also issued his solo debut, 1982's 'Beatitude.' Bad Brains' bassist Darryl Jenifer supplied bass, and recalls the sessions consisting of "Getting a huge daily per diem [and] smoking Hawaiian chronic."

With each of their first four albums being produced by Baker, the Cars opted to enlist the aid of Mutt Lange, who had just produced two of the decade's top-selling rock releases, AC/DC's 'Back in Black' and Def Leppard's 'Pyromania.' As with their debut, the group set up shop in England, but unlike the short amount of time it took to record 'The Cars,' the resulting effort would take nearly a year to complete.

Easton- "It took a long time to make that record, because that's just how Mutt likes to work. I don't know if 'meticulous' even quite describes it. He was trying to get the technical perfection, but he was also trying to make it sound like you picked up the guitar and ripped it off in one take. He was going for the perfect take technically, but also to have spontaneity. They're such contradictory things, so difficult to achieve, that it just takes time."

The wait was certainly worth it, as 1984's 'Heartbeat City' nearly topped the charts, and spawned four hit singles—"You Might Think," "Magic," "Hello Again," and "Drive"—all of which imaginative videos were filmed for the then-burgeoning MTV (it was on the set of the "Drive" clip that Ocasek met his future wife, model Paulina Porizkova). As a result, the band scored Best Video of the Year for "You Might Think" at the first-ever Video Music Awards, while the only other rock album that seemed to keep pace with 'Heartbeat City' in terms of sales, hits, and video play was perhaps Van Halen's '1984.'

With yet another sold out arena tour completed, 1985's best-selling 'Greatest Hits' (which spawned another top ten hit, "Tonight She Comes"), and a well-received performance at Live Aid, there was no reason to assume that the end was fast approaching for the band. Surprisingly, it was.

For reasons no one is exactly sure of, tension grew between Orr and Ocasek during the recording of 1987's 'Door to Door.' Roberts- "It just didn't feel as 'up'—Ben seemed to not be completely present. I think Ben didn't want to tour—he wanted to stay in Hawaii. He liked it there [laughs]."

The photographer can even pinpoint when she realized that not everything was kosher—during another photo shoot in NYC. "There was definite tension between Ric and Ben. Ben didn't seem to be in a good mood—just a lack of energy from Ben, and he had always been great at photo shoots. I did some stuff on a roof of a building, and I also did a thing with a door, where they're lined up near a door. It was a long day and it wasn't working."

Hawkes also offers his take. "'Door to Door' was very unpleasant. It was at that point, Ric and Ben were barely speaking to each other. In fact, I can't even listen to the album, to tell you the truth. All I can hear is bad vibes [laughs]. I haven't even tried to listen to that for at least ten or fifteen years. To me, that was like the 'lost Cars record,' because I'll probably never listen to it again."

Comprised mostly of re-recorded leftovers from earlier albums, 'Door to Door' fizzled on the charts, peaking at a paltry #26 in the U.S.—a far cry from its predecessors. Poor album sales and tour attendance, combined with increased inner-band tensions (Hawkes- "There was getting to be friction all over—everybody was just sort of tired of each other"), led to the tour being scrapped mid-way.

Easton recalls receiving a bombshell from Ocasek shortly thereafter. "I was at Electric Lady with Ric, and we were listening to tapes for a live radio broadcast. It was before the holidays, and at a quiet moment, he said, 'I wasn't going to say anything until after the holidays, but I'm leaving the band.' It wasn't like it broke up in any kind of argument or even formal way with all of us sitting together and saying, 'That's it'."

Looking back at the Cars' split, Ocasek admits that "In the end, it became redundant, and not so fun," while Ocasek's friend, Jenifer, offers his take. "I could tell that rock star shit was taking its toll. Ric is a bad motherfucker white boy from Baltimore—blessed with mad sons, models, [and] mansions."

Although all of the Cars' members went their separate ways (some focusing on solo work, production, and playing with others), it's a little known fact that the group—sans Orr—got back together in the '90s to see about a possible reunion. Hawkes- "We were at the studio for a couple of days, three days tops. But that's all that happened. I think the intention was, 'Let's get together and see what it feels like/see what it sounds like, and see if we should proceed,' which I guess we didn't do."

Even with the friction towards the end, the original line-up buried the hatchet for a group interview that accompanied their 2000 DVD release, 'The Cars Live: Musikladen 1979.' Sadly, Orr had been diagnosed with pancreatic cancer, and the illness had taken its toll on the appearance of a man who once possessed pin-up looks. "That's another thing I can't watch—I can't," admits Hawkes. The keyboardist admits an upside to the taping, however. "[Ocasek and Orr] got along well on that trip. So I think they did kind of reconcile with each other that day." Just a few months after the taping, Orr passed away, on 3 October 2000, at the age of 53.

"He was great—if Ben was your friend, there's nothing he wouldn't do for you," recalls Hawkes about his former band mate. "Ben was very fun loving, liked to party and have a good time—very sweet and warm," adds Roberts, while Jenifer remembers Orr as a "sensitive dude."

Despite the Cars' sedentary state throughout the '90s, the group received a boost when bands—including the Smashing Pumpkins and Nirvana—began covering Cars classics (the Pumpkins tackling "You're All I've Got Tonight" for their 'Aeroplane Flies High' boxset, and Nirvana covering "My Best Friend's Girl" at their last-ever gig). Additionally, Ocasek became a much-sought-after producer (producing both of Weezer's best-selling self-titled releases), and the Cars' albums continued to sell—'The Cars' and 'Greatest Hits' topping six million copies each. Despite Orr's passing, rumors of a Cars reunion gained steam.

Easton- "We tried to get back with the four of us, but ultimately, I think [Ocasek and Robinson] had moved on in whatever way. When Ric made it clear to us that he really no longer wished to tour, and Greg and I wanted to do this thing, we sort of cast about for who we could get to be in the band. I came up with a very short list, and Todd Rundgren was at the top of it. To my very pleasant surprise, he was receptive to the idea, and said he wanted to give it a try."

With Rundgren taking Ocasek's spot, Utopia/Meat Loaf bassist Kasim Sulton taking Orr's spot, and Tubes drummer Prairie Prince taking Robinson's spot, the New Cars were born in late 2005. Playing in front of an invite-only audience this past January on a Los Angeles soundstage, the New Cars recorded a set of hits, which packaged together with three brand new Rundgren-Easton-Hawkes compositions, was recently released as 'It's Alive.'

The New Cars' leader, Rundgren, recounts the first meeting last September. "We learned four songs in three hours, and we all came away satisfied that we could do a reasonable simulacrum of the Cars. We proceeded on with what turned out to be an ass backwards normal life of a band—you record the very first time you play and put out a live album, before you've even got anything [laughs]. Normally, you'd go out and play for a couple of months and then say, 'OK, now we're hot—let's capture this.' Instead, this is kind of the cart that's leading the horse."

"It's just a great fit—it really is," adds Easton. "You know how bands are—if you change one member, the dynamic shifts. [Rundgren] brings to it who he is as a person, as an artist, and that reflects in the music. He brings a little big different set of influences with him. But it just fits great—it sounds terrific. He's a lot of fun to play with."

Hawkes offers his take on the New Cars' chemistry. "Obviously, it's different, but it's great playing with them. Not only is Todd talented and creative, but he's almost got this 'chameleon type quality'—he just drops right into the front position and it works great."

With a U.S. tour of outdoor amphitheaters this summer along with Blondie, the New Cars are planning on expanding their tour itinerary. Easton-"The hopes are after that to do Europe, Australia, Asia, and New Zealand, and then come back, and do another swing of the States. It's going to be predicated about how successful this thing is. If everything works out, after a break, we'll go in and do a studio album."

Since he is filling Ocasek's shoes, one wonders if Rundgren has ever conversed with the ex-Cars leader. "I have never, as far as a I know, had a conversation with Ric. I'm sure we have probably crossed paths and exchanged a pleasantry or two, but Ric and I have never really communicated about anything—not even about this particular thing."

Although Easton and Hawkes have not spoken directly to Ocasek about his thoughts on the New Cars, Easton did come across some encouraging words from his former bandmate. "I read in some press thing that Ric did, where he said he just wanted to see Greg and I be happy. I thought that was a very nice thing to say, and I wish him the same. I don't resent Ric and David for not wanting to tour anymore—they just don't want to do it. And we just do." And that's precisely where the New Cars come in.

Bonus Bit: Cars Discography

Most of the Cars' albums hit the mark—with only one misfire of the bunch. Here's the lowdown:

'The Cars'—1978 (Elektra)

Few albums in rock history have surfaced where every song is a winner—'The Cars' is certainly one of them. Just about every track here has become a U.S. rock radio standard, and with good reason—it's Ric Ocasek's finest batch of songs, and the band sounds like a finely tuned new wave machine.

Standouts: "Just What I Needed," "My Best Friend's Girl," "Bye Bye Love"

Rating: 10

'Candy-O'—1979 (Elektra)

The dreaded "sophomore jinx"—and the Cars avoided it. A continuation of their stellar debut set, three minute, guitar/synth-driven pop ditties abound, while the brief "Shoo Be Doo" served as a preview of the next album's experimental direction.

Standouts: "Let's Go," "Candy-O"

Rating: 8

'Panorama'—1980 (Elektra)

The Cars get artsy here—despite their members denying that was their intention. No radio-ready tracks that jump at you the way "Just What I Needed" did, but definitely a bold move for the band at the time.

Standouts: "Panorama," "Touch and Go"

Rating: 7

'Shake It Up'—1981 (Elektra)

The last Cars album produced by Roy Thomas Baker sees the group return to the radio-friendly new wave style of their first two records. The album's title track became mandatory listening at every U.S. teen party and dance club of the early '80s.

Standouts: "Since You're Gone," "Shake It Up"

Rating: 8

'Heartbeat City'—1984 (Elektra)

The Cars team up with Mutt Lange, and deliver arguably their strongest album since 'The Cars.' The sonics may be a bit dated (the electro drums, the Def Leppard-esque vocals, etc.), but 'Heartbeat City' remains one of the top mainstream rock albums of the '80s.

Standouts: "You Might Think," "Magic," "Drive"

Rating: 9

'Door to Door'—1987 (Elektra)

The band wasn't getting along, and it showed in the grooves of this surprisingly flat release. Proof that the band may have been better off calling it a day after 'Heartbeat City.'

Standouts: "Strap Me In"

Rating: 4

'It's Alive'—2006 (Eleven Seven)
With Todd Rundgren taking over for Ocasek, the New Cars are unveiled with
an album that includes mostly live readings of Cars classics. The three new
studio tracks hint that the band may have a promising road ahead.
   Standouts: "Not Tonight"
   Rating: 6

www.myspace.com/thecarsunlocked
www.thenewcars.com

Classic Rock—June 2006, issue 93

GG Allin

Allin the Family

Having decided he'd taken performances as far as they could go—blood,
broken bones, vomit, feces—GG Allin planned to kill himself on stage.
But he didn't live long enough. Brother and Murder Junkies bandmate
Merle Allin looks back at the 90s' most shocking rocker.

Like his late brother, Merle Allin is covered from head-to-toe in tattoos,
and has an affinity for long, scraggily facial hair. Merle also served as bassist
for GG's last backing band, the Murder Junkies, during the early '90s. As
evidenced in the aforementioned era's classic GG documentary, 'Hated,'
Merle went eyebrow-less during this time, and sported a moustache modeled
after, er, Hitler. "I still have people to this day that are afraid of me," admits
Merle. "I'm sure 'cause GG's my brother, but because of my appearance too.
I'm really not anything like him—I have a lot of the same beliefs that he had,
but I wouldn't go to that extreme to act them out."

Although GG Allin had been making a name for himself in the U.S. punk
underground for over a decade by the '90s, it marked the first time that GG
launched a sustained tour, with a set backing band. The result? Pure mayhem.
"There were shows where we feared for our lives," admits Merle. "People
would love us before we went on, and by the time the show was over, they
wanted to fucking kill us. There were shows where we would finish, somebody
would get the van, everybody [would] sneak out while people were throwing
bottles, breaking the windows, and flattening your tires. We would go through
two or three vans a tour. There were plenty of shows where we got backed in
a corner, in a dressing room with no escape, [or] GG would just be covered in
fucking blood at the end of a show. You'd be like, 'Damn, how the fuck could
he do that to himself?' There was the show at the Space at Chase, which he
wound up breaking two kids' noses—part of that's in 'Hated.' One of them
was underage, and the club ended up closing down a few weeks after. There
were a few clubs around the country that GG was responsible for closing
down! I don't know how we didn't get fucking killed."

When you raise the bar that high with your performance, how do you out-
do yourself? That was a question that GG pondered quite often during the last
few years of his life, as he would openly talk about committing suicide...on
stage. Instead, GG wound up dying from a heroin overdose in mid-1993, at

the tail end of another debaucheries Murder Junkies tour. So what exactly did GG do to get his and fans' blood boiling? It's a wild and wooly tale.

Both GG and Merle were born in the small town of Lancaster, New Hampshire, in 1956 and 1955, respectively, and raised in a log cabin with no running water. Their father was a "maniac recluse, very much a hermit," who named his youngest son Jesus Christ Allin. "It was pretty turbulent the first ten years of our life, before my mom decided to leave my father. I don't even know half the shit that went on. My father was very closed in, tried to keep everybody away from everybody." In the aforementioned 'Hated' film, Father Allin even pondered the idea of killing his entire family and burying the bodies in the basement, before offing himself. He never followed through—dying three years ago, and never traveling far outside his house.

With a new lease on life, the Allins eventually relocated to Williamsburg, Vermont, with Jesus Christ Allin changing his name to Kevin Michael Allin. Both Allin boys became enraptured with the music of the British Invasion in the mid-late '60s, but when glam rock hit in the early '70s, they took it a step further—adopting the gender-bending dress of their heroes. "[GG] took a lot of shit for it, but after a while, people just ignored us, especially him, 'cause people thought he was just out of his fucking mind. We were going to school with a bunch of kids that were coming out of the mountains to go to school everyday—wearing flannels and overalls. We're talking total white bumpkin, there was no mixture of people in our school, it was all white. We'd go out at recess and smoke pot—the derelicts who just wanted to listen to music and party, and go to school when we wanted to. We didn't take it serious because we knew we weren't going to college—we wanted to play music."

And play music they did. With GG on drums and Merle on guitar, the duo plowed through such local bands as Little Sister's Date ("Playing stuff like Aerosmith, Black Sabbath, Alice Cooper") and Malpractice ("Playing Ramones, Iggy"). Eventually, the brothers checked out the Boston and New York City scenes—"There was a world out there that we needed to get into, and get the fuck away from New Hampshire!" Just before their relocation, a collaboration ensued. "Me and GG had been hanging out, writing songs. That's where the very first Jabbers single was written—in Vermont in the basement of the house we were living in. And that was before the Jabbers were even a band. When he stopped being Kevin Michael Allin and became GG Allin was when he came out from behind the drums, took the mic, and was like, 'OK, I'm going to start my own thing.' We didn't really even have a name, we just went up and recorded the three songs—"Beat Beat Beat," "One Man Army," and "Bored to Death"—which eventually came out on 'Always Was, Is, And Always Shall Be' [GG's debut album]. But that was in '78 when I left to go to Boston, and GG moved to Manchester. He got married, moved, [and] put the Jabbers together."

While Merle and GG didn't play together during the '80s, Merle would check out performances by GG, who by now had transformed into a punk rock Tasmanian devil—taking Iggy's confrontational performance style to a whole new level. "He would flip somebody's table over, go up to somebody and take their drink and pour it over their head, roll around on the floor, or grab the pipes and climb up. And that was all it took to get thrown out of a club back then. He pretty much got banned from everyplace. And then it just came to a point that the band would rehearse, get a gig, the show would last ten or fifteen minutes, and the band just got totally fed up. They'd been putting all that time into rehearsing, and got frustrated 'cause GG would say 'OK, tonight we're going to get through the set, I'm not gonna do this and that.' Then they'd get onstage and you couldn't control him. As soon as he got on fucking stage, it didn't matter what he told you, *he just transformed*. I don't think he could help it. The Jabbers couldn't take it anymore, and the band broke up."

Despite having a daughter and being married (up until the early '80s), GG continued on his rock n' shock quest—entirely on his own terms. "He basically lived on the road, or wherever somebody wanted to invite him to do some recording. A tour for GG in the '80s was getting on a Greyhound Bus, riding around the country, and playing two or three shows with bands in different towns that would learn his songs. He was like the 'Chuck Berry of punk.' He never really kept a solid band together." As a result, quite a few band names have been linked to GG's shows and recordings of this era, including the Disappointments, the Toilet Rockers, the AIDS Brigade, and the Holy Men. Some of GG's best known albums surfaced during this time, including such titles as 'You Give Love A Bad Name' and 'Freaks, Faggots, Drunks & Junkies,' while his live shows continued to get more brutal and nihilistic. Case in point, the DVD 'Live and Pissed.' Recorded in late '88 at a San Francisco gig, GG (dressed in only jockstrap and boots) continuously fights with "fans," cuts himself with broken shards of glass, urinates, defecates, and oh yeah, performs several fan favorites, before landing in the hospital.

Despite making a name for himself in the punk underground (receiving accolades from Jello Biafra and Thurston Moore), GG's personal life was in shambles by this point. Due to the nature of his eventual death, many assume heroin was his vice. "People have this idea that GG woke up and fell asleep with a needle in his arm, and that's not true. He was drunk all the time—pissing the bed every night, drinking until he'd fall down." Feeling that he'd reached his limit, GG decided that he was going to take his own life on stage, going as far as announcing the date he was going to do the deed—October 31, 1990. But fate interrupted what would've been GG's most gruesome performance ever—he was sentenced to jail in Michigan. "[GG] got arrested in '89 for 'Intent to Commit Bodily Harm Less Than Murder.' That basically stemmed from some party this chick invited him and his band to, and she wanted to fuck everybody in the band. Then when it got time to get down to what she really wanted, which was for someone to treat her rough, he treated her rough. They didn't have the communication lines open, they were all drunk, and it turned into a night of hell. He ended up burning parts of her body and carving her breasts—fucking her up pretty bad. She called the cops a bunch of times, they came, she would tell them to go. And in the end, she wanted to marry GG and then when he said no, I guess she decided she'd get revenge and turned him in."

While in jail for two years, the date of his planned suicide came and went ("He wasn't going to kill himself in prison, that would have been anticlimactic"). During his prison stay, GG had largely sobered up, and shaved off his long, unkempt hair. By the time he emerged from jail in 1991, he was a new man—albeit meaner and angrier. Merle could sense that GG's pent-up aggression would translate to further on-stage pandemonium, and for the first time since the late '70s, the brothers Allin were band mates once more. The Murder Junkies were formed shortly thereafter, with a chap named Chicken John signing on as guitarist, who recommended a drummer, Dino. "He's notoriously known in New York for being 'the naked drummer.' Dino came into a rehearsal, got naked, started playing, and we were like 'He's the fucking drummer,' 'cause there's nobody like Dino. And that was the Murder Junkies, right there. Then we fired Chicken, 'cause we hated him."

An ad was placed in the Village Voice, which resulted in the hiring of a pair of guitarists—Cincinnati transplant Bill Weber and…Dee Dee Ramone! "Me and GG were just like, 'Man, we gotta have Dee Dee, *'cause he's Dee*

Dee! But you know what, we gotta have Weber, 'cause Weber's a great guitar player.' So were just like, 'We'll turn down Dee Dee's amp down a little bit to make sure Weber drowns him out!'" But the twin guitar Murder Junkies line-up lasted for only a few rehearsals, before Dee Dee flew the coop. It was also around this time that up-and-coming filmmaker, Todd Phillips, began taping GG and his adventures, in hopes of putting together a documentary. That documentary would become the cult classic, 'Hated.'

The Murder Junkies then hit the road, with GG opting to skip parole. What followed was your typical brand of GG-style shows—"Every fucking show was crazy. There was one show in a skate park with 17 kids that got arrested; they were all underage and drinking. Dino and GG both got arrested, so we had to bail GG out, because we couldn't go on without GG, but we didn't have enough money to bail them both out. We bailed GG out, went down to Atlanta, picked up a drummer, and used him to play the show. Then we drove back to Dalton, Georgia, picked up Dino, then drove to New Orleans for our next show!" But it was only a matter of time until GG was hauled in for jumping parole. "During our '92 tour, he got arrested in Austin, for lewd behavior—all the things GG does on stage. The cops came in and arrested him, then they decided they would extradite him back to Michigan, and he served out the remainder of his sentence—another year. So from March of '92 until April of '93, we basically recorded ['Brutality and Bloodshed'], then when he came out of prison, he had the lyrics all written, he just put them to the music. A month later, we were on the road again."

Unlike his first prison stay, when GG was freed, his health appeared to be on the decline. "Me and GG were in Chicago, this was the next to the last date of the tour, in late June [of 1993], and he just looked *bad*. He'd been out on the road for a month abusing himself, and we talked about him dying and about his funeral. And GG was like, 'When I die you guys better have a fucking party'." GG got his wish soon enough, but not before playing arguably his most violent show ever—delightfully, captured on video (and available on the 'Hated' DVD). Playing a hole-in-the-wall NYC venue called the Gas Station, GG got primed and ready beforehand, by snorting cocaine with a photographer friend. "Once he got into the gig and played the two songs and got shut down, he was just wired out of his mind. He was strung out from having so much energy inside that he couldn't release—it just spilled out onto the street, up and down Alphabet City. If you haven't seen the Gas Station show, it's INSANE. You know, you can watch stuff on video, and you can get an idea of what it was like, but it's *ten times* more intense being there."

The next morning, June 28, 1993, Merle got the phone call that he had dreaded for years—GG was dead, from a heroin overdose. "When Johnny Puke called me that morning and said, 'You better get over here, your brother is on the floor, he's not moving,' I knew he was dead. But it shocked me 'cause he wasn't ready to go at that point. I mean, other times of his life it wouldn't have shocked me." Almost immediately after his death, GG's legend grew, thanks largely in part to the popularity of the 'Hated' documentary, issued a year after his death. Then a variety of renowned rockers began voicing their appreciation of GG, namely Faith No More (who covered "I Wanna Fuck Myself" for 1995's 'Ricochet' single), CKY, and Hank Williams III (who have covered the tracks "Bite It You Scum" and "Raw Brutal Rough and Bloody" on stage, respectively).

After GG's death, Merle attempted to continue the Murder Junkies, but when vocalists proved a hard commodity, he shut it down, to concentrate solely on running GG's official website, www.ggallin.com, and selling merchandise, CD's, and video's. To celebrate the ten-year anniversary of GG's passing, the Murder Junkies reunited with Antiseen front man Jeff Clayton for a show in the town where GG is buried, Littleton, New Hampshire (along with a reunited Jabbers), which will be issued as a DVD this year. Also on the horizon is another GG documentary (directed by Chicago filmmaker Mark Hejnar), plus a pair of books that Merle will soon begin work on, one of which will be a scrapbook/photo album.

Strange how rock's all-time anti-mainstream artist is suddenly being embraced by the mainstream. "Everybody's into GG. He's been dead for ten years and he was so far ahead of everybody else. Look at this 'Jackass' stuff, with people doing all this extreme shit. Where the hell did that come from? GG must have influenced these people. GG would never be played on MTV, but at least people that are influenced by him are. And I think that one day maybe the world will catch up enough so GG will get some kind of recognition that he fucking deserves. The kids are getting wiser—they're realizing that there's somebody like GG out there."

www.ggallin.com

Classic Rock—1990s Special III

The Stories Behind the Songs

"Blitzkrieg Bop" The Ramones

Tommy Ramone wasn't considered one of the band's main songwriters. So how come he ended up writing their (and US punk rock's) biggest anthem?

Stop the average geezer on the street and ask them what is punk's all-time great anthem, and the Ramones' "Blitzkrieg Bop" is sure to get most—if not all—the votes. Everything that was great about rock music in the first place—before it became completely forgotten by every bloated arena rock act circa the mid-70's—is included in this two minute and 21 second blast of pure punk perfection. And of course, this divine little ditty contains one of the most instantly recognizable chants in all of rock music history (Are you ready? Everyone, join in!)—"Hey! Ho! Let's go!" Additionally, for the majority of the masses, the song served as their introduction to this New York City quartet, as it kicked off their classic self-titled 1976 debut in glorious fashion.

While the main songwriters of the original Ramones were thought to be Joey, Johnny, and Dee Dee, it was in fact Tommy Ramone (aka Tommy Erdelyi) that penned the majority of the tune by himself. "It's my song—Dee Dee came up with the title, and changed a line from 'They're shouting in the back now' to 'Shoot 'em in the back now.' The rest of the song is mine."

With most mid-70's punkers drawing inspiration from the Stooges and the Dolls, Erdelyi explained that the Ramones were busy studying an unlikely source. "We were looking for a chant-type song, because the Bay City Rollers had a huge hit at the time with 'Saturday Night.' I was trying to think of ideas for something like that. Coming home from the grocery store one day, I just thought of a chant—'Hey! Ho! Let's go!'—which basically comes from a song called 'Walkin' the Dog' by Rufus Thomas, where he goes, 'Hi ho's nipped her toes.' When we were kids we used to goof around—when Mick Jagger sang the song for the Rolling Stones, it sounded like he was saying 'Hey ho.' It was a silly thing, but I remembered that from the past."

Erdelyi figures that the song was written sometime in 1974—shortly after the Ramones formed—and recalls where the germ of the idea for the song came to him. "The actual music and melody, I was fooling around with a guitar at Arturo's loft—Arturo Vega was our lighting guy—and I just started playing the riff. That song slowly came together. I went home, I liked that riff, and just wrote the lyrics."

Which leads to the subject of the song's lyrics. Many have tried to decipher the song's true meaning unsuccessfully over the years, but Erdelyi sets the record straight once and for all. "The lyrics are basically about people going to a concert and having a great time." 'Nuff said.

Up to this point, the other Ramones members thought of themselves as the group's main songwriters. As a result, the arrival of Erdelyi's track caused some anxiety. "They were upset because they thought it was a good song—that was their honest reaction! They thought they were the only ones that could write songs at the time. A lot of ego in the band—they couldn't turn that song down." The song was immediately introduced to the group's live set—probably at CBGB's (along with Television, the Ramones were one of the first rock acts to play at the club)—but Erdelyi doesn't recall the audience's initial reaction. "We go from one song to another—we don't wait for a reaction [laughs]."

It didn't take long for the band to realize "Blitzkrieg Bop" was one of their strongest tracks, however. "The song became pretty much 'the anthem.' We started the album with it—when the album came out, it was the first song. It then became 'the go-to song.' Initially, we used to put it as the third song [in concert]—we'd warm up with two songs, and then hit 'em with 'Blitzkrieg Bop.' Get the audience pumping their hands and all that stuff."

And what does Erdelyi remember about recording the song? "It was kind of strange—we were put into this really interesting studio, that was a beautiful art deco radio station, that was converted into a recording studio in the Radio City Music Hall building. It was a beautiful studio, but we were separated—we were each put in different rooms. It was a strange experience making that record. We knew it was an important song—I think it might have been one of the first songs we recorded, actually. We did that record really fast—that whole record cost $6,000. We did it very quickly and without too much fanfare."

Interestingly, not many know that "Blitzkrieg Bop" was issued as a single in November 1975 in the U.S.—almost six months before the arrival of 'The Ramones' in April 1976. "I'm sure it was a different mix, but it was the same recording," adds Erdelyi.

The song has rightfully since become one of rock's most renowned and enduring anthems—played regularly to this day at U.S. sporting events to get the crowd pumped (Erdelyi's reaction to hearing "Blitzkrieg Bop" played at U.S. football games? "Sort of disbelief—it seems surrealistic").

And we saved the million-dollar question for Mr. Erdelyi last—does he think "Blitzkrieg Bop" is the greatest Ramones song? "No, I don't. There's so many great Ramones songs—'Rockaway Beach,' 'Cretin Hop.' I think 'Blitzkrieg Bop'...it's hard to say, since I wrote the song. I'm very self-conscious about it. But people seem to like it." Quite the understatement.

Bonus Bit: Tommy Ramone...Unplugged?

Think of the Ramones and blaring barre chords, scream-a-long choruses, and leather jackets instantly come to mind. So it may come as quite a surprise to learn that Erdelyi's current musical project is a folk/bluegrass duo—Uncle Monk. Joined by multi-instrumentalist Claudia Tienan, Erdelyi handles mandolin, banjo, fiddle, and guitar duties. But the former punk rock drummer sees some similarities between the two bands. "It's kind of a continuation of what I've been doing all along—what I was doing in the Ramones, the creative ideas and everything. It's just a progression into what we're doing now, as far as certain concepts of our arrangements and aesthetics."

And what have Ramones fans' reactions been to Uncle Monk's live show? "An interesting reaction. But then they see the sort of connection—the underlying framework—and they realize it's a continuation." And like his former group—which just wrapped up live dates in the U.S. on the east coast—Uncle Monk like to keep things simple on stage. "Live, we're kind of a compact duo, that delivers the songs in a very direct way. Slightly different arrangements. The record ['Uncle Monk'] has all this instrumentation on it." To hear for yourself, visit www.unclemonk.com and www.myspace.com/unclemonk.

www.officialramones.com

Classic Rock—December 2007, issue 113

Every Home Should Have One

Living Colour 'Time's Up'

An undervalued or forgotten gem you may have overlooked.

When a band's debut album becomes a hit straight away, their next release is always heavily scrutinized and dissected—as they try to avoid what is known as "the sophomore jinx." That is exactly where New York rockers Living Colour found themselves just as the '90s dawned. "I think it was a very interesting time, because we had just come off of 'Vivid,'" remembers guitarist Vernon Reid, "We were all in different places. I was very much concerned that the band was advancing musically." Reid shouldn't have been that troubled about his band's "advancement," as he and his rhythm section at the time, bassist Muzz Skillings and drummer Will Calhoun, had a heavy-duty jazz/fusion background, while singer Corey Glover was probably the most soulful-sounding in all of rock.

But still, uncertainty surfaced upon entering the old A&M Studios in Los Angeles to work once more with 'Vivid' producer Ed Stasium. "I think different people were dealing with different personal issues. I know that Will Calhoun had a situation in his family that he was trying to come to grips with. Corey Glover had lost his father in the previous tour. There was a lot going on. There was a lot riding on the record. Trying to fit the band into this thing and that thing, and of course now, we were 'The Black Rock Band' that made it." This tension and uncertainty can certainly be felt in the resulting album, 1990's 'Time's Up.' While 'Vivid' was quite a musically diverse rock album, Reid and company took it a step further on 'Time's Up.' Reid—"It goes from "Time's Up," very much a hardcore song, to "Solace of You," which was something that almost could have been on 'Graceland.' It has "Fight the Fight," which is one of my favorite songs that I wrote with Corey."

In addition to those aforementioned tracks, Living Colour absorbed as many styles as possible, tops being such metallic riff monsters as "Pride" and "Type," the soul-pop of "Love Rears Its Ugly Head," as well as a fun jazz-rock romp that Reid still has fond memories of, "Elvis Is Dead." "The two things I recall was Maceo Parker played, and Little Richard [had a cameo]. Little

Richard was living on the Hyatt on Sunset, and we used to stay there. He would talk to us about how important it was that we were doing what we were doing. That was in the middle of making the record! Another funny thing is when we had Mick Jagger and a bunch of other people saying the phrase 'Elvis is Dead' in different languages."

Reid found himself in an interesting situation mid-recording, as well. "One of the background singers on "Solace of You," I believe she sings in Swahili, is Derin Young, my ex-girlfriend. And it was just ironic, because we had broken up during 'Vivid,' and the song "Love Rears It's Ugly Head" was written about her!" While 'Time's Up' wasn't as big a commercial success as its predecessor, it did earn critical raves, as the band took home their second Grammy Award in 1991, for Best Hard Rock Performance, and earned a spot on the inaugural Lollapalooza Tour that summer.

www.myspace.com/livingcolourmusic

Classic Rock—May 2004, issue 66

Q and A's

Hater

*Although ex-Soundgarden bassist Ben Shepherd has been playing on
a somewhat regular basis since the group's split in 1997, many of
his musical ventures have slipped under the radar—the Wellwater
Conspiracy, the Mark Lanegan Band, etc. But you may be hearing
again from Shepherd sooner than you think, as an archival release from
another project, Hater, has finally seen the light of day, in addition to
fronting an all new band, Unkmongoni.*

*Since it was recorded back in 1995, why didn't Hater's 'The 2nd' come
out sooner?*

It was just more or less a demo session that Matt [Cameron] and I were doing,
getting ready to record 'Down on the Upside.' We had the recordings going,
just kind of messing around. Some of the songs were taken off the recording
sessions and put on the Soundgarden record—that's how "demo friendly" it
was. And it wound up being called a Hater session, because the guy that we
were recording with wrote on the cassette 'Hater Sessions Two.' Otherwise,
we wouldn't have even thought of that stuff. Then of course, the band went
defunct. And over the years, just the lack of interest or the gumption on my
part, it was like, "Ah, no one cares." I had all these cockamamie ideas of taking
the tapes and taking all the guitars off and putting strings on it. Then A&M
folded, so it became a process—either shopping it to someone or not, and
finishing mixing. Because I never liked the mixes at all. Everyone just kind of
scattered and left it in my hands. Finally, friends of mine [Burn Burn Burn
Records] said, "Hey, we'll put it out," after being rejected by three different
labels. And it seems fitting to me, that it's local and it's friends, y'know? It
used to be that if you wanted to see Hater, you had to come here.

Two songs from these sessions later appeared on Soundgarden's 'Down on the Upside'—"An Unkind" and "Dusty." How did the Soundgarden versions differ from the Hater versions?

Well, Chris' voice fucking rules and Kim's guitar playing rules. Right there, it makes it ten times better. There's a fine line between being a demo and being a finished thing. "Dusty" was just an instrumental on the Hater stuff, so Chris saved that song right there.

Let's talk about your new band.

The guy Drew Church is the bass player, [and] is partners with Burn Burn Burn Records—he's just a good friend. I always wanted to play in a band with him. I would tell Bubba Dupree, the guitar player of our band, "Someday that guy's going to be our bass player." So Bubba and I always had this kind of joke pact about whoever starts a band first, the other guy gets into it automatically. So I started a band, and now Bubba's the other guitar player. Bubba used to play in that band Void and Earth 18. So that's me, Bubba, and Drew, and we're in-between drummers right now. Our drummer just quit the other night. We have 20 songs recorded already. Every one of them has titles and almost all of them have vocals and everything done. I'm actually at Soundgarden's old building right now, it's called the Space, and downstairs, I've set up my studio and rehearsal room, as a recording room. So we've been recording for *months*. Just whenever we want, we've rolled tape.

Any confirmed song titles?

"Anymore," "Simple," "Hollow Temple of the Other Monkey's Shoe," and "Stone Pale."

And what's the band's name?

Unkmongoni—it's what Tarzan used to yell to the animals to run and be free. He'd yell "Unkmongoni!" and they'd all run away through the jungle.

Has the band recorded yet?

We're getting our demos done, and we're going to see if there's any interest anywhere. We were about a week away from being able to play live as far as I was concerned, and then the drummer quit. Now we're just trying out new drummers.

I remember reading a rumor last year that you were working with Kim Thayil [ex-Soundgarden guitarist] again...

No, we always lie about stuff like that. Somebody's always coming up with weird rumors about that stuff. And I have no idea how they get that idea.

You were friends with Kurt Cobain. Despite how the media portrays him...he was a just regular guy, right?

Yep. They like to say that he had charisma. *Bullshit.* He didn't have any...he was just "Kurt," and that was that endearing quality. I met him in Olympia, I don't even think he'd started Nirvana yet, or Bliss, they'd change their name all the time. I met him at a party—we were both sitting on the end of a couch—and I go, "Oh, you're like me, huh? You always wind up at this spot at the party." And he says, "Yep." Everyone else is partying and we're sitting there, being loners on the end of a couch. There was thankfully a guitar, and we'd swap it back and forth. That's how we met, because we were both kind of shy weirdos, y'know? Well, I'm the weirdo, I don't think he was, I think he was more shy. Like even that guitar, he said, "Yeah, I always find a guitar and then I'll just sit alone and play guitar at a party." We were just smoking cigarettes, talking, and kicking back. [Through the years] there was always a rumor through our grapevine that we were going to play music together—me, him, and Buzz [Osborne, of the Melvins]. I'd always hear that from people, because our friendship from touring and everything, it turned into a grapevine.

Classic Rock—May 2005, issue 79

Ric Ocasek

One-time Cars man returns with a new album, production projects, and news of a new Cars documentary DVD.

Former Cars leader Ric Ocasek has returned with his first solo release in eight years, 'Nexterday,' quite possibly the must "under-produced" album of his career. With possible forthcoming live dates, producing other artists, the formation of his own label (Inverse), and finishing up a Cars documentary ('The Cars Unlocked'), Ocasek has his work cut out for him. Ocasek recently discussed all the projects on the eve of his latest release.

How did 'Nexterday' come about?

I kind of recorded it all in the basement. I was writing the songs and intending to re-record everything. But once I started putting things on tape, I decided to keep what I had. So it's a pretty simplistic record for me, it's pretty under-produced—but I like it that way.

How did the recording go?

I did do it here, so it was pretty much a personal record. I used a couple of musicians here and there. I went in the studio and did a couple of drum tracks. Darryl Jenifer [Bad Brains] played bass on a song or two, I think I had Greg Hawkes [ex-Cars] play on a cut or two on keyboards, but besides that, there was a guy named Rob Johansen who played drums. It went pretty good. I was sitting on the record a while because I was doing a lot of productions—I kind of let it sit there before I got involved with Sanctuary, and decided to put it out on my own label.

How did you hook up with Sanctuary and form your own label through them, Inverse?

Sanctuary came and wanted to put out my records, do production work, and also wanted to give me my own little label. Which is kind of what I wanted to do anyway. So that's how that came about. It's been good so far.

What are your future plans?

For my label, Inverse, I produced a band called the Hong Kong—they're from New York. I love them. I just finished a record by a band called the Pink Spiders—they're a Nashville band, for Geffen. Productions…there's many, I'm just deciding which ones to do. But that's my love really, listening to new music. Demos are kind of like listening to albums of the future, so I like doing that more than buying albums and listening to those.

Any updates regarding the Cars documentary DVD that was first talked about a few years ago?

I've had little run-in's getting that out, but I think it's going to come out pretty soon. Right now it's in the works. It's completely done, I really like the documentary, it's kind of cool. All kinds of gigs from '78 to '88, and a lot of backstage foolery. Some clubs, some big concerts, it's kind of a potpourri—it's more like a "home movie thing," y'know? It's kind of neat.

Any specific songs that stand out on it?

There's probably like 25, 30 songs on it. From all over the world, really. Certainly, people wouldn't have gotten to see all this stuff. It's much more than anything that's been out. Much more fun—just a much better retrospective of the Cars than what I've seen. I haven't seen any actually that are as comprehensive as this. It just has to be packaged up and put out. There's a couple of people that want to put it out, so I guess it's just a matter of who we're going to pick to do it.

Any companies in particular?

Well, I'd like Sanctuary to put it out. So I'll see.

www.ricocasek.com

Classic Rock—October 2005, issue 85

The Dictators

30 years on from being a big noise at the birth of US punk, the Dictators release their first new album in 20 years.

If you slap on the Dictators' 1975 cult-classic debut, 'The Dictators Go Girl Crazy,' you'll hear a sound/approach quite a kin to the Ramones, a full year before Joey, Johnny, Dee Dee, and Tommy debuted on vinyl. The group's contribution to punk is often overlooked, but they're still rocking and singing about their favorite pastimes (TV, burgers, girls, wrestling, fast cars)—going on 30 years strong. Bassist and chief songwriter Andy Shernoff recently talked about the group's legacy, and their new live release, 'Viva Dictators.'

Let's talk about the new live album...

We put out our first record in 20 years in 2001 ['D.F.F.D.'], and every time we'd play New York, I'd have a friend of mine record the shows. One in particular, at Maxwell's, sounded the best. So the majority of ['Viva Dictators'] was from Maxwell's, and some from the Bowery Ballroom. I'm afraid people are going to think we did some overdubbing—all live records these days are fixed up in the studio. Outside of editing a few mistakes, this is the performance.

What was the New York scene like when the Dictators started?

First of all, we started before the Ramones. Our first record was recorded in 1974 and released in 1975. It was a vast wasteland out there if you were a rock n' roll fan. There was no MTV, no Sex Pistols, no Nirvana. There was CBGB's—drugs, prostitutes, and alcoholics. You were able to get your shit together out of the gaze of the media, which is hard today. The bands we were playing with were Television, Blondie, Talking Heads, the Ramones, the Heartbreakers. Every weekend, a band would headline at CBGB's. You'd play Thursday, Friday, Saturday, two shows a night, and just alternated. The first time I saw the Ramones, they played for 15 minutes—I used to go to shows and there were drum solos longer than their show! It was exciting to be part of something new.

Memories of opening for Kiss in 1977?

We did a tour of the Midwest—they were pretty pompous. [Singer Dick Manitoba] would imitate Paul Stanley, and they didn't dig that. We were sarcastic wise guys—like the Beastie Boys were on their first few records. Wise guy New Yorkers making fun of everything, and Kiss were very serious—they were rock stars, and didn't want anyone making fun of them. They already had a few hits, and they were playing 18,000 seat places. They knew how to work the audience, and we didn't—we'd been playing clubs for 2-300 people. Basically, [the audience] ignored us!

Memories of touring Europe in the '70s?

Great experience. We were in England the week that the Sex Pistols' record came out, and were touring with the Stranglers, who at the time, were the biggest band in England. The Sex Pistols had the impact, the Clash had the longevity, but the Stranglers had hit single after hit single. We did like five nights at the Roundhouse, then we went to Europe. We came back, and we headlined at the Roundhouse. Got to meet all the guys in the Sex Pistols, Billy Idol, Brian James, and also at the same time, the Dead Boys were touring with the Damned, and Richard Hell and the Voidoids were touring with Elvis Costello, I think, so we had a bunch of friends over there. It was a real kick in the ass to see that enthusiasm. Huge audiences all over the country—spitting, po-going, kids with the safety pins through their mouths.

What do you think of modern day punk?

If it's drivin', I like it. I like guitars, I like catchy hooks. I'm all for teenagers liking rock n' roll. When I was a kid, music was more of a 'cultural influence'— how you wore your hair, how you dressed, what kind of music you listened to. If you listened to rock n' roll, it was a statement that you were a rebel. Now, rock n' roll is used to sell cars. It plays a different role in society, but I still prefer it to most other forms of music.

www.thedictators.com

Classic Rock—October 2005, issue 85

Mudhoney

They rode the front crest of grunge's first wave, but now they risk brassing off fans by using lots of horns on their records.

Mudhoney remains one of the last group's left standing from "grunge's first wave." The group that single handedly popularized second-hand guitars and vintage stomp boxes is back with 'Under a Billion Suns,' their seventh full-length overall. Mudhoney will curate a day of the 'All Tomorrows Parties Festival' in May, as well as play additional Euro dates that month. Singer/guitarist Mark Arm recently gave Classic Rock the lowdown.

Why did it take four years between the last album and 'Under a Billion Suns'?

We hoped to do the record sooner. Originally, we were going to start work on it the summer before last. But I got asked to tour with the DKT/MC5, and Steve [Turner] the year before had done a solo record—he was doing a lot of touring and wasn't in town that much. But we did get together a couple of times and worked on a few things. One of the earliest songs we had was "Hard-On for War."

Lyrically, that song is bound to come under scrutiny.

It was written in the run-up to "Gulf War II." Maybe just a couple of months after 9/11 when they started talking about Iraq, you knew that was the next thing that was going to happen. We recorded it on the same day as there were those worldwide anti-war protests, against the invasion of Iraq [February 15, 2003]. You knew they were so eager to fuckin' get in there. They weren't letting the weapon inspectors do their job—they had this timetable. They already had the troops over there, they had to get in there before it got too hot, or else it would be miserable for the troops, and they didn't want to keep them over there for that long—for like another year 'til it became "seasonably OK" to fight a war again. So they just rammed all this propaganda and shit down people's throats. Instead of marching in the streets, I guess we just recorded that song that day.

Like the last album, horns appear on 'Under a Billion Suns.'

There are horn arrangements for two songs, and there's some saxophone on a third song. This time around, we asked Craig [Flory], who did the horns on the last record, to come up with horns on as many songs as he wanted. There was actually a lot more horns recorded than we ended up using. I don't think we could use horns on the whole record, or else it would turn into something that we couldn't approximate live.

How were the South American shows with Pearl Jam last year?

One of the thoughts we had was in one of Pearl Jam's encores, maybe we'll break out a Green River song. We were going to do "Come on Down." None of us had it on us—someone finally found it online. Jeff [Ament] heard it, and just went, "Nah, that sucks" [laughs]. So we ended up doing "Kick out the Jams" and "Rockin' in the Free World," both of which are much better songs [laughs]. Usually if we play with Pearl Jam, if we're playing a shed or an arena, the crowd is there to see Pearl Jam. They don't give a shit about who is playing first. But in South America, they [utilized] festival seating. So whoever's the most interested is going to come up front, and despite the fact that these people were waiting for Pearl Jam—and probably a good percentage of them never heard us—they were really open to us and receptive. It was great.

Classic Rock—May 2006, issue 92

Mike Patton

The second *hardest working man in show business, Mike Patton, is back with his latest venture, Peeping Tom. Long in the making, Peeping Tom's self-titled Ipecac debut sees Patton offer his most straight-ahead/ pop-minded compositions since his Faith No More days, loaded with special guests (Massive Attack, Norah Jones, etc.). Patton was more than willing to fill in the gaps.*

How did Peeping Tom come about?

Way back in 2000 I started writing a few innocent sounding pop songs. It was all downhill from there! All of a sudden I had three, and then all of sudden I had ten. It sat on my shelf, and as it gathered dust, it kind of shined through the dust, and I decided I'd better do something with it. That process probably took a year or so, because I wasn't taking it very seriously. A lot of things you write and they do just sit on your shelf, and you never end up doing anything with them. This seemed like something worth exploring and would be a nice detour, and provide some balance for me, with all the other things I was doing. Next phase was, "OK, how am I going to execute this? Do I hire a band like I always do? Do I hire a bunch of musicians-for-hire?" The more I lived with the stuff; I realized I liked the sound of everything. The one weak link in all the tunes was the programming was awful—I am not a very good programmer. A light bulb went off at some point, saying to me, "Fuck the band, let's just keep everything the way it was, with all the true instrumentation/self-played stuff, but let's get some real programmers, beat makers, and maybe a few guests to spice thing up." So that started a whole new phase of sending out files—quite a learning process there too, find the right people and once I did, making sure I stayed on top of them and got the stuff back that I wanted in a timely fashion. So that being a new process to me took quite a bit of time.

I heard major labels were interested...

From that point, somewhere in there, I did a little two-step with major fucking labels, which ate up another good six to eight months of indecision and general disillusionment. All together I'm glad that I investigated it, but I let it go on a little too long. That contributed to some more time being lost. I would say that during that whole process, I was busy doing a bunch of other things too, and it became a "backburner thing" for me. But when I finally cleaned my plate and was able to focus on it, I probably worked on it for a year solid...and here we are.

Special guests appear throughout.

The Anticon guys I worked with pretty head-to-head. They were in The Anticon guys I worked with pretty head-to-head. They were in the Bay Area, so they would come over and we would work together on stuff—they were probably the guys I worked with the most. The other being Dan the Automator, who's kind of family by now, and we worked together as well. The rest of it was phone calls, emails, letters. I think I met with Amon Tobin once up in Montreal; I did go up to Montreal also and record Kid Koala. But most of it was "the dating game."

Touring plans?

Yeah, at some point. We're doing a TV appearance on Conan O'Brien, so I'm actually assembling a "New York band" for that date, and we'll see—that will probably lead to a more solid live formation. A few guests from the record, a few non—take it from there. For the appearance, I've got the Dub Trio guys,

Dan the Automator is going to be doing the electronics, Rob Swift from the X-Ecutioners is DJing, Rahzel is going to be doing his thing, and myself and Miho Hatori from Cibo Matto are going to the vocalists. If I could take that out on the road, believe me, I'd be tickled pink.

www.myspace.com/peepingtomispatton
www.ipecac.com

Classic Rock—August 2006, issue 95

Eagles of Death Metal

With his band set to unleash a second album of "sex boogie," frontman Jesse Hughes recounts his X-rated exploits.

Eagles of Death Metal are trying to rekindle listeners' lust. Led by mustachioed jive-talker/guitarist Jesse Hughes (aka J. Devil Huge), the EODM are about to drop their sophomore effort, 'Death By Sexy.' Once more featuring Queens of the Stone Age leader Josh Homme behind the drum kit, the album also includes a gaggle of guests, and promises to be another rockin' good time. Hughes recently discussed the album with Greg Prato, as well as his apparent popularity with the opposite sex.

How's the new album?

I make it easy on myself by only writing hits…I'm just kidding! No, it's awesome man. We recorded at Sound City, and it was one of the most fun things I did in my life. Josh is one of my dearest friends—he's kind of my mentor too, y'know? It's got an all-star cast on it—a couple of songs Joey Castillo from Queens is playing on, Mark Lanegan came in, Wendy Ray, this hot little vixenous siren singing on it, Brody Dalle, who just killed it. We had Liam Lynch in there directing a DVD, documenting the whole process. The DVD includes all my imaginary friends and Josh beating up a digitally rendered banana. It's rad—it's going to come with the CD. Basically it's three concept videos we made for the album, and then a documentary detailing the fucking—pardon my language— the *incredible* weirdness going on in the studio.

Who will be in the touring band?

For the tour, Samantha Maloney, who was formerly in Hole and Mötley Crüe will be playing drums, me on the lead magic, Brian "Big Hands" O'Connor is the new bass player, and David Catching on guitar. By the way, I want to say that Samantha Maloney, for the record—she's not only one of the most smoking hot girls I've ever seen in my life, she's one of the most kick ass fucking drummers I've ever played with. To have her in our band is like a glorious bonus.

How does the new album compare to the debut?

It's kind of like a graduation—the same sort of philosophy about rock n' roll, which is I kind of look at it as the Quentin Tarantino-izing of classic rock. But this one steps up. I was really worried on this album because we were going to use bass on everything. The first album, we didn't set out *not* to use bass. It's just the way I tune my guitars, it achieved a bass frequency and sounded cool, but I didn't want this album to come off sounding like, "Now we got bass in your face!" But it's awesome man. I mean, I stole from some of the best classic rock songs of all-time, so technically, this is just the greatest rock album *ever made*. I lift heavily from the Stones, T. Rex, the Sonics—I actually lift a lot from Josh, because he's there and I can steal from him easier.

Any plans to tour Europe?

Yeah, we do. We're going to hit the summer festivals, [and] we do a major tour with Queens of the Stone Age—we're going to do the entire North American tour with Queens. We intend to be really busy. There's a general exciting feeling around this album because it feels good, it sounds good—it's a dance rock album, y'know? It's straight sex boogie. I didn't come here to save whales, I came here to get laid and make rock n' roll!

Is your solo album, 'Fabulous Weapons,' still coming out?

Yeah, I'm actually going to try and buffer some of that up right now. I'm a hillbilly kind of, and I love hillbilly rock—it's a real tribute to my roots, if you will. Right now I have a couple of labels interested in putting that out. I'm up in Joshua Tree right now with Biblical Proof of UFO's, producing a seven-inch single for them. We ended up recording a little bit, and I think Kim

Fowley may actually come in and check us out, to see what we're doing. They have a great classic rock sound, and I'm not afraid of saying that's what I want to hear. This was kind of my "test" to see if everything Josh has taught me and shown me, if I can pull it off myself.

I caught a smoking EODM show last December in Brooklyn, New York—any memories of that particular performance?

Yeah, yeah, yeah. [To someone else in the car] "It was the Brooklyn show where those three chicks from Gwen Stefani's design team went back to my room with me, right?" [Back to the interview] THREE GIRLS AT ONE TIME, MY FRIEND! It was *hot* action to the fucking max. And they were all these little hot nineteen-year-old lovelies who were design girls for Gwen Stefani's fashion line.

Any other interesting touring stories?

Well, New York is an amazing town, man. I was cruising into this club where they had on karaoke—I kid you not—"Is It My Body" by Alice Cooper. And I sang "Is It My Body" to a table full of kind of stuffy, upper crusty-looking girls, and one followed me into the bathroom and gave me the hottest blow job of my life. Just for singing "Is It My Body." Apparently, *the answer was yes.*

What about memories of recording 'Death By Sexy'?

This chick, we wanted to get stoned a little bit, so we needed some weed. So I called this girlfriend of mine, this six foot one amazon with huge, beautiful breasts. I had her come all the way down to the studio to bring me weed. I marched her up into the upstairs parking lot of Sound City, nailed her on top of a car, and then I heard a noise. When I looked up to the left, there was this dude standing in the parking lot, and he dropped his coke. And then I looked at her, and said, "OK baby, we're done!" And I sent her on her way.

How is Josh recovering from his illness [resulting in the cancellation of several QOTSA/Euro gigs]?

He got the European strain of the flu right as he landed, and it developed into a lung infection. So it was serious business. But he's home, he's with his girl. Yeah, he's wonderful man. That was a rough tour for him. The press on him—y'know, he's really getting a bad rap in the press. The European press seems to be acting like he's some kind of control freak Nazi, and I can see that it was bumming him out. I mean, I have a great relationship with him—he's not just my mentor, he's not just in my band, he's the dearest friend I ever had. The most "just" person I've ever met in my life. I'm starting to get a little personally mad at the bad rap that he's taking, because it just ain't fair man. He's a decent guy—he's always kept his word. I've been in situations with Joshua where there's been no paperwork at all concerning royalties I might be due, and on the day that everyone gets paid, the full amount comes to me. He's a stand-up guy. He and Brody Dalle—they have the coolest relationship, and they've kind of saved my ass from myself. I can't tell you how many times I've stumbled into his home like after a fight in the Beauty Bar in Hollywood, or after having someone's boyfriend chase me out into the fucking alleyway and beating the fuck out of me! Other than that, he's doing great, his voice is back. His voice dropped to three octaves low because he was sick. It was wild man. You can't have fans at a gig and not be able to deliver what you're promising them, especially with someone with the perfection and standard that Joshua has.

www.eaglesofdeathmetal.net

Classic Rock—Summer 2006, issue 96

Radio Birdman

Had their 1978 US tour with the Ramones not been cancelled, the Aussie garage punks coulda been real contenders.

After a hiatus of nearly 20 years, the greatest garage/punk band to ever hail out of Australia, Radio Birdman, reunited for performances in their native land in 1996. But it would be another decade until the core of the group—guitarists Deniz Tek and Chris Masuak, plus vocalist Rob Younger—got around to issuing their first all-new studio release since 1978, the just-released 'Zeno Beach.' With Euro dates (and the group's first-ever U.S. tour) on the horizon, Tek gave Classic Rock the lowdown.

How did Radio Birdman reunite?

The promoter Ken West contacted me in mid 1995, and made a lucrative offer for the band to get back together to play the Big Day Out. It so happened that Chris Masuak and his family was visiting my family in Montana when the call came. He was on a road trip, and was only around for a couple of days—we were drinking beer, barbequing, sitting around in the hot tub and so forth. We had worked together fairly recently on the Hitmen's last album, 'Moronic Inferno,' and on my solo project, 'Take It To The Vertical,' and I was still trying to recover from the financially disastrous 'Vertical' tour I had done with Chris and Scott Asheton. So Chris and I knew we could work together well, and we rang the others and got the go-ahead. So the initial impulse was a suitcase full of cash, but once we got together, we saw that the old magic seemed to survive the hard years. And we reclaimed something worth a lot more than cash.

How was it playing together again?

We are all writing now so it's more collaborative and allows more scope for new directions. I used to write almost everything for the band, but in those days something like "The Brotherhood of Al Wazah" wouldn't have been possible. The recording is like recording always is—tedious and hard work. We've all made lots of albums, both playing and producing, probably close to 80 or 100 albums between us if you added them all up. The studio is familiar to us all, and it's no different now. Both Rob and Chris are accomplished producers. We were well rehearsed for this album so the tracking went pretty smooth and not a lot of fooling around. On stage we fight the same battles as ever with the sound, but we generally don't fight each other much any more.

Memories of the 'Zeno Beach' sessions?

I was having so much personal trauma in my life during the sessions that I almost can't stand to think about it. It was rough on me, and on Chris too. The recording sessions were actually a bit of respite from the world outside, which seemed a rather hostile place at the time. I was homeless, and living part time at Pip's house, and elsewhere. I was trying to stay immersed in the work except for when sleeping. You tend to recall the peripheral things like the food you ate, the coffee, etc. Greg Wales, our engineer for the album, happens to be an expert chef of Mexican food and a connoisseur of fine tequila. He introduced us to some of the most outstanding stuff—beyond the imagination.

Favorite tracks?

I like all of them—otherwise, they wouldn't be on there. I think "Heyday" came out especially well. "Brotherhood" is great, for the experimentation, and it's a wonderful piece of writing. "You Just Make It Worse" works great as a single. I love the riff. "If You Say Please," which started life as "Seminole," is the sleeper—the last track written and learned at the last minute. [It's] amazingly modern sounding and would be a good radio tune. We started with 25 good songs and ended up with 13.

Looking forward to the group's first-ever U.S. tour?

Well, of course we are. We should have toured there with the Ramones in 1978, which would have sent us on a very different trajectory if it hadn't been cancelled when we were dropped from Sire. We've been wanting to go ever since, although none of us expected that we ever would.

What can fans expect?

The real thing. Authentic 200-proof Radio Birdman.

Future plans?

We plan to keep on playing. But the future is never knowable. And in this world there is no such thing as permanence. Better get it while you can.

www.radio-birdman.com

Classic Rock—September 2006, issue 97

Bad Brains

From a Rastafarian jazz fusion outfit to what many cite as the first hardcore band, with reggae, funk, and metal twists.

The on-again/off-again Bad Brains are once again 'on,' with 'Build A Nation'—an album overseen by Beastie Boy Adam Yauch, and their first all new studio release since 1995's 'God of Love.' One of the first bands to speed up punk's tempo and create hardcore (and embrace reggae/dub, as well), the original Bad Brains line-up—singer H.R., guitarist Dr. Know, bassist Darryl Jenifer, and drummer Earl Hudson—are back in business. Dr. Know recently gave Classic Rock the scoop.

How did the band hook up with Adam Yauch?

Adam has always been a very good friend of ours—from way, way back. He didn't produce it—nobody produces our music, first of all. God produces our music, then we produce it, and then we work with other people. Adam's take was just like, "Why don't you all play some old school shit?" Me and Darryl wrote the songs—we sat down like we always do, and we riff out the riffs. All the stuff was kind of like that.

Did Adam introduce any interesting gadgets?

One of the cool things was that Adam had were these drum seats that have a speaker in the bottom of them. So therefore, a drummer and a bass player can feel that bass in their ass—for real! When you're dealing in a sterile recording environment with headphones, you don't hear or feel any bass, and that effects how you play. I didn't have one [laughs]. I play guitar, so it's different frequencies.

How does the album compare to the classics?

Everything that we do is what we do—we always do what we do when we do how we do what we do. That's who we are. I just listened to it the other day, and I was like, "This shit is *bad*." We are true to who we are—that's a blessing, and I don't take that shit for granted at all.

Tour plans?

We're going to do some gigs. We're not going to do like, "tours," but we're going to do some strategic shows. Do an L.A. show, do a New York show, go to Europe and do a couple of shows in England. Strategic shows—not tour.

I understand you're working on a solo album.

Last night I sat down and wrote a little riff. As of last night, like, "OK, let me get back into my solo world." I just need to document and express myself—for myself. I haven't touched on dub yet or anything like that, I've been kind of feeling jazz-y a little bit. I might just bug out and program everything. I have a MIDI guitar set-up, and play horns, trumpets, and bells and whistles—who knows? I'm trying to keep myself open. There's going to be total, crazy special guests—whoever I can get. A lot of people said they would participate—Flea, Mos [Def], the Living Colour guys, Darryl, Earl and H.R.

Plans for another Bad Brains album?

I want to start working on the next one, is what I really want to do—because we did that one two years ago already. We'll do that in the next six months—go back in the studio hopefully. We all want to sit down together. Which is a thing that I am really missing—for all of us to sit down and write some songs. Not me write songs, or Darryl write songs, or H.R. write songs, or Earl write songs. This next venture, sit down in a room—let's go back to '79 and play. Get that spontaneity.

How was it playing at CBGB's their final week?

It was tremendous. We hadn't played in that place in a long, long time. Did you see the DVD [the recently-released ëLive at CBGB 1982']? That shit was like that! There was so much friends and family—it was a bit much, actually. It was really an honor and a privilege to have so many good friends and see them all.

www.badbrains.com

Classic Rock—February 2007, issue 102

Show Review

The Stooges/Sonic Youth

Jones Beach Theater, Wantagh, New York—August 8, 2003

Gimme Danger

Iggy and the Ashetons reunite and bring their Funhouse to New York for the first time in well over a quarter century.

"How's my band?" the singer asked the crazed audience. An appropriate question for a young group finding their "stage legs," but when it's Iggy Pop asking (backed by Detroit punk-pioneers the Stooges), he's pulling our leg. For years, Iggy has been asked about a reunion with the Ashetons (no chance of bassist Dave Alexander showing up, he joined the great "jam session in the sky" back in 1975). Despite rumors, no reunion materialized…until now.

With ex-Minutemen/fIREHOSE bassist Mike Watt replacing Alexander, a successful Stooges show went down at last April's Coachella Festival. Fans hoped for more, and New Yorkers celebrated when a Jones Beach date was announced, with Sonic Youth added to the bill—resulting in a once-in-a-lifetime event.

The weather gods must be Stooges fans—despite thunderstorms forecast, not one raindrop fell during the performance at the open-air venue. Up-and-comer's Thursday got things started, but their emocore shtick proved out-of-place. After being treated to '60s garage rock over the sound system, Sonic Youth took the stage.

Opening with harmony feedback, Sonic Youth embarked on an hour-log set—featuring "Drunken Butterfly" (bassist Kim Gordon went instrument-less to sing and jump around like a cheerleader), "Teen Age Riot," "100%," and "Eric's Trip." Guitarists Thurston Moore (still modeling the "librarian look"—floppy hair, baggy long-sleeved shirt) and Lee Renaldo displayed their oddball guitar collection—one of which Moore played with a drumstick. Another highlight was a "feedback duel," with both scraping their guitar necks against the stage.

With the main attraction nearing, a soundtrack of old-time blues played. Around a quarter to ten, the Ashetons and Watt assumed their spots, and launched into 'Loose,' with Iggy waiting until the last second to run up to the mic. While Iggy looked eerily 1969/70-era (shirtless, long hair, hip-hugger jeans), the Ashetons looked more "mature" (Scott- backwards white baseball cap and long scraggily hair, Ron- army fatigue jacket with "Stooges" and a skull scrawled across the back), Watt wore a "Germs" t-shirt. It didn't take Iggy long to become the focus—Watt stood by his amps (staring intensely at Iggy throughout), while Ron manned his effects pedals.

Iggy's specialty remains breaking down barriers between performer and audience, as he leapt into the crowd, threw his mic stand (eventually sailing into the seats), twirled the mic so it narrowly missed the front-row, and even attempted to reach the balcony by foot. More so than most, Iggy reaches an unfazed "zone" when he performs—the Easter Bunny could deliver him a deviled egg on stage, and Iggy would simply gyrate, slap him upside the head, and get back to the mic in time for the next verse. The majority of the audience was in "worship mode," yet some remembered how old-time audiences treated the band—by spitting and hurling objects (a bag of popcorn).

The setlist was stellar—comprised of selections from 'The Stooges' and 'Funhouse,' save for a track from Iggy's new release, 'Skull Ring.' Despite the period of inactivity, the quartet sounded spot-on, especially on "Dirt," "No Fun" (concluding with a noise jam), "1969," "1970" (with sax player Steven MacKay), and "Funhouse," the latter finishing with Iggy screaming "I AM YOU" and "I AM HAPPY" repeatedly. Ron is still a wah-drenched solo master, while Scott's barebones time-keeping was a revelation (his rarely utilized cymbals could be returned to the Drum Center for a refund), and Watt recreated Alexander's lines on his weathered Gibson SG bass.

After their exit, Iggy reappeared, demanding his bandmates follow. What better way to close than with a second thrashing of "I Wanna Be Your Dog," with Iggy handing the mic to front-row fans. After feedback from Ron's abandoned guitar had subsided, and a tape of the MC5's "Kick Out the Jams" came on, it became clear what the several thousand-strong throng had just witnessed—the gig of a lifetime.

Setlist:
Loose
Down on the Street
1969
I Wanna Be Your Dog

TV Eye
Dirt
Real Cool Time
No Fun
1970
Funhouse
Skull Ring
Not Right
Little Doll
I Wanna Be Your Dog

www.iggypop.com
www.sonicyouth.com

Classic Rock—October 2003, issue 58

Lollapalooza

Jones Beach Theater, Wantagh, New York—July 30, 2003

Lollapa-Snoozer

*Perry Farrell invites you to take a magic carpet ride back to the early
'90s. Sometimes, memories are best left undisturbed.*

Back in the early '90s, a wind of change was sweeping across rock music. All it took was a handful of alt rock acts to flush teenybopper pop and overblown rock stars down the toilet, but as it turns out, they didn't do a good enough extermination job. The early 21st century is a replica of the pre-Nirvana landscape, where the majority of new bands merely copy each other for a paycheck. What better time for Perry Farrell to resuscitate his Lollapalooza road show with a reunited Jane's Addiction, right?

They couldn't have picked a better day for the show at New York's Jones Beach Theater—sunny with a touch of clouds. And the venue's scenic beauty is extraordinary—entirely outdoors, and on the edge of the beach (besides watching the performance, you get a beautiful view of the Atlantic Ocean). With the stage scaffolding obscured by a design that resembled the Statue of Liberty's crown and a computer's motherboard, a giant "yellow golf ball" curtain covered the stage between bands.

On the mainstage, things got off to a rocky start with punk revivalists the Distillers, Kiss-worshippers the Donnas, and rappers Jurassic Five. Courtney Love-clone Brody Armstrong led the Distillers through a set of forgettable punk, with a horrible mix making it sound like 'Live Through This' blasting in a wind tunnel. The Donnas didn't fare much better—screeching their way through a set only memorable for their cover of Kiss' "Strutter." Jurassic Five's entrance turned out to be their highpoint (one-by-one through a glittering 'J5' logo swaying door), as they relied heavily on "Wave your hands in the air" shenanigans.

One thing about festivals, it's easy to spot which bands belong in the big leagues and which don't, as shown by the mighty Queens of the Stone Age. With an absolutely roaring sound, the multi-membered band hit the crowd hard with "Millionaire," while large red and white panels flashed cutout symbols (a pitchfork, sperm, etc.) behind them. Led by singer/guitarist Josh Homme (who sported a cut-off Eagles of Death Metal shirt and a whisper of a mullet) and singer/bassist Nick Oliveri (who should be commended for wearing black pants and biker boots in the heat), QOTSA was the first band to be embraced by the audience—as they received a loud ovation for their set-closing "No One Knows."

In addition to the mainstage, there was also a second stage in the parking lot (Burning Brides being a bright spot) plus booths. At past Lollapalooza's, booths were occupied by thought-provoking organizations and topical debates. This year, it was disheartening to see mostly advertisements.

The girls needed a sex symbol, and Incubus' shirtless/beefcake singer Brandon Boyd was this year's model. Although their set was enthusiastically received, it's hard to take a band seriously that began as one-dimensional funk-metallists, and now come off as serious/spiritual rock philosophers. Once more, a Lolla-band utilized covers—snippets of Lionel Richie's smaltzy "Hello" and '90s art-rockers Shudder To Think's "X-French Tee Shirt." However, the spotty sound mix returned (Boyd bopping a djembe drum and the group's DJ were inaudible), which turned Incubus' set into a snoozefest.

With the sun setting, several Bob Marley hits preceded Audioslave, before Woody Guthrie's "This Land is Your Land" signaled the quartet's entrance. With a stage adorned with mirrors, drummer Brad Wilk's back was surprisingly to the audience for the entire performance. The day was soon becoming a battle of cover songs, and Audioslave's choices took the prize—Funkadelic's

"Super Stupid" and the White Stripes' "Seven Nation Army." This was clearly an "Audioslave audience" (evidenced by the day's largest turn-out), as they played spot-on renditions of "I Am the Highway" (which singer Chris Cornell played half of solo with an acoustic guitar), and the set-closing "Cochise." Cornell clearly enjoyed himself throughout—hoisting a tape recorder before requesting cheers (so he could listen to it when he's "75 years old"), and even jumping into the crowd and running around the aisles.

After scantily clad Asian dancers entertained the crowd (embarrassingly called "the Lolla Girls," it all came off like an '80s-era Paula Abdul video), headliners Jane's Addiction finally appeared. Jane's set-up was the day's most elaborate—a silver, space age stage that had curving ramps on both sides of drummer Stephen Perkins, while two artsy platforms adjourned both corners of the front of the stage. Present-day Jane's Addiction is a lot different than the junkie art-punks circa 1990—the glitzy stage, designer duds (Farrell—'Mad Max'-ish, Dave Navarro—'Liberace'-ish, with feather boa) and re-appearances by the dancers transformed the performance into a Vegas revue. With tracks from their latest, 'Strays,' kept to a minimum, Jane's focused on the classics, with the epic "Ted, Just Admit It" being a standout. But "Ocean Size" was the highpoint—to hear a song about the ocean's vastness and to actually look directly into it behind the band was quite awe inspiring. A rough version of the acoustic sing-a-long "Jane Says" (which was hindered by a guitar malfunction) wrapped up the long day.

Lollapalooza remains a sign of the times. 1991—a climate of change. 2003—corporate and commercialized.

Setlists:
Queens of the Stone Age:
Millionaire
Do It Again
First It Giveth
Quick and to the Pointless
Go with the Flow
Gonna Leave You
Mexicola
Hangin' Tree
Another Love Song

A Song for the Dead
The Sky is Fallin'
Monsters in the Parasol
No One Knows

Audioslave:
Gasoline
Set It Off
Light My Way
Like a Stone
Super Stupid
new song
Shadow on the Sun
I Am the Highway
Seven Nation Army
Show Me How to Live
Cochise

Jane's Addiction:
Stop!
Ain't No Right
Just Because
Been Caught Stealing
Strays
The Riches
Ocean Size
Up the Beach
Mountain Song
Ted, Just Admit It
Jane Says

www.lollapalooza.com

Classic Rock—October 2003, issue 58

The New Cars/Blondie

Jones Beach Theater, Wantagh, New York—June 9, 2006

"They're not going to rain on our parade!" Never have truer words been spoken—courtesy of Todd Rundgren—on the night that the New Cars/ Blondie double-bill rolled into Jones Beach Amphitheatre. Mother Nature failed to take pity on the crowd of old-school new wave fanatics, as rain and a crisp breeze nearly froze the crowd.

Despite the mini-typhoon, both re-hauled acts delivered. Yet when Blondie hit the stage with "Call Me," it looked/sounded as though Debbie Harry would rather be anywhere than the soggy stage. Harry's demeanor soon warmed up however, as Blondie handed in strong renditions of "Heart of Glass" and "Rapture," and on "Dreaming," Clem Burke proved to still be a drumming madman.

Now led by Rundgren (taking over for Ric Ocasek), the New Cars setlist focused on the classics—"Drive," "Let's Go," "Shake It Up"—as well as a few oft-overlooked gems ("Bye Bye Love") and Rundgren solo tracks ("I Saw the Light"). And the "best dressed performer award" went to drummer Prairie Prince—who was covered from head to toe in a white polka dot on black ensemble…and a matching drum kit.

Even with the uncooperative natural elements, both the New Cars/ Blondie partied like it was 1979.

www.blondie.net
www.thenewcars.com

Classic Rock—September 2006, issue 97

Buyer's Guide

Grunge

The music that killed glam metal, or a movement that breathed new life into music? Whichever, it threw up lots of real gems.

Love it or hate it, you've got to give credit to the early '90s grunge movement. Without it, we would have remained stuck in the quagmire of unbearable hair spray and make-up bands, singing about fast cars and fast women. But a trio of bands—Nirvana, Soundgarden, and Pearl Jam—helped change it all in one fell swoop, along with a few other similarly styled acts.

Up until then, Seattle had already spawned a few renowned names (most notably Jimi Hendrix), but 1991 truly put the Emerald City on the rock n' roll map. By mixing the detuned, snail-paced riffs of Black Sabbath with the punk energy of Black Flag, the birth of grunge could be traced back to when a Kiss-obsessed/afro-haired gentleman, Buzz Osborne, formed the Melvins, in the logging town of Aberdeen, Washington. From there, it seemed like a light bulb went off over the head of every local musician, as grunge's first wave soon came fast and furious.

A select number of non-Seattle groups also got into the swing of things, including Dinosaur Jr. (an obvious influence on Nirvana), as well as the Courtney Love-led Hole (back when Courtney was more concerned with music rather than movies/modeling), and Smashing Pumpkins (whose early recordings fit in well with grunge—until Billy Corgan shaved off his hair and lost his superhuman strength).

Something else that made grunge stick out from the form of music it replaced on radio and MTV—it was completely unglamorous. With most bands possessing a look that was equal parts lumberjack (flannel shirts) and thrift store (ripped jeans), grunge put the emphasis back on music, as well as a return to live-sounding recordings.

Another difference was that most grunge bands were vocal about their political beliefs and pro-feminist stances, as evidenced by interviews and benefit shows (Nirvana and Pearl Jam in particular).

As with any musical movement, it wasn't long until record labels took note, and started cranking out horrific impersonators (something that can still be detected today—the amount of bands with guitarists aping Nirvana riffs and singers karaoke-izing Eddie Vedder's baritone remains staggering).

However, one thing that first wave grungers were not prepared for was success—drug abuse, deaths, break-ups, and battles with Ticketmaster effectively ended the movement almost as quickly as it began.

But the focus was always the music, and the following albums are plucked straight from grunge's magnet tarpit trap.

Essential: The Classics

Nirvana, "Nevermind"

DGC, 1991

Ask anyone "Which album is synonymous with grunge?" and the answer will probably be Nirvana's landmark 1991 release, 'Nevermind.' And there's good reason—Kurt Cobain assembled a set of songs that appealed to headbangers, punks, and pop fans a like. The fact that 'Nevermind' includes the song that single handedly ignited the grunge revolution, "Smells Like Teen Spirit," would be reason enough for the album's "essential" status. But the hits just keep coming—"Come As You Are," "Lithium," and "In Bloom"—in addition to tracks that could have easily been issued as singles ("Drain You," etc.). Also, 'Nevermind' popularized the now done-to-death quiet verse/raging chorus style of songwriting. The holy grail of grunge.

Pearl Jam, "Ten"

Epic, 1991

Although they eventually rejected the mainstream, Pearl Jam's best release is their most mainstream-sounding one, 1991's 'Ten.' Instead of wallowing in their misery following Mother Love Bone's tragic demise, guitarist Stone Gossard and bassist Jeff Ament put together Pearl Jam, a much more back-to-basics affair (both musically and visually). San Diego native Eddie Vedder manned the mic, who in addition to climbing lighting rigs during shows, had a knack for singing songs in a part news reporter/part sitting-round-the-campfire style, as evidenced by the hits "Alive," "Evenflow," and "Jeremy."

You also have to love that the album's best song, "Black," was never issued as a single. Along with 'Nevermind,' 'Ten' made "grunge" a household word.

Superior: The Albums That Built the Genre
Soundgarden "Badmotorfinger"
A&M, 1991

Along with the Melvins, Soundgarden was one of the first Seattle bands to specialize in slow/murky riffs, and possessed one of the genre's best singers, Chris Cornell. By the time that the quartet's third full-length rolled around, 1991's 'Badmotorfinger,' the band had transformed into quite a musically adventurous beast, as evidenced by the overabundance of prog-esque song structures, as well as the presence of blaring saxophone (a la the Stooges' 'Funhouse') on several cuts. But 'Badmotorfinger' also contained "Outshined"—a radio/MTV hit that propelled the album up the charts. Although Soundgarden had been around for seven years by 1991, it wasn't until 'Badmotorfinger' that it finally all came together in the recording studio.

Temple of the Dog "Temple Of The Dog "
A&M, 1991

It has been said that misery can inspire great work. Case in point, the self-titled debut by Temple of the Dog. Shortly after the death of Mother Love Bone singer Andrew Wood, Soundgarden singer Chris Cornell penned two songs as a tribute to his former roommate/friend. Enlisting members of Soundgarden and Pearl Jam (two of which were ex-MLB members), a few songs soon turned into a full-on album. Taking their name from a Wood lyric, TOTD's one-and-only album was a roots rock affair, as evidenced by such tracks as "Say Hello 2 Heaven" and "Hunger Strike." A year after its 1991 release, 'TOTD' scaled the charts, thanks to Pearl Jam and Soundgarden's enormous success.

Mother Love Bone "Apple"
Polydor, 1990

Grunge was the antithesis of glam. But interestingly, one of the genre's early favorites, Mother Love Bone, was fronted by an outrageous singer from the Freddie Mercury/Marc Bolan school of camp. After Green River's break-up, the inseparable team of Stone Gossard and Jeff Ament looked to move in a more metallic direction, and hooked up with ex-Malfunkshun frontman Andrew Wood. But before Mother Love Bone's full-length debut could be issued, Wood died from an overdose. Issued several months later, 'Apple' showed what could have been, especially such potential stadium stompers as "Stardog Champion." Along with Soundgarden, Mother Love Bone was picked by many to introduce the world to grunge. 'Apple' is the proof.

Alice in Chains "Facelift"
Columbia, 1990

Whereas most grunge bands had obvious punk influences, Alice In Chains was a tried and true heavy metal band. Originally a glammed up Guns N' Roses clone; Alice received a musical and visual makeover, which move paid off immediately. 1990's 'Facelift' was the first grunge album to leave an impression on the charts (thanks to the success of "Man in the Box"), paving the way for 'Nevermind,' 'Ten,' and 'Badmotorfinger'—all of which would follow Alice's debut up the charts in the ensuing months. However, it turned out that 'Facelift' only hinted at the band's potential—they were about to deliver a knockout blow with their 1992 dark classic, 'Dirt.'

Good: Worth Exploring

Mudhoney "Superfuzz Bigmuff"
Sub Pop, 1990

In addition to heavy metal and punk, elements of garage rock could be detected in grunge, and no other Seattle band embraced that style more than Mudhoney. With Jeff Ament and Stone Gossard splitting Green River to explore a more arena rock-based direction (Mother Love Bone), the group's ex-singer Mark Arm and guitarist Steve Turner opted to go in the completely different direction—fuzzy guitar riffs and lo-fi production. Collecting singles, covers, and an EP spanning 1988-1990, 1990's 'Superfuzz Bigmuff' contains grunge's first true anthem, "Touch Me I'm Sick." Their early recordings are considered to be their best (and certainly most classic) work, and that's precisely what 'Superfuzz Bigmuff' focuses on.

Screaming Trees "Uncle Anesthesia"
Epic, 1991

Psychedelia was not usually associated with grunge, but one of the genre's originators, the Screaming Trees, clearly had a thing for the '60s. Led by the Jim Morrison-esque Mark Lanegan (who can be spotted nowadays intermittently singing for Queens of the Stone Age), the group also featured a pair of larger-than-life brothers, Van and Gary Lee Conner, who supplied bass and guitar, respectively. Along with Soundgarden, the Screaming Trees were one of the first grunge bands signed to a major, and 1991's 'Uncle Anesthesia' is their finest, as evidenced by such standouts as "Ocean of Confusion." Also scores extra points on the grunge-o-meter for being co-produced by Chris Cornell.

Dinosaur Jr. "Bug"
SST, 1988

Along with the Pixies, Dinosaur Jr. was one of the biggest influences on a then-fledgling Nirvana. Led by the mumble-mouthed J. Mascis, Dinosaur Jr. did not hail from Seattle (they called Amherst, Massachusetts their home), but were certainly grunge worthy, especially such early releases as 1988's 'Bug.' With a sound modeled largely after Neil Young's cranked-to-ten work with Crazy Horse, Mascis was one of the few guitar heroes to emerge from the '80s indie rock underground. With tracks like "Freak Scene," the group also helped spawn another niftily named musical style—slacker rock. Interesting grunge trivia—'Bug' was the last Dinosaur Jr. album to feature a pre-Sebadoh Lou Barlow on bass.

Stone Temple Pilots "Core"
Atlantic, 1992

There's no way to get around it—Stone Temple Pilots were unanimously slammed by critics as "Pearl Jam clones" upon their 1992 arrival with 'Core.' But looking back on it years later, STP was certainly not the Judases they were made out to be at the time (especially after experiencing such true Pearl Jam clones as Creed and Nickelback). While their subsequent albums would see the group scale greater heights from a songwriting standpoint (especially their sophomore effort, 1994's 'Purple'), 'Core' is definitely their most grunge-friendly album, especially such MTV favorites as "Sex Type Thing," "Plush," and "Creep." The only STP album that wasn't overshadowed by drama surrounding Scott Weiland's prevalent drug problems/arrests.

Avoid

Silverchair "Frogstomp"
Epic, 1995

It's happened time and time again throughout the history of rock—a style becomes popular, and a slew of imitator acts crash the scene with dollar signs in their eyes. Hence the arrival of Australia's then-teenaged Silverchair in 1995, with 'Frogstomp.' It doesn't get much more "by the numbers" than "Tomorrow" (a now-thankfully forgotten massive hit) and "Pure Massacre." Singer Daniel Johns took copycatting to a whole new level—not only did he sound like Kurt Cobain, but he even looked like the bugger! Anyone have the courage to admit buying 'Frogstomp' ten years later? Didn't think so, but a zillion copies didn't just disappear off the shelves by themselves...

A Starter

Singles Motion Picture Soundtrack "Epic", 1992

Director Cameron Crowe has a way of perfectly capturing specific eras in his films, whether it is a '70s touring rock band ('Almost Famous') or grunge-era Seattle ('Singles'). For the latter's soundtrack, Crowe expertly assembled a collection that told the history of Seattle rock, where veterans like Jimi Hendrix and Heart (under the alias the Lovemongers) merged with the new regime. But what really made 'Singles' such a dandy was the presence of previously unreleased gems from Pearl Jam ("Breath"), Soundgarden ("Birth Ritual"), and Smashing Pumpkins ("Drown"), as well as a taster from Alice in Chains' sophomore full-length ("Would?"). The only thing that prevents 'Singles' from being a definitive grunge compilation is Nirvana's absence.

The Rest

Want to sample some proto-grunge? Then be sure to check out a pair of compilations—garage grungers Green River's 'Rehab Doll/Dry As A Bone' (which features future Mudhoney and Pearl Jam members) and glam grungers Malfunkshun's 'Return to Olympus' (which features Mother Love Bone's

Andrew Wood). And if you dig heavy riffs/heavy frontmen, another early grunge favorite was Tad, and their 1991 release, '8-Way Santa.' Although hard to imagine because of their latter-day schizoid/electronic direction, the Smashing Pumpkins once specialized in psychedelic grunge, especially on their exceptional debut, 1991's 'Gish.' And males weren't the only grunge acts to flourish during the early '90s, as evidenced by raging releases by L7 (1992's 'Bricks Are Heavy') and Hole (1991's 'Pretty on the Inside'). And lastly… the forgotten and the best forgotten. Featuring an early member of Alice in Chains, My Sister's Machine enjoyed their 15 minutes of fame with the Alice-esque "I'm Sorry" off 1992's 'Diva,' while Bush plumbed Silverchair-esque depths with 1994's 'Sixteen Stone.'

Classic Rock—January 2006, issue 88

www.ingramcontent.com/pod-product-compliance
Lightning Source LLC
Chambersburg PA
CBHW060230050426
42448CB00009B/1378